Published by Ockley Books Limited, Huddersfield, England

First published November 2019

ISBN - 978-1-910906-194

Layout & design by Michael Kinlan,
edited by David Hartrick

Printed & bound by:

Biddles Printing, King's Lynn

Icons made by Freepik from www.flaticon.com

All statistics and records supplied by

To Don,
Enjoy being the 3rd best team

RICHARD FOSTER

PREMIER LEAGUE NUGGETS

ONE LEAGUE, 27 SEASONS, 49 CLUBS:
A WORLD OF FACTS & FIGURES

OCKLEY BOOKS
.com

FOREWORD
BY MARTIN TYLER

Attention to detail was one of the first lessons I was taught when I started out in television many moons ago. Richard Foster has a rare gift in that respect and Premier League Nuggets is another example of his ability to share those details in an engrossing and entertaining way.

The book is all encompassing but also full of the titbits of trivia that we football fans absolutely adore. It is a great way to test out the memory of your mates. That the number of clubs which have appeared in the Premier League is 49 is a typical statistic which draws you in. Which team will round it up – and give the author a perfect excuse for a re-print?

I have been very fortunate to commentate on Premier League matches for Sky Sports since the League's inception in 1992. I have always maintained that English football is the most watchable in the world and the universal viewing figures support that belief. As a broadcaster every game is an adventure. My mantra is always to look forward . There is not too much time to look back. But Premier League Nuggets is an extremely handy, very entertaining and totally reliable reference point to have by my side.

INTRODUCTION

Going to Selhurst Park for the opening day of the Premier League season did not feel too different to the hundreds of games that I had already attended since my first foray into live football back in 1969. The fact that it was a top flight game was a bonus as for most of the intervening 23 years Palace had been loitering without much intent in the Second Division for eleven pretty inglorious seasons, with a brief dip into the Third Division for a dose of harsh reality, interspersed by nine seasons in the First Division to give an all too brief glimpse of life among the sunnier uplands. Much of the football was pretty poor and traipsing up and down the country following the likes of Trevor Aylott and John Lacy was possibly good for the soul but did not do much for one's self respect. The beautiful game seemed an alien and distant concept throughout most of this period.

So on Saturday the 15th of August 1992 it was Blackburn at home, a team that Palace had beaten a few years before in a dramatic Play-Off Final to secure the club's latest tilt at trying to establish themselves in the upper echelons of league football. Things had gone well since, with a first ever FA Cup Final appearance in 1990, followed by the club's highest ever position of 3rd in 1991, behind Liverpool and the champions Arsenal. Then there was a solid, respectable 10th position in 1992, the last season before the advent of the Premier League. Blackburn themselves had just been promoted via the Play-Offs so were back in the big time for the first time since England had lifted the World Cup. And so both clubs were part of the Whole New Ball Game, which was how the original Premier League announced itself in August 1992 to an unsuspecting audience.

As ever with the opening day of any season the tingling mixture of optimism and anticipation accompanied by a warm, sunny day had the juices flowing for what lay ahead. The match did not disappoint as it was a cracking encounter, with the fortunes swaying to and fro before the satisfaction of Simon Osborn's 90th minute equaliser nullified the disappointment of losing an early lead. The quality of the goals added to the excitement of the 3-3 draw with the second Palace goal a particular highlight as the ball was expertly lobbed into the net from the edge of the penalty area. It was a combination of fine judgment, excellent vision and was beautifully executed. The man responsible was destined to go far in the sport and indeed it was appropriate that Gareth Southgate, the future England manager, should score on the opening day of the Premier League.

But that accomplished strike was overshadowed by two equally good goals for the visitors from their new centre forward who had just arrived from Southampton for just over £3.5m, a transfer record at the time. Step forward Alan Shearer. His first Rovers goal was similar to Southgate's, as he brought the ball down with his chest before nonchalantly lobbing Nigel Martyn from the edge of the box. His second was even better as he picked the ball up near the left touchline, forged inside before unleashing a measured effort inside the far post. Little did we know then that those two fine goals were the precursor to another 258 that the Premier League's record goalscorer would accumulate over the next fourteen seasons but we had seen an early glimpse of his undoubted prowess.

So it proved to be quite an auspicious start to Premier League life at Selhurst although there were plenty of disappointments in the offing, not least the sorry statistic that Palace's staying power was not the most robust in managing to last only one season in their first four spells in the Premier League era. Starting with the trauma of that first season when a healthy total of 49 points was somehow not enough to ward off relegation. Having established the record number of points for a relegated club in the very first season, Palace followed it up with the second highest points total to be relegated in 1994/95 with 45. These two totals for a relegated club are now pretty much unassailable in a 20-club division so Palace's place in the record books, even if it is for less than joyful reasons, is pretty much assured.

Even taking into account the reduction to 38 games, averaging 1.16 points per game would yield 44 points and no team since 1994/95 has ever accrued that many points and gone down, West Ham came closest with 42 in 2002/03. If you are going to set a record for glorious failure you might as well make it one that will last. You can tell that I am neither bitter nor resentful over those relegations, not one little bit.

There is a whole gamut of such facts and figures in this book for every club that has graced, or sometimes disgraced the Premier League with dismal defeats rubbing shoulders with valiant victories and Invincibles cheek by jowl with incompetents. Each of the 49 clubs that have taken their bow in the Premier League are featured. I do feel just a tad conflicted in writing this book as I and many others have often railed against those who consider that 1992 represents year zero. The glossing over of more than 100 years of league football that preceded the advent of the Premier League borders on the sacrilegious.

As the Premier League has only been in existence since 1992 and with over a century of league football beforehand, the Premier League can be viewed as the insolent pup in the grand scheme of things and there are those who have a blind spot covering anything before 1992, which is clearly wrong and misguided. There is a vociferously supported argument that all that is rotten with modern football should be laid at the door of the Premier League as its arrival triggered a massive change in the fortunes of top-flight clubs. As the television money started to flow into the clubs' coffers courtesy of Sky's determination to build a subscriber base many have argued that this was the beginning of the end and that football's soul has been steadily eroded since.

The following quote sums up the attitude of those who could be termed as contrarians. "Nearly everything possible had been done to spoil the game: the heavy financial interest; the absurd transfer and player-selling system; the absurd publicity given to every feature of the press; the monstrous partisanships of the crowds." This could have been uttered by any of those who find the most recent changes in the way the game is run, both distasteful and destructive of the very spirit of the game. In fact this expression of disdain was from that curmudgeonly Yorkshireman JB Priestley back in 1933. Plus ça change. Priestley died in August 1984 but his words are still very much alive and kicking today,

There are indeed many aspects of the game today that are unwelcome, including the inconvenience suffered by supporters at the hands of the television schedulers, the anodyne atmosphere at many grounds and the chasm that has opened up between the big clubs and their lesser rivals. By becoming the principal paymaster, broadcasters have wielded too much influence and some checks and balances are needed. Having said that, great strides have been made, with the television coverage itself having advanced in leaps and bounds, the pace of the game has increased as have the levels of skill and the athleticism, assisted by the improvement in the quality of the pitches and impressive stadia. All these factors have led to the Premier League becoming the most watched and watchable league in the world.

I do have sympathy with the argument that the new stadia have rather sucked the life out of the atmosphere and it is certainly true that some of the passion has been eroded with the steady gentrification of football at the top level. But the eventual opening of the Tottenham Hotspur stadium in April 2019 hinted that building a new ground does not necessarily lead to the eradication of the noise and colour that has marked out English football. Furthermore, it cannot be denied that the wealth of the Premier League and its clubs has attracted some of the greatest football talent from around the world so we have been blessed with a host of stars, from Aguero to Zola and a whole lot in between, which cannot be sniffed at even by the sniffiest critics.

The Premier League is often portrayed as the great pariah of the game and while the technical quality may not match some of the other European leagues there is no denying its global popularity. Some will scoff at this and criticise the relentless pursuit of money and rapaciousness but as somebody who witnessed much of what went on in the previous two decades I have enjoyed both periods for different reasons. Charles Dickens' words at the start of A Tale of Two Cities are strangely appropriate when describing the birth of the Premier League: "It was the best of times, it was the worst of times, it was the age of wisdom, it was the age of foolishness, it was the epoch of belief, it was the epoch of incredulity, it was the season of Light, it was the season of Darkness, it was the spring of hope, it was the autumn of despair." Many supporters will recognise seasons of Darkness and the autumn of despair, while the lucky few will have experienced seasons of Light and the odd spring of hope. The full range is encapsulated here.

Much has been written about the Premier League, including a rash of books to celebrate the 25th anniversary back in 2017 so this book is coming from another perspective. In Premier League Nuggets I have aimed to elicit some of the more unusual and idiosyncratic facts and statistics rather than attempt to write a comprehensive history although there is a standard set of facts and figures for each club. There is a natural bias towards more recent records as they are freshest in the memory and many have not been covered by the aforementioned 25th anniversary titles. Also it is worth reflecting on the last few years, which have generated some extraordinary achievements and underlined the polarisation of the top tier of English football, such as Manchester City's century of points in 2017/18, the gripping title race of the following season, which also featured Tottenham's draw aversion as well as some epic failures such as Fulham's porous defence and Huddersfield's allergy to goal scoring at home. That the runners-up in 2018/19 Liverpool secured more points than all but one of the previous winners while for the first time two clubs had been relegated by early April 2019 points to the growing disparity between top and bottom. Mind the Gap.

Despite this growing inequality and indeed partly inspired by it, I was keen to show that every single one of the 49 clubs have made their own mark irrespective of their size, their stature and the length of their tenure. Even though they only lasted one season Blackpool and Barnsley had their moments and for the most part, enjoyed their season in the sun and have as much right to be featured as the behemoths of the two Manchester clubs, Chelsea and Arsenal, who between them have gobbled up 25 of the 27 titles available and I hope I have struck the right balance in the coverage of each club.

Writing a book is often a lonely task and I have been lucky enough to enlist the help of some very supportive people. I have had the good fortune of meeting Martin Tyler as well as interviewing him a few times. He has always been extremely generous with his time and has always shown his uncomplicated love for the game without a hint of superiority. I was therefore delighted when he agreed to write the foreword for this book. He is indisputably the doyen of football commentary in this country, as illustrated by the fact that he has been voted the Football Supporters Federation Commentator of the Year for six consecutive years up to 2018. His encyclopedic knowledge allied with his inimitable style and perfect delivery have rightly made him the voice of the Premier League. Tyler commentated on the very first live Sky Sports game when Nottingham Forest beat Liverpool on Sunday the 16th of August 1992 and since then I would estimate he has racked up in the region of a thousand live matches up to and including the 2018/19 season. There was nobody else I would have chosen to write this foreword, and I am eternally grateful to Martin for his kind words.

I am also indebted to the fans, or at least observers, who contributed on their respective clubs as this forms an important aspect of this book. Ultimately the fans are the lifeblood of the game, who often get a raw deal from the Premier League in its thirst for commercial growth and so their perspective is important. As Jock Stein said all those years ago "Without fans who pay at the turnstile, football is nothing." There is always a slight risk in asking for external contributors especially when there is no financial remuneration but every single one of them has been more than willing to write their pieces, which made the lives of my publisher and myself appreciably easier. We could not have done it without you, so many thanks to the magnificent club contributors. There are a handful of exceptions including Blackpool, Coventry and Newcastle, whose fans are united in their opposition to the dastardly owners they have had to suffer. We felt it was best to allow them to grieve privately. As a Palace fan I may at some points during the book, veer into partiality towards the gods of SE25 so you will have to forgive me for that indulgence and this is where having a Brighton fan as not only the publisher but also as the editor brings its advantages.

I hope you find enough of interest and the odd surprise amongst these nuggets and I am grateful to Simon Gleave, Head of Analysis, Sports at Gracenote, who has provided some of the more well-hidden and obscure facts and figures within these pages. Also his colleagues Grant Fisken and Ernst Wark (no relation to John) were masterful at mining out some of the more obscure and arcane facts from the coalface. Also a quick mention of my other fact checker, Tristram Foster. Thanks, son.

The Premier League is clearly not the be-all and end-all of English football as there is plenty of life in the EFL and beyond, which provides exciting, dynamic and gloriously unpredictable football on a regular basis. By coincidence John Nicholson, a regular contributor to the excellent Football 365 site has had a book published recently, in which he takes up the cudgels on some of the less beneficial effects of the Premier League. I am sure "Can We Have Our Football Back?" will be an entertaining read and may well be the Yin to this book's Yang. There is certainly room for a healthy debate over the advantages and disadvantages without needing to fall out.

The Premier League has given us some magical moments and some startling statistics over the last quarter of a century or so and plenty of them are collected here. Naturally, I will have missed a fair few as the odd one will have slipped through the net and I would be delighted to hear from anybody who has any of their own Premier League Nuggets that are not featured here but you feel are worthy of inclusion. They might well end up either in the sequel to this book or at the very least provoke some debate or discussion in the future via the maelstrom that is social media.

Finally, I finished writing this book in June so the line has been drawn at the end of the 2018/19 season for any records, facts or statistics, some of which will undoubtedly be broken in the forthcoming season.

Thanks and happy reading.

Richard

RICHARD FOSTER

PREMIER LEAGUE NUGGETS

ONE LEAGUE, 27 SEASONS, 49 CLUBS:
A WORLD OF FACTS & FIGURES

All statistics and records supplied by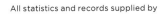

ARSENAL STATS

NUMBER OF SEASONS:

27

1992/93-2018/19

NUMBER OF MATCHES:

1,038

Wins 565 (Home 337 Away 228)
Draws 260 (Home 119 Away 141)
Losses 213 (Home 63 Away 150)

[Win ratio 54%]

Goals F 1,845
(Home 1,059 Away 786)

Goals A 1,013
(Home 427 Away 586)

Goal Difference: +832

TOTAL POINTS

1,955

Home 1,130: 58%; Away 825: 42%
Av per season: 72

BEST POSITION:

1st (3)

Champions
1997/98, 2001/02, 2003/04

WORST POSITION:

12th

(1994/95)

BIGGEST WIN:

7-0

v Everton (11th May 2005)
v Middlesbrough (14th Jan 2006)

BIGGEST LOSS:

8-2

v Manchester United
(28th Aug 2011)

LONGEST UNBEATEN RUN:

49 matches

(23rd Mar, 2003 - 16th Oct, 2004)

LONGEST WITHOUT A WIN:

8 matches

(21st Nov, 1992 - 9th Jan, 1993)

ALL TIME RANKING

2nd

MOST GOALS SCORED IN A SEASON:

87

2004/05

FEWEST GOALS SCORED IN A SEASON:

40

1992/93

FEWEST GOALS CONCEDED IN A SEASON:

17

1998/99

MOST GOALS CONCEDED IN A SEASON:

51 (2)

2017/18 & 2018/19

TOP GOALSCORER:

175

Thierry Henry

MOST APPEARANCES:

333

Ray Parlour

OWN GOALS:

41

RED CARDS:

88

LOWEST ATTENDANCE:

18,253

v Wimbledon
(10th Feb, 1993)

HIGHEST ATTENDANCE:

60,161

v Manchester United
(3rd Nov, 2007)

ARSENAL NUGGETS

DID YOU KNOW?

In the 75th minute of Arsenal's game at White Hart Lane on May 5th, 1999, Nwankwo Kanu replaced Dennis Bergkamp and ten minutes later the Nigerian scored Arsenal's third to seal a 3-1 win. Beyond an impressive win over Tottenham there was added significance behind the substitution. This was the first of the most common substitution made in Premier League history as over the next five years it happened 27 times. To round things off nicely Kanu scored the winning goal in Bergkamp's testimonial in 2006 which officially opened the Emirates Stadium.

FIRST PREMIER LEAGUE MATCH: 15TH AUGUST, 1992
ARSENAL 2 (BOULD, CAMPBELL)
NORWICH CITY 4 (ROBINS 2, PHILLIPS, FOX)

HIGHBURY 24,030

David Seaman, Nigel Winterburn, Lee Dixon, Steve Bould, Tony Adams, John Jensen, Paul Merson (Ian Wright), David Hillier, Anders Limpar, Alan Smith, Kevin Campbell, Manager: George Graham

The 2019/20 season will be Arsenal's 100th consecutive season in the top flight, which is by some way the longest spell (Everton are next with 66). They have never really been threatened by the spectre of relegation and their 12th position in 1994/95 was their only foray into the lower half of the table. Manchester United are the only club to have not finished lower than 10th in Premier League history.

Arsene Wenger's arrival in 1996 has been rightly hailed as the watershed moment, which propelled Arsenal to 20 consecutive top four finishes. Le Professeur's influence was felt throughout the club and was primarily responsible for a Gallic invasion with the Gunners fielding 28 of his fellow countrymen, many of whom had a massive bearing on their success, such as Patrick Vieira, Emmanuel Petit and Robert Pires. This is the highest number of non-British players from a single nation. The Foreign Legion were in town.

For a club that became the only credible challenger to Alex Ferguson's Manchester United over the first dozen years, Arsenal's opening day record started off pretty dismally. They lost their first two at home - conceding four to Norwich in the last 20 minutes on the very first day of Premier League action and then allowing Coventry City's Micky Quinn to become the first player to notch a hat-trick on the opening day in the space of just over half an hour on the first day of the 1993/94 season. Since then 28 hat-tricks have been scored in Arsenal home games and Quinn's remains the only one scored by an opposition player. Arsenal can lay claim to the best final day record of recent times, winning their last eight in succession and they have not lost a game on the last day since 2005 when they succumbed in the very last minute to Emile Heskey's winner for Birmingham.

The Invincibles' unique achievement in 2003/04 has still not been emulated and has been rightly lauded as it will probably remain the only unbeaten season for the foreseeable future. During that momentous season they were behind in only nine games and for an aggregated total of just 223 minutes, the equivalent of less than two and a half matches. The longest spell they were behind in any game was 64 minutes at home to their North London neighbours, Tottenham after Darren Anderton scored in the fourth minute and Robert Pires did not equalise until the 68th. At least Spurs' fans could take that as the most infinitesimal crumb of comfort available in a season of torture and torment.

Only against Liverpool at home were they in arrears more than once after Sami Hyypia's opening goal in the fifth minute was cancelled out by Thierry Henry and then after Michael Owen put the visitors back in front, Pires brought them level seven minutes later before Arsenal went on to win 4-2. On the back of that season Arsenal hold the record unbeaten streak of 49 matches, which lasted for over 18 months between March 2003 and October 2004. It was apposite that the last game of Arsenal's unbeaten run was a comfortable win over Aston Villa at Highbury as the original Invincibles of Preston's last game was a 2-0 victory over none other than Aston Villa on 9 February 1889 with England international striker, Fred Dewhurst scoring both goals. Fast-forward 115 years and it was a French international, Robert Pires, who scored two of Arsenal's goals in their 3-1 win on 16 October 2004.

But for Tottenham fans and assorted nitpickers there will be that Achilles heel of too many draws, a dozen of them amounting to over 30% of their matches. Only Leicester have drawn that many matches and won the Premier League title. Their closest encounter with defeat was "The Battle of Old Trafford", as the match when Ruud van Nistelrooy and Martin Keown had a difference of opinion has been dubbed.

KEOWN KICKS OFF

SUNDAY 21 SEPTEMBER 2003

MANCHESTER UNITED 0 (0) **ARSENAL 0** (0)

OLD TRAFFORD - (67,639)

There are goalless draws and goalless draws and this one was most certainly on the more entertaining and significant end of the scale. There was already a fairly long charge sheet of fiery, feisty incidents from the previous decade when these two slugged it out for Premier League supremacy and certainly neither party held back when it came to standing up and being counted. The ill feeling between the clubs dated back to about the time Ferguson took over at Old Trafford in 1986 with the 21-man brawl of 1990 being probably the epitome of this particular brand of malevolence, points deductions and fines flying around along with the odd haymaker.

More recently, the previous fixture in April 2003 was a game that featured a couple of flying elbows - one from Bergkamp that floored Mikael Silvestre went unpunished, and one from Sol Campbell that took out Ole Gunner Solksjaer that did end up with a red card. Naturally there was a yellow for Roy Keane when he scythed down Freddie Ljungberg. There were also four goals shared between the two sides, but they were a sideshow.

So it was, with the sort of baggage that sets off alarm bells at airport check-in desks, that this match imbued with a sense of dark foreboding that this was not going to be a quiet Sunday afternoon. The first yellow arrived halfway through the first half as Roy Keane established himself in the match but things only really got interesting as the second half unfolded. Patrick Vieira collected two bookings in the space of three minutes with the second sparking some serious handbags at dawn as Arsenal players took exception to Ruud van Nistelrooy's response to being kicked by Vieira.

A smattering of yellow cards followed but the final act of this battle/ match was played out after van Nistelrooy missed this third successive penalty by smashing his added-time spot kick against the crossbar. As the ball rebounded into play, the sheer relief of not conceding a late winner got too much for a baying Martin Keown, who jumped into the Dutchman's face and did not hold back with his candid assessment of natural justice.

That was one of four goalless draws for the Gunners in that season. Arsenal won 26 matches and in the 15 seasons since only twice have the champions won fewer than 26 matches—Manchester United in 2010/11 and Leicester in 2015/16—12 title winners have won more games as did Liverpool in 2018/19 who won four more but still finished 2nd.

As such the sense of achievement for Arsenal has been a little overshadowed by the feats of some other clubs in subsequent seasons. Arsenal's record points tally of 90 for a 38-game season was immediately beaten by Jose Mourinho's Chelsea which accrued 95 in 2004/05 and 91 in 2005/06. It was also surpassed by Antonio Conte's Chelsea in 2016/17 (93 points), as well as by Pep Guardiola's centurions in 2017/18 and by both Manchester City and Liverpool in 2018/19. The Invincibles' goal difference of +47 is not even in the top 20 and they even achieved a better goal difference of +51 the following season when finishing second.

Despite the recent paucity of European success Arsenal did become the first Premier League club to win European silverware when they beat Parma in the 1994 Cup Winners Cup in Copenhagen. They also contested the following year's final but lost out to Real Zaragoza and Nayim's 120th minute winner from the halfway line, as the popular ditty of the day reminded us on countless occasions.

One of the fundamental changes that Wenger brought to English football was the introduction of European training methods as well as attracting the cream of European players and those from further afield. And so almost inevitably on 14 February 2005 Arsenal became the first club to pick an all-foreign 16-man squad when they beat Crystal Palace 5-1 at Highbury. The 14 players used consisted of six Frenchmen, two Dutchmen, two Spaniards, and single representatives from Brazil, Cameroon, Cote d'Ivoire and Germany.

Their reputation for functional football pre-Wenger was supported by the fact that they had only six different scorers in a 42-game season. In the 1993/94 season a total of 53 goals were shared between Ian Wright (23), Kevin Campbell (14), Paul Merson (7), Alan Smith (3), Ray Parlour (2), Steve Bould (1) and three own-goals. Averaging just over 1.25 goals per game they finished fourth while notching seven of their most favoured wins; 1-0 to the Arsenal no less. In the last two seasons, 2017/18 and 2018/19, Arsenal have conceded the same number of goals (51), which is the equal highest number over their 27 seasons. By contrast in 1998/99 they let in a mere 17, one of the lowest in Premier League history (see Chelsea Footnote).

ONE HIT WONDER

David Bentley spent five seasons at Arsenal before moving to Blackburn initially on loan and famously scored a hat-trick for Rovers against Manchester United in his first match after signing permanently. Not many Arsenal fans will remember his fleeting appearance for The Gunners, when he started in a 1-1 draw with Portsmouth and was substituted just after the hour towards the end of the Invincibles season. But they will almost certainly be able to recall one of his first games for Tottenham when he scored one of the more outrageous goals to light up the North London Derby in October 2008, hitting a dipping volley from around 40 yards which left a flailing Manuel Almunia in a sorry heap at a stunned Emirates. Bentley was playing in his first North London derby, which made it all the sweeter and the fact that it was the opening goal of a memorable 4-4 draw exacerbated his joy. That Bentley only scored one other goal for Spurs makes this ridiculous strike stand out even more.

Disillusioned by the sport Bentley retired from football at the age of 29, investing in a restaurant business in Spain and in Essex.

FOOTNOTE

Arsenal's 107 goals against Everton is the most
by a club against another team.

FIXTURES	GOALS	PLAYED
Arsenal v Everton	107	54
Man United v Everton	100	54
Liverpool v Newcastle	98	48
Chelsea v Tottenham	98	54
Man United v Newcastle	97	48

A VIEW FROM THE STANDS

Adrian Clarke, talkSPORT

As one of the select clubs that is an ever-present throughout Premier League history your club has enjoyed prolonged success so what is your favourite moment from the last 27 years?

In early June 1995 a meeting held almost 600 miles away from the pristine Marble Halls of Highbury, changed the course of Arsenal's history forever.

It was a summit requested by Dutch football agent Rob Jansen, who travelled to northern Italy armed with an ultimatum for Inter Milan's new president Massimo Moratti.

His client was 26-year-old Dennis Bergkamp.

A world-class talent on the precipice of his peak, 'The Iceman' had somehow become an isolated, disconsolate and under-performing figure at the San Siro.

And the playmaker's message to the Inter chief was a simple one... Sack Ottavio Bianchi, the head coach he despised, and rebuild the side with a batch of new players—or sell him.

Moratti, not a man to be pushed around, took up the latter option and within weeks the new Gunners boss Bruce Rioch was stood alongside his superstar signing posing for pitch-side photographs. It was a £7.5m acquisition that transformed Arsenal Football Club.

I was there as a player at the time, and inside the dressing room there was a feeling of genuine euphoria. Training and playing alongside such a gifted No.10 was an unashamed pleasure, and we all felt the same way.

Raising the bar with his velvet touch, consummate skill and pitch perfect technique; all of the pros at Arsenal knew they needed to up their game. And standards quickly rose.

Tripling their own transfer record and in turn smashing George Graham's notoriously tight wage structure with a £25,000 a week contract that had made Bergkamp British football's top earner, the club had also instantly propelled itself into the big league.

This was a signing that was dripping with ambition. Overnight the team's style and image would immediately change. Out went the 'boring boring Arsenal' tag, and in came a swashbuckling brand of attacking football that was taken up several levels 15 months later when Arsene Wenger's revolution began.

Enticed by this, and the prospect of being a teammate of the gifted Netherlands international, a flurry of top signings soon piled through the door and the rest, as they say, is history.

Wenger's arrival as manager in October 1996 was of course a monumentally important sliding doors moment for the club. But it was the signing of Dennis Bergkamp that had already set them on the path to greater glory.

The next ten years would be the most successful in Arsenal's history.

ASTON VILLA STATS

NUMBER OF SEASONS:

24

1992/93-2015/16

NUMBER OF MATCHES:

924

Wins 316 (188 Home, 128 Away)
Draws 275 (139 Home, 136 Away)
Losses 333 (135 Home, 198 Away)

[Win ratio 34%]

Goals F 1,117
(604 Home, 513 Away)

Goals A 1,186
(491 Home, 695 Away)

Goal Difference: -69

TOTAL POINTS

1,223

(Home 703: 57%; Away 520: 43%)
Av per season: - 51

BEST POSITION:

2nd

1992/93 (RUNNERS-UP)

WORST POSITION:

20th

2015/16 (RELEGATED)

BIGGEST WIN:

7-1

v Wimbledon
(11th Feb, 1995)

BIGGEST LOSS:

8-0

v Chelsea
(22nd Dec, 2012)

LONGEST UNBEATEN RUN:

14 matches

(2nd May, 1998-14th Nov, 1998)

LONGEST WITHOUT A WIN:

19 matches

(14th Aug, 2015-2nd Jan, 2016)

ALL TIME RANKING

9th

MOST GOALS SCORED IN A SEASON:

71

2007/08

FEWEST GOALS SCORED IN A SEASON:

27

2015/16

FEWEST GOALS CONCEDED IN A SEASON:

34

1996/97

MOST GOALS CONCEDED IN A SEASON:

76

2015/16

TOP GOALSCORER:

74

Gabriel Abgonlahor

MOST APPEARANCES:

365

Gareth Barry

OWN GOALS:

45

RED CARDS:

56

LOWEST ATTENDANCE:

16,180

v Southampton
(24th November, 1993)

HIGHEST ATTENDANCE:

45,347

v Liverpool
(7th May, 1994)

All statistics and records supplied by

ASTON VILLA

FIRST PREMIER LEAGUE MATCH: 15TH AUGUST, 1992
IPSWICH TOWN 1 (JOHNSON)
ASTON VILLA 1 (ATKINSON)

PORTMAN ROAD 16,977

Nigel Spink, Earl Barrett, Steve Staunton, Shaun Teale, Paul McGrath, Kevin Richardson (Cyrille Regis), Tony Daley, Garry Parker, Ray Houghton, Dalian Atkinson, Steve Froggatt, Manager: Ron Atkinson

Villa are one of only three clubs to be both founding members of the Football League and the Premier League, alongside Blackburn Rovers and Everton. Following their Play-off final win over Derby, Villa will be back in the Premier League in 2019/20 after a three-season absence. However, they have still spent 24 seasons in the Premier League, more than any other Midlands club. Leicester are the closest but are quite a way behind, having completed 13 by the end of 2018/19. They are just two seasons short of reaching 1,000 matches and having secured promotion under Dean Smith they are in touching distance of that magical landmark. If they do not get relegated straight away, they would be the seventh club to achieve that feat.

They will be pleased that Sheffield United gained automatic promotion as they are the club against whom they have the best record, with five wins and a draw out of six, collecting 16 points out of a possible 18. The Villans will also be happy that Swansea are still in the Championship as they have only won one game against the Swans out of eight, picking up just six points from a possible 24.

Their unbroken run from the very first season came to a juddering halt as their last season in the Premier League was little short of a disaster. Having been one of seven ever-present clubs over the first 23 years of the Premier League Villa hit the buffers in 2015/16. Although they hold the record for the longest completed spell of any club to subsequently be relegated, their end was an inglorious stain on their longevity. They had been in steady decline since their 9th position in 2010/11, which was their fifth consecutive season in the top 10. In the four seasons between 2011/12 and 2014/15 they finished 16th twice, 15th and 17th. The writing had been on the wall for a while but nobody anticipated such a dramatic fall from grace.

Not only did they suffer relegation for the first time from the Premier League they only managed to win a paltry three matches, and with Tim Sherwood, Kevin McDonald, Remi Garde and Eric Black in charge at various points they had more managers than victories. There was no hint of what was to come when they won the opening game of the season away to Bournemouth but that proved to be a false dawn and they were soon at the wrong end of the table and failed to mount any recovery. They dropped into the relegation zone in late September and did not poke their head above the parapet again. They were 20th by the end of October and never got off the canvas for the remainder of the season, ending up 22 points short of survival.

They scored a measly 27 goals and never scored more than two in a single match. After that first victory on 8th August they had to wait over five months until 12th January to record their next win, against Crystal Palace. Then after winning their third game, against Norwich, on the 6th February they lost their next match 6-0 at home to Liverpool. That was their biggest Premier League defeat at Villa Park and it started a run of 13 games until the end of the season in which they picked up a single, solitary point. Their final total of 17 points is the third lowest in Premier League history.

This is all a very long way from the inaugural season when Ron Atkinson's team were the only credible challengers to Manchester United and took four points off them. The team's twin spearhead of Dean Saunders and the late Dalian Atkinson were as good as any front line. Atkinson not only scored Villa's first Premier League goal but also arguably their best ever in that first season against Wimbledon. The combination of his muscular run, brushing off several defenders having picked up the ball in his own half, with the delightfully judged delicate chip over the keeper was rightly voted the Premier League's first Goal of the Season in 1992/93.

Significantly Atkinson was injured at the wrong time as his namesake Ron pointed out: "And then, just before Christmas, Dalian got injured, he couldn't come back until Easter and we lost a bit of momentum." Indeed Villa suffered their heaviest defeat of the season in the next match on Boxing Day at Coventry and lost a couple more before Atkinson's return and those dropped points proved to be decisive in the end as United overhauled them with comparative ease.

In that inaugural season Villa were a single point behind the leaders with four games to go however they ran out of steam at the end of the campaign, losing their last three games including a defeat against Oldham that was as damaging as it was surprising. This limp finish effectively handed the trophy to Ferguson's men, who ended up with a comfortable ten-point margin, the fourth highest of their 13 Premier League titles, but it could and probably should have been a great deal closer but for Villa's late collapse. They never got that close again but they can claim to be the most consistent side in Premier League history. In their 924 matches they have won 34%, drawn 30% and lost 36% - the divergence of just 6% is the smallest of any club.

In July 2001 Peter Schmeichel moved to Villa Park having spent a couple of years in Portugal following his successful time at Old Trafford. His spell at Villa was marked by him becoming the first goalkeeper to score in a Premier League match on 20 October away at Goodison Park. Four other keepers have followed in Schmeichel's large footsteps (see Footnote below). Of those five keepers there is only one Englishman, Paul Robinson who scored for Tottenham and he is also the only scorer-keeper to finish on the winning side.

There is a strong connection between Villa and the number six. Along with Newcastle, Villa have finished in the top six on nine occasions, including finishing sixth six times, and on three consecutive occasions between 2007/08 and 2009/10. Up to the 2017/18 season this was the sixth highest of any club and as many times as Manchester City had achieved over that period. In 2011/12 they only recorded seven victories but managed to survive whereas Bolton who were relegated, won ten times. Villa notched 17 draws, a record number for a 20-team season alongside Sunderland in 2014/15, who also survived after only winning seven games, as did Newcastle in 2003/04 and Villa again in 2006/07.

Gareth Barry, who began his career at Villa, holds the record for number of appearances for the Villans with 365 between 1997/98 and

2008/09, a rather apposite number for such an evergreen player—one for each day of the year. Of course Barry also holds the record for the most appearances in the Premier League overall with 653. None of those 365 appearances for Villa were as a substitute and the only season in which he was an ever present for Villa was his last. After leaving Villa he clocked up over 100 appearances for both Manchester City and Everton before that one last hurrah at West Brom in 2017/18, which ended rather sadly in the only relegation of his career. A valiant but vanquished Villan.

ONE HIT WONDER

At the opposite end of the spectrum to Barry's widely lauded achievement is Jonathan Bewers who was a graduate of the Football School of Excellence at Lilleshall. He spent five years at Villa between 1999/2000 and 2003/04 but even the most diehard Villa fans would struggle to remember him. Bewers managed to make it on to the pitch just once during his time there, as a substitute in the 89th minute of a 4-2 win at White Hart Lane when he replaced Mark Delaney who had himself been a half-time substitute.

Bewers eventually left for Notts County in 2004 after that one fleeting appearance back in 2000.

FOOTNOTE

THE FIVE GOALKEEPERS WHO HAVE SCORED IN THE PREMIER LEAGUE

Peter Schmeichel: Everton 3 Aston Villa 2	20 Oct 2001
Brad Friedel: Charlton Athletic 3 Blackburn 2	22 Feb 2004
Paul Robinson: Tottenham Hotspur 3 Watford 1	18 Mar 2007
Tim Howard: Everton 1 Bolton Wanderers 2	6 Jan 2012
Asmir Begovic: Stoke City 1 Southampton 1	2 Nov 2013

A VIEW FROM THE STANDS

Chris Nee

What was your club's 'Sliding Doors' moment, that seemingly inconsequential action, which actually became a turning point in their fortunes, for either good or bad?

In the Premier League's first season, 1992/93, Aston Villa fell short of Manchester United not because of an irretrievable difference in quality, but a collapse at the most inopportune time.

Over the winter Ron Atkinson's Villa side won eight of their ten Premier League games. Two draws followed, and then came the week that could, maybe should, have set them up for a real go at the championship.

Villa's home win over Sheffield Wednesday is remembered for an extraordinary team goal tapped in by Dwight Yorke at a packed Villa Park. Four days later Villa played Norwich City, themselves with plenty to play for at the top end of the table. Garry Parker should have put Villa ahead but it was Norwich's John Polston who settled the game, stealing in to rifle home a rebound from a late corner.

The loss didn't immediately knock Villa off course. But, with Manchester United flying above them courtesy of a run of four wins—one of them a controversial late victory against Wednesday that many Villa supporters would identify as the day the title race was lost—Villa soon faltered. United just kept on winning.

Villa never again got a chance like it. Had they beaten Norwich the shape of the run-in might have been different. United reaped the benefits of winning the new league. Villa faded into mediocrity.

BARNSLEY STATS

NUMBER OF SEASONS:

1

1997/98

NUMBER OF MATCHES:

38

10 Wins (7 Home 3 Away)
5 Draws (4 Home 1 Away) 23
Losses (8 Home 15 Away)

[Win ratio 26%]

Goals F 37
(25 Home 12 Away)

Goals A 82
(35 Home 47 Away)

Goal Difference: -45

TOTAL POINTS

35

(25 Home: 71%;10 Away: 29%)
Av per season: 35

BEST POSITION:

19th

RELEGATED

WORST POSITION:

19th

RELEGATED

BIGGEST WIN:

2-0

v Coventry City
(Oct 20th, 1997)

BIGGEST LOSS:

7-0

v Manchester United
(Oct 25th, 1997)

LONGEST UNBEATEN RUN:

3 matches

(28th Feb, 1998-4th Mar, 1998)

LONGEST WITHOUT A WIN:

6 matches

(30th Aug, 1997-4th Oct, 1997)

ALL TIME RANKING

48th

MOST GOALS SCORED IN A SEASON:

37

(1997/98)

FEWEST GOALS SCORED IN A SEASON:

37

(1997/98)

FEWEST GOALS CONCEDED IN A SEASON:

82

1997/98

MOST GOALS CONCEDED IN A SEASON:

82

1997/98

TOP GOALSCORER:

10

Neil Redfearn

MOST APPEARANCES:

37

Neil Redfearn

OWN GOALS:

1

RED CARDS:

4

LOWEST ATTENDANCE:

17,172

v Wimbledon
(28th Feb, 1998)

HIGHEST ATTENDANCE:

18,694

v Newcastle (13th Dec, 1997)
v Manchester United (10th May, 1998)

All statistics and records supplied by  gracenote.
A NIELSEN COMPANY

BARNSLEY

FIRST PREMIER LEAGUE MATCH: 9TH AUGUST, 1997
BARNSLEY 1 (REDFEARN)
WEST HAM 2 (HARTSON, LAMPARD)

OAKWELL 18,667

David Watson, Nicky Eaden, Darren Barnard, Peter Shirtliff (Clint Marcelle), Adie Moses, Arjan De Zeeuw, John Hendrie, Neil Redfearn, Paul Wilkinson (Georgi Hristov), Eric Tinkler, Martin Bullock (Andy Liddell), Manager: Danny Wilson

Barnsley's one and only season in the top flight ended in relegation as they finished 19th, five points below safety. They are one of only three clubs, alongside Blackpool and Swindon Town, who have only been in the Premier League for a single season. Barnsley are one of only nine clubs who have spent more seasons in the Premier League than in the top flight in the pre-Premier League era. The others are Bournemouth, Crystal Palace, Hull, Reading, Swansea, Swindon, Wigan and Wimbledon.

In conceding 82 goals they share the second worst record for a 38-game season with Burnley in 2009/10 and Wolves in 2011/12. Only the woeful Derby County in 2007/08 have let in more—89. (Swindon and Ipswich conceded 100 and 92 goals respectively but in 42-game seasons.) Of the ten matches Barnsley won, nine were by a single goal and their only victory by two goals was against Coventry City, which rather bizarrely came just five days before their heaviest defeat, a 7-0 thumping at Old Trafford. Barnsley did complete one double, over Crystal Palace beating them 1-0 both times and they did also beat Palace's tenants Wimbledon once. However they didn't generally fare well against London clubs, going pointless against Arsenal, Chelsea and West Ham, whom they faced in their opening match. Their aggregate score against those three clubs does not make for pretty reading: 1-21.

Barnsley drew only five of their 38 matches, giving them a ratio of 13%, which is among the lowest of any team. The lowest number of draws is Spurs in 2018/19 with just two and then Chelsea in 1997/98 and 2016/17 with three. Alongside Swindon in 1993/94 this is the lowest number of draws for a club only spending one season in the Premier League although Swindon's five draws did come in a 42-game season, so at an even lower ratio of 12%.

Barnsley's highest attendance of 18,694 against Manchester United was for their last match of the season when they were already relegated, which says something for the loyalty of their fans combined with the attraction of hosting United. With a lowest crowd of 17,102 for the match with Wimbledon, the difference between the two was just over 1,500, which is amongst the smallest variances at just over 9%.

Having scored Barnsley's first ever Premier League goal in the 9th minute of their Premier League debut at home to West Ham, Neil Redfearn also scored the only goal of the game in their first Premier League win, against his former club Crystal Palace. Additionally the Yorkshireman gained the twin accolade of racking up the most appearances in that season, missing only one of their 38 fixtures, as well as being the leading goal scorer with 10 of the 37 goals that the team scored. And apart from being responsible for more than a quarter of Barnsley's goals he was also the club skipper. Truly, a Captain Fantastic.

If there is one match that will stick in the memory of Barnsley supporters more than any other, but not for any positive reasons, it is their clash with Liverpool as detailed below.

THE OAKWELL THREE

SATURDAY 28 MARCH 1998

BARNSLEY 2 (1) REDFEARN 37', 85' (PEN)
LIVERPOOL 3 (1) RIEDLE 44', 59', MCMANAMAN 90'

OAKWELL (18,684)

"We have always felt it was us against the world and Saturday has proved that." Barnsley's chairman John Dennis' comments after the game against Liverpool were perfectly understandable after three Barnsley players were sent off in just over 30 minutes of the second half. Throughout the rest of the season they only received one other red card.

Barnsley had sprung a huge surprise by winning 1-0 at Anfield in November 1997, one of only three away wins all season. Therefore the game at Oakwell in March had a bit of added heat, which was entirely appropriate as the Tykes took on The Spice Boys. Also, Barnsley had won their previous three games prior to this match, giving themselves a real chance of escaping the drop.

The scoreline hardly does justice to the events of that day. Eight minutes after the break referee Gary Willard dismissed Barnsley's Darren Barnard for tripping Michael Owen when the Liverpool striker was bearing down on goal. Twelve minutes later Willard produced a second red, sending off Chris Morgan after his raised arm appeared to hit Owen in the face.

At this point Willard owes a huge debt of gratitude to Norwegian striker Jan-Age Fjortoft who spotted a fan making a beeline for the referee seemingly intent on having a lively debate about his dismissal of Morgan. Fjortoft ran full pelt to intercept the intruder and rugby tackled him before he could reach Willard.

Fearing for his safety, Willard took the teams off and the game was held up for a few minutes until some semblance of order was restored and Willard felt safe enough to return to the pitch. He did not hang around after the final whistle either, beating a hasty retreat to the safe haven of the changing rooms having also sent off Darren Sheridan in the aftermath of Steve McManaman's last-minute winning goal.

This is still the only Premier League match in which three players have been sent off from the same team. To make matters worse for an already fuming home crowd, Liverpool won 3-2 through a goal in added time, after Barnsley had fought back with nine men. They had equalised through Neil Redfearn's penalty, his second goal of the game, with only a few minutes remaining, only to be denied by McManaman's last gasp winner.

It was not quite like watching Brazil but it certainly did not lack drama or incident.

ONE HIT WONDER

Laurens ten Heuvel arrived in South Yorkshire in 1996 as one of a trio of Dutchmen to bolster Barnsley's squad for their promotion push from what was then the Second Division. Following in the footsteps of Arjan de Zeeuw who had arrived the year before, striker ten Heuvel was accompanied by Carol Van Der Velden from Eerste Divisie outfit FC Den Bosch. His Premier League baptism came in September 1997 as a substitute in a 3-0 home defeat to Aston Villa when he replaced Georgi Hristov for the last 20 minutes. He had to wait another couple of months for his only other appearance in a 4-1 defeat at Southampton when he got over 30 minutes as a replacement for John Hendrie.

By January 1998 manger Danny Wilson had seen enough and ten Heuvel was considered surplus to requirements leaving Oakwell on a free transfer to Northampton, before eventually ending up back in the Netherlands, taking in a couple of other Yorkshire clubs, Sheffield United and Bradford City, on the way. During his career in English football he featured in 22 matches but did not score a single goal.

FOOTNOTE

SINGLE SEASON SYNDROME

There are only three clubs that have spent just a single season in the Premier League, Swindon were the first, followed by Barnsley and then Blackpool. Between the three of them they collected a total of 104 points through 25 wins and 29 draws:-

CLUB	SEASON	POSITION	PTS
Swindon Town	1993/94	22nd	30 points
Barnsley	1997/98	19th	35 points
Blackpool	2010/11	19th	39 points

A VIEW FROM THE STANDS

Dan Williams

Your club's spell in the Premier League was brief and while there was the odd glorious moment ultimately it was short-lived. Looking back now, one question remains - Was it really worth it?

It's a period that defines my childhood and the memories are still clear as day. We may have lost 7-0 at Old Trafford, 6-0 at Upton Park and 5-0 at Highbury, but many Barnsley fans could close their eyes and relive Ashley Ward's* winners at Anfield and Villa Park, describe Scott Jones' two goals against Manchester United under the lights at Oakwell in minute detail, or go off on a 40-minute rant about Gary Willard's refereeing performance in our 2-3 defeat to Liverpool.

We became everyone's second team in that season, and despite relegation being confirmed with a game to play, it was worth every pound spent following the team up and down the country. Hindsight suggests money would have been better spent on established English players, given the success Darren Barnard and Ashley Ward enjoyed compared to players such as Gjorgji Hristov, but the market at the time dictated Danny Wilson's decisions.

We came within a saved Barnard penalty of returning to the big time two years later in 2000, but it was ultimately the demise of ITV Digital, rather than our season in the sun, that was the precursor to the problems we've experienced since.

* *Ashley Ward - one of the most relegated players see list*

BIRMINGHAM CITY STATS

NUMBER OF SEASONS:

7 (3 spells)

2002/03-05/06;
2007/08; 2009/10-2010/11

NUMBER OF MATCHES:

266

Wins 73 (Home 50 Away 23)
Draws 82 (Home 46 Away 36)
Losses 111 (Home 37 Away 74)

[Win ratio 27%]

Goals F 273
(Home 162 Away 111)

Goals A 360
(Home 140 Away 220)
Goal Difference: -87

TOTAL POINTS

301

(Home 196: 65%; Away 105: 35%)
Av per season: - 43

BEST POSITION:

9th

2009/10

WORST POSITION:

19th

2007/08 RELEGATED

BIGGEST WIN:

5-0

v Portsmouth
(21st Jan, 2006)

BIGGEST LOSS:

5-0

v Manchester United
(22nd Jan, 2011)

LONGEST UNBEATEN RUN:

12 matches

(24th Oct, 2009–9th Jan, 2010)

LONGEST WITHOUT A WIN:

10 matches

(3rd Apr, 2004-21st Aug, 2004)

ALL TIME RANKING

31st

**MOST GOALS SCORED
IN A SEASON:**

46

(2007/08)

**FEWEST GOALS
SCORED IN A SEASON:**

28

(2005/06)

**FEWEST GOALS
CONCEDED IN A SEASON:**

46

2004/05

**MOST GOALS
CONCEDED IN A SEASON:**

62

2007/08

TOP GOALSCORER:

29

Mikael Forssell

MOST APPEARANCES:

150

Damien Johnson

OWN GOALS:

9

RED CARDS:

27

LOWEST ATTENDANCE:

13,556

v Southampton
(9th Mar, 1993)

HIGHEST ATTENDANCE:

30,895

v Liverpool
(24th Feb, 1996)

BIRMINGHAM CITY

FIRST PREMIER LEAGUE MATCH: 18TH AUGUST, 2002
ARSENAL 2 (HENRY, WILTORD)
BIRMINGHAM 0

HIGHBURY 38,018

Nico Vaesen, Jeff Kenna, Martin Grainger, Kenny Cunningham, Darren Purse, Olivier Tebily (Darren Carter), Damien Johnson, Stern John, Geoff Horsfield (Stan Lazaridis), Aliou Cisse, Bryan Hughes, Manager: Steve Bruce

With 29 goals, Mikael Forssell is Birmingham's Premier League top scorer however he is not the only Finn to be lauded at St. Andrews, although the other one was for very different reasons. If beating your fiercest rivals 3-0 was not quite enough pleasure for Blues' fans the night of 16th September, 2002 provided perhaps their most exquisite moment of the last 25 years. City had regained their top-flight status for the first time since their relegation in 1985/86 so this was their first top-flight league meeting with Villa for almost 20 years, a game that they had won 3-0 in March 1986 at Villa Park. So it would be an understatement to say this game 'was eagerly anticipated' at St. Andrew's. Birmingham were already enjoying the best of the Second City derby after Clinton Morrison had given them the lead on 31 minutes and they were holding on to that lead when with 13 minutes remaining the incident that would be forever associated with this game unfolded.

As Villa's left back Olaf Mellberg prepared to take a throw there was no hint of any calamity, soon the ball was rolling innocuously towards goalkeeper Peter Enckelman who was under no pressure whatsoever. Inexplicably Enckelman seemed to freeze and got caught in between controlling the ball and hitting it first time. The result was he did neither and the ball rolled apologetically and humiliatingly over his foot and dribbled into the corner of the net. The Finnish No.1 was mortified, placing his hands on his head with a mixture of apology and horror at what had just happened.

The St. Andrew's crowd quickly got over their disbelief and roared their approval of the decisive second goal. Amidst the celebrations a couple of fans encroached on to the pitch and made sure that the poor keeper was left in no doubt about his culpability. One in particular goaded him with a well-known vigorous hand gesture as well as cuffing him on the cheek. Enckelman did well to avoid being provoked into a response although he was probably too shell-shocked to react.

Not content with handing Birmingham their second goal, Villa then compounded their own humiliation. Turkish defender Ozalan Alpay decided he would try to employ some of his silky skills to play out from the back but lost possession to Geoff Horsfield who then went on to shoot past the still rattled keeper. The game ended in a flurry of yellow cards as tempers flared with a handful of players booked for an 89th minute stramash.

To ensure this game would be writ large in the annals, Birmingham fans commemorated the evening with a chant to the tune of The Four Seasons' *December 1963 (Oh What a Night)*, and who could blame them for such showboating. Bragging rights were definitely dressed in blue and white ribbons as Birmingham followed up this victory with a 2-0 win in the return fixture and at Villa Park which had a sense of déjà vu.

There was another Enckelman error, although not on the same scale as the St. Andrew's debacle, when he failed to collect a nodded pass back, allowing Horsfield to nick it off him and walk the ball into the unguarded net. This doubled Birmingham's lead in the second half after Stan Lazaridis had opened the scoring 10 minutes earlier.

The abiding memory of this game was not a keeper's howler nor was it a Horsfield goal, but a head-butt from Dion Dublin on Robbie Savage, which was as understandable as it was minimal. Dublin has always maintained that there was no contact but there was certainly intent and Savage made the most of it and Dublin was sent off. That was not the end of the disciplinary issues as Joey Guðjónsson also got his marching orders for a vicious two-footed lunge at Matthew Upson that left Villa with nine men and the embarrassment of Birmingham completing a comfortable double over their neighbours with an aggregate score of 5-0. To make things even better for Birmingham they ended the season three points above Villa and it is the only time in their seven Premier League seasons that they have finished above their Second City rivals and must have been over the Blues moon.

ONE HIT WONDER

Richard Kingson arrived at St. Andrew's in 2007 after spending most of the previous ten years in Turkey. He represented Ghana 90 times between 1996 and 2012, including being their keeper in the 2010 World Cup when they reached the quarter-finals. On 24th November, 2007 he played his one and only match for Birmingham in a 2-0 defeat at home to Portsmouth. This was also caretaker manager Eric Black's only match in charge and as soon as the new manager Alex McLeish was in place Maik Taylor was restored as the No.1. Kingson did see a little more Premier League action with both Wigan and Blackpool, where he played in more than half of their matches in their only season.

Kingson is currently the goalkeeping coach for the Ghanian national team.

FOOTNOTE

RED CARD/LETTER DAY
Three players have been sent off in their club's PL debut match.

PLAYER	MATCH	DATE
Richard Rufus	Charlton vs Newcastle	5 August 1998
Derek McInnes	West Brom vs Man Utd	17 August 2002
Aliuo Cisse	Birmingham vs Arsenal	18 August 2002

A VIEW FROM THE STAND

Dean Gripton

What was your club's 'Sliding Doors' moment, that seemingly inconsequential action, which actually became a turning point in their fortunes, for either good or bad?

It is the 87th minute of the Blues' final Premier League game on 22nd May, 2011 – just weeks after they had beaten Arsenal 2-1 in the Carling Cup, courtesy of an Laurent Koscielny and Wojciech Szczęsny comedy assist for Obafemi Martins' late strike.

The Blues were away at Tottenham, and drawing 1-1 thanks to a Craig Gardner 79th minute equaliser. In that same minute Hugo Rodallega had put Wigan ahead at Stoke and were now two points clear and it was a straight battle between Birmingham and Midlands rivals, Wolves. Birmingham were ahead, on goal difference by one goal, of Wolves who were 3-1 down at home to Blackburn. Stephen Hunt then scored for Wolves to make the score at Molineux 'Wolves 2 Blackburn 3', meaning Wolves no had an identical goal difference and were ahead of Birmingham on goals scored.

This changed the dynamic and we needed to secure the three points. As we pile forward to try to win the game, Roman Pavlyuchecnko breaks and nets a 94th minute winner for Tottenham, and we are relegated.

Had we stayed up, with Europe the following season, we may have been able to progress. Clearly, we will never know. We were relegated, and after a play-off semi-final defeat the next season under Chris Hughton, Birmingham fell into the inevitable financial difficulties that have ended up with us spending three of the last four seasons fighting a further relegation, this time from the Championship.

BLACKBURN ROVERS STATS

NUMBER OF SEASONS:

18 (2 spells)

1992/93-1998/99; 2000/01-2011/12

NUMBER OF MATCHES:

696

Wins 262 (Home 169 Away 93)
Draws 184 (Home 85 Away 99)
Losses 250 (Home 94 Away 156)

[Win ratio 38%]

Goals F 927
(Home 545 Away 382)

Goals A 907
(Home 381 Away 526)

Goal Difference: +20

TOTAL POINTS

970

(Home 592: 61%; Away 378: 39%)
Av per season: - 54

BEST POSITION:

1st

1994/95 (CHAMPIONS)

WORST POSITION:

19th

1998/99 & 2011/12 (RELEGATED)

BIGGEST WIN:

7-0

v Nottingham Forest
(18th Nov, 1995)

BIGGEST LOSS:

7-1 (2)

v Manchester United (27th Nov, 2010)
v Arsenal (4th Feb, 2012)

LONGEST UNBEATEN RUN:

12 matches

(5th Dec, 1993-22nd Feb, 1994
& 29th Oct, 1994-14th Jan, 1995)

LONGEST WITHOUT A WIN:

11 matches

(17th Aug, 1996-26th Oct, 1996
& 4th Oct, 2008-13th Dec, 2008)

ALL TIME RANKING

11th

MOST GOALS SCORED IN A SEASON:

80

(1994/95)

FEWEST GOALS SCORED IN A SEASON:

32

(2004/05)

FEWEST GOALS CONCEDED IN A SEASON:

36

(1993/94)

MOST GOALS CONCEDED IN A SEASON:

78

(2011/12)

TOP GOALSCORER:

112

Alan Shearer

MOST APPEARANCES:

261

Brad Friedel

OWN GOALS:

26

RED CARDS:

77

LOWEST ATTENDANCE:

13,556

v Southampton
(9th Mar, 1993)

HIGHEST ATTENDANCE:

30,895

v Liverpool
(24th Feb, 1996)

All statistics and records supplied by  gracenote.
A NIELSEN COMPANY

BLACKBURN ROVERS

DID YOU KNOW?

Having beaten Leicester in the Division Two Play-Off Final in 1992 Blackburn are the only club to have won the Premier League following promotion via the Play-Offs. But of all the champions, Blackburn are the lowest ranked club currently and the only one that is not in the Premier League, as of 2019/2020.

FIRST PREMIER LEAGUE MATCH: 15TH AUGUST, 1992
CRYSTAL PALACE 3 (BRIGHT, SOUTHGATE, OSBORN)
BLACKBURN 3 (RIPLEY, SHEARER 2)

SELHURST PARK 17,086

*Bobby Mimms, David May, Alan Wright (Chris Price),
Tim Sherwood, Colin Hendry, Kevin Moran,
Stuart Ripley, Mark Atkins, Alan Shearer, Mike Newell,
Tony Dobson, Manager: Kenny Dalglish*

Blackburn's debut Premier League match, a 3-3 draw at Selhurst Park, was the joint highest-scoring game of all the opening day fixtures of that first season (along with Norwich's 4-2 win at Highbury) and was lit up by a double from their new signing from Southampton which set the tone for a record-breaking career that lasted until 2006. Alan Shearer would have surely gone on to become the leading goalscorer in that inaugural season if he had not been injured in December. Despite missing the rest of the season and playing only half the games he was only six goals behind the eventual top marksman, Teddy Sheringham.

Shearer is not only the all-time leading Premier League scorer, he is also the only player to be the top scorer for two clubs and is so by some margin, scoring 112 for Blackburn, comfortably ahead of his strike partner Chris Sutton's 47. To put that into perspective the total for the leading scorers for the lowest-scoring ten clubs is 126, only just ahead of Shearer's figure for Blackburn alone and behind his tally for Newcastle. The distance between him and his nearest challenger is even more marked at Newcastle where his tally of 148 is over 100 goals more than the second highest scorer, Peter Beardsley.

Shearer's record haul of 260 Premier League goals is unlikely to be rivalled with second placed Wayne Rooney, who scored 208 goals, the only other player to score more than 200. The closest active players are Sergio Aguero with 164 and Jermain Defoe with 162. Also, Shearer's achievement of scoring at least 20 goals in seven out of his 14 seasons is testament to his relentless consistency.

The famous SAS combination of Alan Shearer and Chris Sutton led Blackburn to their title win in 1994/95, scoring 49 goals between them, 61% of the team's total of 80. Only one other striking partnership in a league-winning team has ever been so dominant, when Jamie Vardy and Riyad Mahrez scored 42 of the 68 goals that secured Leicester's unlikely triumph in 2015/16, which equates to 62% of the champion's tally.

Clinching the title at Anfield could not have provided a more ideal setting for former Liverpool icon Kenny Dalglish to secure his one and only Premier League title as a manager. Emotions were running high for the Scot as he returned to the ground where he had justifiably earned the title of King Kenny after his achievements as player and manager. Blackburn were 1-0 up at half time through the inevitable Shearer strike after 20 minutes following a neat exchange with Stuart Ripley. However, a goal from John Barnes and a Jamie Redknapp free-kick in the 93rd minute looked to have killed off their title hopes.

Within a few seconds of that potentially devastating blow news filtered through that Manchester United could not muster the win they needed at Upton Park that would have given United a clean sweep of the first five PL titles and Blackburn were champions. Of all the seven titles decided on the last day of the season this was the only one where the eventual winners actually lost the game but Dalglish did not care a jot as the sweetest of celebrations began as "Always Look on the Bright Side of Life" reverberated around a joyous Anfield.

Every title-winning team needs a strong, reliable goalkeeper and Tim Flowers was just that. He only let in 39 goals in the 42 matches but on 1st February 1995 he almost scuppered Blackburn's challenge when he was sent off after just 72 seconds of the home game with Leeds. This remains the fastest red card in Premier League history. But Blackburn got away with a draw, in fact they took the lead only five minutes after Flowers' dismissal through a Shearer penalty and conceded the equaliser with just five minutes remaining via another penalty, this time by Gary McAllister.

Having been promoted via the play-offs in 1992 Blackburn finished their first Premier League season in an impressive 4th place. They followed that by being runners-up in 1993/94, which paved the way for their title-winning season in 1994/95. In the first four seasons of the Premier League Blackburn were clearly the second best team in England, with an average position of 4th and even after Dalglish surprisingly resigned as manager in the wake of winning the title, they finished 7th under Ray Harford, so they were the only club to be in the top seven in all those four seasons apart from the dominant Manchester United.

However, Blackburn could not maintain their place at the top and four years after their triumph, in 1998/99, they became the only Premier League champions to be relegated. In this season they also managed to register the best goal difference of any relegated club with -14, by contrast there have been 77 occasions when clubs with a worse goal difference than that have survived. To put this into even sharper perspective in the 2016/17 and 2017/18 seasons a dozen clubs had a worse goal difference and did not get relegated and in 2009/10 Rovers themselves had exactly the same goal difference of -14 when finishing tenth.

They did return two years after their first relegation and lasted a further 11 years before being relegated in 2012. Having spent 18 seasons in total in the Premier League they are 12th in the overall list, having competed in 696 games. With an accumulated goal difference of +20 Blackburn are one of only ten teams to have a positive goal difference throughout PL history and they are also one of ten clubs to have more wins than losses.

In his eight seasons at Ewood Park between 2001/02 and 2007/08 Brad Friedel only missed five matches and was an ever-present for the last five seasons. Overall he made 261 appearances for Blackburn and is one of two American keepers to be the record holder for appearances at a club alongside Tim Howard, whose 354 appearances for Everton is still the most by any American player. Friedel continued his remarkable run of not missing a game after he moved to Aston Villa, where he was ever-present for all of his three seasons, and Tottenham, where he was ever-present in his first season.

Both Howard and Friedel are members of an elite group of only five keepers to have scored a Premier League goal with Friedel doing so against Charlton in 2004. Friedel scored in the last minute at The Valley to make it 2-2 after Charlton had been 2-0 ahead. Then in added time Claus Jensen regained the lead for Charlton by lobbing the ball over Friedel, whose joy was short-lived. Well before the birth of sweeper-keepers, this pair had been heavily involved in the novel concept of scorer-keepers.

ONE HIT WONDER

Nick Blackman joined Blackburn in January 2009 and soon went out on loan to Blackpool. Over the next couple of years he was also loaned out to Oldham as well as Motherwell and Aberdeen. But he returned to Ewood Park in 2011 and in the very first game of the 2011/12 season he came on as a substitute in the 84th minute so he must have felt that his career with Rovers was about to start. But unfortunately for him those solitary six minutes were it as far as his Blackburn Premier League appearances were concerned and he joined Sheffield United in August 2012.

He did get to play in the Premier League again, having joined Reading in January 2013.

FOOTNOTE

COALS, (OR COLES, OR EVEN GOALS) TO NEWCASTLE
Most goals by a striking partnership in a season

SAS are the best for a title-winning club but ironically they are pipped by the Newcastle pair of Andy Cole and Peter Beardsley and SAS Mark 2 - Daniel Sturridge and Luis Suarez. Shearer also appears in the top scoring chart courtesy of his partnership with Les Ferdinand at Newcastle.

PLAYERS	CLUB	GOALS	SEASON
Cole/Beardsley	Newcastle	55	1993/94*
Sturridge/Suarez	Liverpool	52	2013/14
Shearer / Sutton	Blackburn	49	1994/95*
Shearer/Ferdinand	Newcastle	49	1996/97

*42-game season

A VIEW FROM THE STANDS

What was the club's 'Sliding Doors' moment, that seemingly inconsequential action, which actually became a turning point in their fortunes, for either good or bad?

For younger generations of fans Blackburn's Premier League title in 1995 will always be the answer to a pub quiz question. For those who were there it was an unforgettable season, jab and counterpunch throughout between Manchester United and Rovers, champions verses underdogs culminating on an incredible Agüerooooooooo-rivalling final day.

All of this was built on the ambition, the dream, the finances, and the love for the club of one man: Jack Walker. Blackburn Rovers' sliding doors moment came in 1988, way before the Premier League existed, when the steel magnate began a relationship with the club he adored by donating the materials needed for a new stand at Ewood Park. It would be three more years before he would eventually become chairman and set about building a team which could win the title, a notion that seemed like a fantasy as Blackburn were facing relegation from the Second Division.

A quick injection of funds, a change of manager which saw Kenny Dalglish take the reins, and a promotion via the play offs in 1992 gave them the platform. With the club in the Premier League, Walker really flexed his financial muscle by signing first Alan Shearer and then Chris Sutton, in 1994, both for then-record fees. In that title-winning season they scored 49 goals between them, well over half Blackburn's total, and Walker had his crowning glory.

BLACKPOOL STATS

NUMBER OF SEASONS:

1

2010/11

NUMBER OF MATCHES:

38

Wins 10 (Home 5 Away 5)
Draws 9 (Home 5 Away 4)
Losses 19 (Home 9 Away 10)

[Win ratio 26%]

Goals F 55
(Home 30 Away 25)

Goals A 78
(Home 37 Away 41)

Goal Difference: -23

TOTAL POINTS

39

(Home 20: 51%; Away 19: 49%)
Av per season: -39

BEST POSITION:

19th

2010/11 (RELEGATED)

WORST POSITION:

19th

2010/11 (RELEGATED)

BIGGEST WIN:

0-4

v Wigan
(14th Aug, 2010)

BIGGEST LOSS:

6-0

v Arsenal
(21st Aug, 2010)

LONGEST UNBEATEN RUN:

5 matches

(13th Nov, 2010–28th Dec, 2010)

LONGEST WITHOUT A WIN:

9 matches

(15th Jan, 2011–7th May, 2011)

ALL TIME RANKING

47th

MOST GOALS SCORED IN A SEASON:

55

-

FEWEST GOALS SCORED IN A SEASON:

55

-

FEWEST GOALS CONCEDED IN A SEASON:

78

-

MOST GOALS CONCEDED IN A SEASON:

78

-

TOP GOALSCORER:

13

DJ Campbell

MOST APPEARANCES:

38

Ian Evatt

OWN GOALS:

5

RED CARDS:

2

LOWEST ATTENDANCE:

14,550

v Birmingham
(4th Jan, 2011)

HIGHEST ATTENDANCE:

16,116

v Manchester City
(17th Oct, 2010)

All statistics and records supplied by

BLACKPOOL

FIRST PREMIER LEAGUE MATCH: 14TH AUGUST, 2010
WIGAN 0
BLACKPOOL 4 (TAYLOR-FLETCHER, HAREWOOD 2, BAPTISTE)

DW STADIUM 16,152

Matty Gilks, Alex Baptiste, Stephen Crainey, Charlie Adam, Ian Evatt, Craig Cathcart, Gary Taylor-Fletcher (Jason Euell), Brett Ormerod (Ludovic Sylvestre), Marlon Harewood (Chris Basham), Elliot Grandin, David Vaughan, Manager: Ian Holloway

Blackpool's only Premier League season was encapsulated in their first two games. Their opening fixture was a 4-0 win away to Wigan Athletic, which still stands as the largest Premier League debut victory of any club. The optimism generated by that amazing game was quickly swept away by their next match when they were ruthlessly dispatched 6-0 by Arsenal. Within their first two matches the Tangerines managed to secure their biggest Premier League win and then followed it up immediately with their record loss. Their third match was a 2-2 draw at Fulham, which meant that there had been 14 goals in their first three games and this set the pace for a giddy ride. Their most notable scalp was doing their only double over Liverpool, both by 2-1 with the victory at Anfield on 3rd October, 2010 the high point.

In a season littered with plenty of goals Blackpool scored 55, which is still the most by any relegated club and in conceding 78, their 38 matches generated an impressive 133 goals, at an average of 3.5 per match. Their cavalier attitude, fostered by the ever-ebullient Ian Holloway, won them many friends but not enough points and their final fixture was as symptomatic of their approach as those opening games.

Needing a win at Old Trafford the Tangerines were a goal down after 21 minutes, equalised through Charlie Adam just before half-time and then had the audacity to take the lead at the home of the champions in the 57th minute through Gary Taylor-Fletcher. That turned out to be Blackpool's last goal in the Premier League and a neat top and tail as he had also scored their first in their handsome 4-0 opening day win against Wigan. Only one other player has scored the first and last Premier league goal for their club, the redoubtable Neil Redfearn for Barnsley. Salvation seemed within Blackpool's grasp only for it to be snatched from them as they conceded three goals inside the last 30 minutes including an own goal by club stalwart Ian Evatt, who was an ever-present that season.

And so Holloway's buccaneers were cast off again to the waters of the Championship, but everyone had enjoyed the ride. Holloway described his unfashionable team with his customary panache: "I might be in a bit of a Skoda garage rather than a Mercedes garage, but I am telling you some old bangers don't half polish up great." Blackpool's penchant for goals led them to only two goalless draws all season and only two other games featuring just one goal. Their fearless approach was part of the reason that this Premier League season boasted the highest overall goal ratio of 2.8 per game until 2018/19 just nudged ahead with 2.82 with a total of 1,072, nine more than 2010/11. Blackpool proved to be the rock in this high-scoring festival.

ONE HIT WONDER

Ishmel Demontagnac had a troubled career, he was a rising star at Walsall but after he was arrested on suspicion of a breach of the peace he was released in November 2008. After various trials he ended up at Blackpool at start of 2009/10 season and was part of the squad that gained promotion under Holloway although he encountered more disciplinary problems after being caught in a nightclub and was suspended. He took his Premier League bow in the 57th minute of Blackpool's second match, at Arsenal. He was joining a lost cause as they were already 4-0 down and within a minute of his introduction Arsenal scored their fifth. At least he was on the pitch to witness Theo Walcott complete his first Arsenal hat-trick.

By January he was packed off to Stockport County on loan and then joined Notts County on a permanent transfer at the end of the season.

His last port of call in 2014 was the now-defunct Thurrock FC, who were then in the Isthmian League.

FOOTNOTE

HIGH-SCORING LOSERS

The six highest-scoring relegated clubs are headed by Blackpool who impressively scored the most, 55 in a 38-game season.

CLUB	SEASON	GOALS
Blackpool	2010/11	55
Middlesbrough	1992/93	54*
Middlesbrough	1996/97	51**
Crystal Palace	1992/93	48*
Leicester City	2003/04	48
Blackburn Rovers	2011/12	48

* 42-game seasons   ** 3-point deduction

A VIEW FROM THE STANDS

What was the club's 'Sliding Doors' moment, that seemingly inconsequential action, which actually became a turning point in their fortunes, for either good or bad?

Blackpool ended 2010 on the crest of a wave, having comfortably beaten Sunderland 2-0 at the Stadium of Light on the 28th December, courtesy of a DJ Campbell brace. They had reached the giddy heights of eighth and with 25 points after 17 games survival, if not guaranteed, looked very possible. Only Norwich had previously been relegated after being that high in the table at the turn of the year.

Blackpool's steady, relentless decline started with a 1-0 loss at Manchester City on New Year's Day. Over the next 21 matches they did not win another match away from home and only gathered three more wins altogether, collecting a mere 14 points. This left them needing to get a result at Old Trafford on the last day of the season.

The Tangerines' goose was cooked although naturally they went down fighting, eventually losing 4-2 to the champions. They ended up just one frustrating point shy of Wolves in 17th and have never been close to returning to the Premier League. A disastrous few seasons led to the club dropping down to League Two within just six short years. All this was played out against a backdrop of fan protests against the club's owners, the Oyston family. The supporters' anger was understandable as those heady days in the Premier League seemed as far away as the glory days of Matthews and Mortensen.

BOLTON WANDERERS STATS

NUMBER OF SEASONS:

13 (3 spells)

1995/96; 1997/98;
2001/02-2011/12

TOTAL POINTS

575

(Home 354: 62%; Away 221: 38%)
Av per season: 44

NUMBER OF MATCHES:

494

Wins 149 (Home 93 Away 56)
Draws 128 (Home 75 Away 53)
Losses 217 (Home 79 Away 138)

[Win ratio 30%]

Goals F 575
(Home 319 Away 256)

Goals A 745
(Home 313 Away 432)

Goal Difference: -170

BEST POSITION:

6th

2004/05

WORST POSITION:

20

1995/96 (RELEGATED)

BIGGEST WIN:

5-0

v Stoke
(6th Nov, 2011)

BIGGEST LOSS:

0-6

v Manchester United
(25th Feb, 1996)

LONGEST UNBEATEN RUN:

7 matches (2)

1st Jan, 2005–12th Feb, 2005 &
2nd Jan, 2006–26th Feb, 2006)

LONGEST WITHOUT A WIN:

12 matches (2)

(6th Dec, 1997–7th Mar, 1998 &
24th Nov, 2001–2nd Feb, 2002)

ALL TIME RANKING

18th

MOST GOALS SCORED IN A SEASON:

52

(2010/11)

FEWEST GOALS SCORED IN A SEASON:

40

(2009/10)

FEWEST GOALS CONCEDED IN A SEASON:

41

(2005/06)

MOST GOALS CONCEDED IN A SEASON:

77

(2011/12)

TOP GOALSCORER:

68

Kevin Davies

MOST APPEARANCES:

379

Jussi Jaaskelainen

OWN GOALS:

23

RED CARDS:

44

LOWEST ATTENDANCE:

16,216

v Wimbledon
(13th Jan, 1996)

HIGHEST ATTENDANCE:

29,504

v Newcastle
(24th Aug, 2005)

All statistics and records supplied by  gracenote.
A NIELSEN COMPANY

BOLTON WANDERERS

FIRST PREMIER LEAGUE MATCH: 19TH AUGUST, 1995
WIMBLEDON 3 (EKOKU, EARLE, HOLDSWORTH)
BOLTON 2 (THOMPSON, DE FREITAS)

SELHURST PARK 9,317

*Keith Branagan, Gundi Bergsson (David Lee), Jimmy Phillips,
Chris Fairclough, Alan Stubbs, Scott Green, Mark Patterson,
Mixu Paatelainen (Owen Coyle), Fabian De Freitas, Alan Thompson,
Manager: Roy McFarland*

It was a case of third time lucky for Bolton, after two bites of the cherry had led them to just a pair of single season spells in 1995/96 and 1997/98 (see Footnote). In that 1997/98 season they went into the last day just above the relegation zone, a point ahead of Everton. They fell to two late Chelsea goals at Stamford Bridge and Everton drew with Coventry so despite finishing on 40 points, Bolton were relegated on an inferior goal difference of -20 compared to Everton's -15. They eventually found stability in the formidable shape of Sam Allardyce who moulded them into a solid Premier League outfit before he moved to Newcastle in April 2007, just as Bolton secured qualification for the UEFA Cup, their first foray into European football. Their third spell in the Premier League spanned 11 seasons and to date that is the longest that a team being promoted from the Play-Offs, as Bolton were in 2001, has lasted in the Premier League.

Nothing was more impressive than the way they began their campaign in 2001 as they recorded the biggest victory of a newly promoted side in their opening fixture away to Leicester. Coming out of the blocks with an alacrity that surprised the Foxes they were 4-0 up by half-time as a Kevin Nolan double was complemented by goals from Michael Ricketts and Per Frandsen. When Frandsen added his second with seven minutes to go, the most consummate performance of any newly-promoted club was complete.

They followed up this stunning opener with two further victories at home, the second a commendable 2-1 victory over Liverpool courtesy of a last-minute winner from Dean Holdsworth that squirmed through Sander Westerveld's grasp. An away draw at Elland Road meant that the Trotters were top of the table with 10 points from four games, scoring eight goals and only conceding one. But despite a notable 2-1 win at Old Trafford in October they could not maintain such heady form and they dropped down the table, finishing with three straight defeats after a draw, mirroring their start and ending 16th just four points above the relegation places.

Under Allardyce Bolton developed into a tough, uncompromising team who enjoyed cocking a snook at the bigger clubs, none more so than Arsene Wenger's Arsenal. The game that encapsulated their ability to upset the Gunners came in the season after Arsenal's 'Invincibles' season. Arsenal had started the season at a canter, winning the first five games while scoring 19 goals, and were looking likely to exert the same dominance as the previous campaign.

Despite being pegged back to 1-1 early in the second half Arsenal appeared to have restored order when Robert Pires scored in the 66th minute. Bolton refused to buckle and with five minutes remaining, Henrik Pedersen punctured the home team's 100% record and showed there was a vulnerability about this all-conquering team. Allardyce revelled in the role of curmudgeonly party-pooper and not for the last time Wenger bristled at their rather rudimentary approach.

This draw proved to be the first spoke in the wheels of Arsenal's dominance and a few games later that unbeaten run stretching over 49 matches was brought to a halt at Old Trafford. When Bolton won the reverse fixture 1-0 in January, Arsenal knew their defence of the title was pretty much over as they ultimately surrendered to Chelsea by 12 points in Jose Mourinho's first season at Stamford Bridge. Wenger would have noted the irony that the new champions, who lost only once in the league, secured their first top-flight trophy with a 2-0 win at Bolton.

Over the following two seasons Bolton did indeed prove to be the Gunners' nemesis with two more victories, one draw and just one loss. This series of results affected Arsenal's psychology more than anything else and significantly after Allardyce, Wenger's nemesis, left Bolton only secured one draw and lost seven of their next eight fixtures against the Gunners.

Jussi Jaaskelainen joins the long list of foreign keepers who hold their club's record number of appearances. The Finn amassed an impressive 379 games over his 15 years at Bolton, with six seasons as an ever-present and nine seasons where he appeared at least 30 times and with a few years at West Ham, where he joined Sam Allardyce after Bolton were relegated, he is in the top 30 for overall Premier League appearances with 436, squeezed in between Alan Shearer and Richard Dunne. Like Dunne, Jaaskelainen holds a record for red cards. While Dunne has the joint highest number of dismissals of any player, Jaaskelainen collected more red cards than any other keeper with four, the same number as Tony Adams, Sol Campbell, Ben Thatcher and Cristiano Ronaldo.

He is just behind another Bolton stalwart Kevin Davies in the all-time appearances list as Davies played more than 100 games for Southampton before joining Bolton and racked up 444 in total. Davies is second in the Bolton list behind Jaaskelainen and is the leading marksman for the Trotters with 68 goals, which puts him 12th equal in top scorers for a club alongside Romelu Lukaku who is Everton's No.1. Davies also makes the overall Top 40 scorers with 88 goals, neatly tucked in between a pretty decent pair of strikers in Ole Gunnar Solksjaer and Dennis Bergkamp.

ONE HIT WONDER

There are not many better names in the world of football or any other sport, than Blessing Kaku who made one substitute appearance for Wanderers in 2004. The Nigerian international came on in the 65th minute of the 2-1 loss to West Brom on 10th February, 2004, replacing Ivan Campo. His fellow Nigerian Nwankwo Kanu had scored the Baggies' first goal. It was not the most glorious 25 minutes and Kaku is perhaps better known for being one of those transfers which aroused the suspicions of Lord Stevens' 2007 enquiry into bungs, which included the dealings of Sam Allardyce's son Craig, who was responsible for the transfer of Kaku to Bolton from Israeli club FC Ashdod.

After being found surplus to requirements at Bolton Kaku joined Derby County briefly and then returned to Israeli club football in 2005 before retiring four years later.

FOOTNOTE

The 1997/98 season is unique as it is the only season when all three promoted clubs were immediately relegated and with added synchronicity Bolton, Barnsley and Crystal Palace went down in exactly the same order they came up.

1996/97 DIVISION ONE TABLE

1st	Bolton	98 points
2nd	Barnsley	80 points
6th	Crystal Palace	71 points (promoted via the Play-Offs)

1997/98 PREMIER LEAGUE TABLE

18th	Bolton	40 points
19th	Barnsley	35 points
20th	Crystal Palace	33 points

A VIEW FROM THE STAND

Joe Crilly, William Hill

What was your club's 'Sliding Doors' moment, that seemingly inconsequential action, which actually became a turning point in their fortunes, for either good or bad?

Bolton Wanderers experienced a number of highs during their time in the Premier League but they now feel like a hazy memory given how far the club have fallen since Big Sam and his team were bloodying the noses of the big boys.

Bolton dropped out of the Premier League at the end of 2011/12 however, the sliding doors moment came the season before.

Some would argue that the FA Cup semi-final humiliation (0-5) at the hands of Stoke on 17th April 2011 was the beginning of the end, however the descent began a month earlier.

On Saturday 19th March, during a 1-0 defeat at Old Trafford, Stuart Holden was caught by a rash challenge from Jonny Evans. The Manchester United defender saw red, the Bolton Wanderers midfielder saw his season cut short due to a fractured femur and a cut to his knee that required 26 stitches.

Up until that point, the USA international had been the best player in a side that sat seventh in the Premier League, and he would go on to win the club's Player of the Year at the end of the season.

That FA Cup semi-final defeat followed and the club slipped down the table and finished in 14th place.

His absence in the Wanderers side in 2011/12 was compounded by long-term injuries sustained by Chung Yong Lee, Tyrone Mears and Fabrice Muamba—four players who certainly would have helped the side win the requisite two points to keep the club in the Premier League for at least another year.

AFC BOURNEMOUTH STATS

NUMBER OF SEASONS:

4

2015/16-2018/19

NUMBER OF MATCHES:

152

Wins 47 (Home 29 Away 18)
Draws 36 (Home 19 Away 17)
Losses 69 (Home 28 Away 41)

[Win ratio 31%]

Goals F 201
(Home 114 Away 87)

Goals A 265
(Home 118 Away 147)

Goal Difference: -64

TOTAL POINTS

177

(Home 106: 60%; Away 71: 40%)
Av per season: 44

BEST POSITION:

9th

2016/17

WORST POSITION:

16th

2015/16

BIGGEST WIN:

6-1

v Hull
(15th Oct, 2016)

BIGGEST LOSS:

5-1

v Manchester City
(17th Oct, 2015)

LONGEST UNBEATEN RUN:

7 matches

(26th Dec, 2017–3rd Feb, 2018)

LONGEST WITHOUT A WIN:

8 matches (4)

(26th Sept, 2015–28th Nov, 2015;
17th Apr, 2016–27th Aug, 2016,
3rd Jan, 2017–4th Mar, 2017, 25th
Nov, 2017–26th Dec, 2017)

ALL TIME RANKING

38th

MOST GOALS SCORED IN A SEASON:

56

(2018/19)

FEWEST GOALS SCORED IN A SEASON:

45 (2)

(2015/16 & 2017/18)

FEWEST GOALS CONCEDED IN A SEASON:

61

(2017/18)

MOST GOALS CONCEDED IN A SEASON:

70

(2018/19)

TOP GOALSCORER:

42

Josh King

MOST APPEARANCES:

139

Steve Cook

OWN GOALS:

9

RED CARDS:

6

LOWEST ATTENDANCE:

9,980

v Huddersfield Town
(4th Dec, 2018)

HIGHEST ATTENDANCE:

11,388

v Burnley
(13th May, 2017

AFC BOURNEMOUTH

FIRST PREMIER LEAGUE MATCH: 8TH AUGUST, 2015
BOURNEMOUTH 0
ASTON VILLA 1 (GESTEDE)

GOLDSANDS STADIUM 11,155

Artur Boruc, Simon Francis , Steve Cook, Tommy Elphick, Charlie Daniels, Dan Gosling (Eunan O'Kane), Andrew Surman, Marc Pugh (Max-Alain Gradel), Matt Ritchie, Callum Wilson, Josh King (Yann Kermorgant), Manager: Eddie Howe

At the end of the 2018/19 season Bournemouth completed their fourth successive season in the Premier League and are one of only eight clubs that have never been relegated alongside the six ever-presents and Brighton. This is an eye-catching achievement considering the Cherries had been on the verge of extinction only ten years previously when after two successive seasons of points deductions for falling into administration and breaching insolvency rules they finished 21st in League Two. At one stage of the season they had been 10 points adrift of safety and this was the moment that Eddie Howe took over as manager.

Howe was the chief architect for the club's renaissance over the next decade as he initially steered the club away from the threat of dropping out of the League and then got them promoted to League One before moving to Burnley for a brief spell from 2011 to October 2012. Following his departure from Turf Moor, Howe, the prodigal son, returned and led Bournemouth from the lower reaches of League

One to the Championship and then followed this with promotion to the top flight for the first time in their existence in 2015. In his second spell at the club Howe has now been in charge longer than any other current Premier League manager and in a neat juxtaposition of continuity the man who replaced him at Burnley, Sean Dyche is the second longest-serving manager.

Considering they took over 115 years to reach the top flight for the very first time and had a pretty tortuous journey getting there, including being on the brink of exiting the Football League altogether, Bournemouth's consistency in terms of points gained in their four seasons is pretty impressive from a low of 42 to a high of 46. In a similar vein their high of 56 goals scored in 2018/19 is only 11 ahead of their lowest and their goals against is even tighter with a low of 61 in 2017/18 compared to 70 the following season.

In their match at home to Manchester City on 2nd March, 2019 Bournemouth managed to do something unique. In what turned out to be one of the most comprehensive 1-0 defeats they became the first home side to not muster a single shot, either on or off target, in the dozen years since Opta started gathering Premier League data in the 2006/07 season.

Considering how good City had been in winning 15 of their previous 16 games and their imperious form over the previous season it is hard to blame an opposition manager for playing conservatively and effectively launching a damage limitation exercise. Added to which, Bournemouth's previous seven league meetings with City had all ended in defeat resulting in a rather chastening aggregate score of 24-3, so Eddie Howe's cautious approach made perfect sense.

Despite those caveats there was a flood of remarkable statistics that emanated from this match. Bournemouth's timid approach meant that they did not even force a single corner and their possession percentage of 18% was amongst the lowest ever recorded for a side playing at home. At least the Cherries matched their opponents in the number of fouls, with seven apiece. As a team City out-passed Bournemouth by a ratio of slightly over 7:1 and to put this into even sharper focus City's right back, Kyle Walker completed more successful passes (106) than the entire Bournemouth team put together (100). Having said that, John Stones completed 71 passes and was only on the field for 48 minutes.

Howe did try to freshen things up towards the end of the game by bringing on three attack-minded substitutes Lys Mouset, Jordan Ibe and Diego Rico. But that did not shift the momentum as between them they played for a total of 41 minutes and amassed just a single completed pass. After all this noble rearguard action, Bournemouth succumbed to a Riyad Mahrez goal in notching up their eight successive loss to City and in so doing became the first club in the top-flight to lose eight on the trot to the same opponent. It was a truly bruising afternoon for the Cherries.

ONE HIT WONDER

Baily Cargill joined Bournemouth as a 13-year-old in 2008 and made his debut in a League Cup tie in 2014 but did not quite make the step up to regular first team action. During his 10-year spell at the club he was loaned out seven times but finally in March 2017 he made it on to the pitch at no less a stage than Old Trafford. Replacing Tyrone Mings in 78th minute he helped Bournemouth to a battling 1-1 draw with Manchester United, after they had been reduced to ten men following Andrew Surman's dismissal just before half-time.

Cargill was released by Bournemouth at the end of the 2017/18 season and moved to Milton Keynes Dons where he was part of the squad that gained promotion from League Two in 2019.

FOOTNOTE

TO YOU, TO ME, TO ME, TO YOU

When Callum Wilson converted a Ryan Fraser cross during a 3-3 draw at St. Mary's on 27th April 2019 the Bournemouth pair came close to matching the long-standing record of Alan Shearer and Chris Sutton who combined together to score 13 goals in 1994/95. Wilson and Fraser's dozen in the 2018/19 season is the highest during a 38-game season and although FAW does not have quite the same ring as SAS they are almost as potent as the pair who spearheaded Blackburn's title-winning side.

Top five goal combinations in a season

PLAYERS	CLUB	SEASON	GLS
Shearer/Sutton	Blackburn	1994/95	13
Fraser/Wilson	Bournemouth	2018/19	12
Gallen/ Ferdinand	QPR	1994/95	11
Shearer/Newell	Blackburn	1995/96	11
Fowler/Collymore	Liverpool	1995/96	10
Bergkamp/Anelka	Arsenal	1998/99	10

A VIEW FROM THE STANDS

What was the club's 'Sliding Doors' moment, that seemingly inconsequential action, which actually became a turning point in their fortunes, for either good or bad?

As sliding doors moments go some are more obvious than others. Eddie Howe's decision to join Burnley in early 2011 was met with universal disappointment on the south coast but things weren't to go the manager's way up north. Results were okay and he never came under huge pressure, but it always seemed an uncomfortable marriage.

He left Burnley for 'personal reasons' in 2012 and was welcomed back to Dean Court with open arms. When he took over from Paul Groves, Bournemouth were languishing in 21st place in League One and a Premier League future for the club seemed like a mere pipe dream. Getting Howe was a coup as a mid-table Championship manager rarely swaps that safety for a League One relegation battle, but he admitted "there was only one club I'd contemplate leaving Burnley for". The homecoming was complete.

Cue some serious investment in the squad backed by some extremely clever picks, and two promotions in three seasons including a Championship title. Bournemouth dared to dream and it paid off. Howe's stock has risen to the point where he's now seen as an England manager in waiting, and Bournemouth are currently in their fifth relatively drama-free Premier League season.

Sometimes a manager and a club are destined to be together for success. Could Howe have done it at Burnley longer-term? We'll never know, and furthermore Bournemouth fans will never care.

BRADFORD CITY STATS

NUMBER OF SEASONS:

2

1999/2000–2000/01

NUMBER OF MATCHES:

76

Wins 14 (Home 10 Away 4)
Draws 20 (Home 15 Away 5)
Losses 42 (Home 13 Away 29)

[Win ratio 18%]

Goals F 68
(Home 46 Away 22)

Goals A 138
(Home 58 Away 80)

Goal Difference: -70

TOTAL POINTS

62

(Home 45: 73%; Away 17: 27%)
Av per season: 31

BEST POSITION:

17th

1999/2000

WORST POSITION:

20th

2000/01 (RELEGATED)

BIGGEST WIN:

3-0

v Wimbledon
(30th Apr, 2000)

BIGGEST LOSS:

6-0

v Manchester United
(5th Sep, 2000)

LONGEST UNBEATEN RUN:

3 matches (2)

(21st Apr–30th Apr, 2000 &
25th Nov, 2000–9th Dec, 2000)

LONGEST WITHOUT A WIN:

13 matches

(26th Aug, 2000–25th Nov, 2000)

ALL TIME RANKING

45th

MOST GOALS SCORED IN A SEASON:

38

(1999/2000)

FEWEST GOALS SCORED IN A SEASON:

30

(2000/01)

FEWEST GOALS CONCEDED IN A SEASON:

68

(1999/2000)

MOST GOALS CONCEDED IN A SEASON:

70

(2000/01)

TOP GOALSCORER:

13

Dean Windass

MOST APPEARANCES:

71

Stuart McCall

OWN GOALS:

5

RED CARDS:

2

LOWEST ATTENDANCE:

15,523

v Coventry
(2nd Dec, 2000)

HIGHEST ATTENDANCE:

22,057

v Liverpool
(1st May, 2001)

All statistics and records supplied by

BRADFORD CITY

FIRST PREMIER LEAGUE MATCH: 15TH AUGUST, 1992
MIDDLESBROUGH 0
BRADFORD CITY 1 (SAUNDERS)

RIVERSIDE STADIUM 33,762

Gary Walsh, John Dreyer, Wayne Jacobs, Gunnar Halle, Andy O'Brien, David Wetherall, Neil Redfearn, Dean Windass (Dean Saunders), Lee Mills, Gareth Whalley, Peter Beagrie, Manager: Paul Jewell

Bradford achieved what few promoted teams have done in their first match - they won away courtesy of substitute Dean Saunders' late strike at the Riverside for a 1-0 win over Middlesbrough. The Bantams had not been in the top division since 1922 so their survival that first season was an achievement in itself. They also managed an unusual double by scoring four goals twice but still not winning either game.

They drew 4-4 with Derby a game in which top scorer Dean Windass scored a first half hat-trick. However, the disappointment of not taking three points in that game, having been 4-3 up at half-time was nothing compared to what had happened at Upton Park earlier in the season when they were 4-2 up with 25 minutes remaining and ended up losing 5-4. This was the game where Paolo Di Canio asked Harry Redknapp to be substituted after a penalty appeal was turned down and also where he battled Frank Lampard to take a penalty that was awarded a little later. Lampard had the last laugh when he scored the fifth and deciding goal, from a Di Canio pass.

These games were indicative of a topsy-turvy season and led to a dramatic denouement for the Citizens. Of all the last day escapes Bradford's in 2000 takes some beating. With 14 games to go they were 18th and in the next nine games they picked up just two points. However, they gave themselves a fighting chance when in their next four games they won two and drew one - that high-scoring extravaganza with Derby. And so it came down to their last match, at home to Liverpool, and they came out on top via the unlikely route of a David Wetherall goal, as emphatic a header as you could wish to see. It was a goal worthy of its impact as it secured their safety at the expense of Wimbledon who notched up their 10th defeat in 11 matches, away at Southampton, a run which included a crucial 3-0 loss at Valley Parade at the end of April.

This was Wetherall's second ever goal for Bradford and he was the most appropriate scorer as he was the only Bradford player to play every minute of the season and he spent a dozen years as both player and coach at Valley Parade. He stayed with the club through thick and thin as the Bantams dropped down the divisions, ending in the bottom tier six years after their relegation from the Premier League in 2001. Wetherall was in charge as caretaker manager when they were relegated to League Two. His other claim to fame was that he was the first footballer to graduate with a first class degree with a BSc in Chemistry from Sheffield University in 1992.

Neil Redfearn joined Bradford at the same time as Wetherall as the Bantams became Redfearn's third club in three consecutive seasons and when he scored in the 3-1 win over Leicester City on 23rd October, 1999 he became one of the few players to score for three different teams in the space of three years.

At the time of their survival in their first season, Bradford's total of 36 points was the lowest of any team to avoid relegation but the bar dropped considerably in the following 14 years and between 2004/05 and 2017/18 a total of 36 points or fewer proved to be enough to avoid relegation on seven occasions.

Ironically Bradford's first match in their second season pitted them against Liverpool but this time they succumbed 1-0 at Anfield. In their first home match they secured a famous 2-0 victory against Chelsea but then did not win any of their next 13 games and it was not until early December that this winless run came to an end, by which time they were mired in the relegation places and never climbed off the bottom after dropping to 20th in mid-December, eventually ending cast adrift and 16 points shy of safety. The Bantams' feathers were well and truly ruffled and they never recovered.

ONE HIT WONDER

On 12th March, 2000 at the grand old age of 41, Bradford's goalkeeping coach came to the club's rescue when all three first-team keepers—Aidan Davison, Matt Clarke and Gary Walsh—were out injured. So it was that Neville Southall came out of retirement to face City's West Yorkshire rivals Leeds. Although not at his peak physically, Southall's performance was respectable enough as he was only beaten twice and in the process he became the fourth oldest player to appear in the Premier League and still remains in the top 10.

In recent years Southall has worked at a special needs school in Ebbw Vale has been an active campaigner over mental health issues.

FOOTNOTE

A QUESTION OF DEGREES - SELECTED GRADUATES

David Wetherall, Bradford City 1999/2000 - 2000/01
First class honours degree in Chemistry (Sheffield University) 1992

Duncan Watmore, Sunderland 2013/14 - 2018/19
First class honours degree in Economics and Business Management (Newcastle University) 2015

Barry Horne, Everton 1992/93 - 1995/96
First class honours degree in Chemistry & Materials Science (Liverpool University) 1984

Steve Palmer Ipswich 1992/93 - 1994/95, Watford 1999/2000
Software Engineering (Christ's College, Cambridge University) 1989

A VIEW FROM THE STANDS

Jamie Allen

Your club's spell in the Premier League was brief and while there was the odd glorious moment ultimately it was short-lived. Looking back now, one question remains - Was it really worth it?

I'll take the obvious question first, what were the long-term consequences of Bradford City's fleeting spell in the Premier League?

The history is there for all to see to be honest and the consequences of the way the club was managed during the 2000/01 season reverberated throughout the best part of a decade. Following our relegation in 2001, the downward spiral almost saw the club disappear into oblivion on more than one occasion. We'd made it all the way to League Two in the six seasons since the heady days of the Premier League. We'd twice survived periods in administration and narrowly avoided relegation from the Football League entirely in 2010/11 thanks to a late Dave Syers winner against Aldershot which all but secured our Football League status for another season. But as they say, that's history.

What would I do differently? A difficult question to answer really, it was a great time to be a City fan, especially the two seasons from 1998 to 2000. However, there was some serious financial mismanagement during City's Premier League years which I'd almost definitely change. Or at least I'd have developed a better long-term plan.

The Stadium expansion was certainly a bit premature and at a high cost when Premier League status wasn't even assured during the 2000/01 season. Although the expansion was spread over a couple of seasons, the first spell of administration in 2002 saw much of the stadium and associated premises sold off to new owners which the club, to date, still don't own outright.

Secondly, the classic issue of playing staff on unsustainable wages and high transfer fees. We spent £2.5m on David Hopkin from Leeds, another £1.5m on Ashley Ward* from Blackburn, Benito Carbone arriving on £40k a week from Villa, a troubled Stan Collymore arriving from Leicester, none of which worked out and weren't sustainable in the long-term. To be fair to Carbone, the lad waived somewhere in the region of £1m in wages he was owed by the club when we went into administration which contributed to our survival as a club. So, was it worth it?

Probably the toughest question of the lot! Some of the best memories of my childhood come from watching Bradford City in the Premier League. Stan Collymore's bicycle kick against Leeds. Dean Windass netting a hattrick against Derby and goals against Arsenal, Leeds and Liverpool. Jamie Lawrence's red or blonde hair (depending on what day of the week it was back then) bounding effortlessly down the wing. A historic win over Arsenal and battling for a point against Chelsea. David Wetherall powering home a header against Liverpool on the final day of the season and celebrating with that famous belly flop, thus securing Premier League status for another year. Watching your team's first foray into European competition—the Intertoto cup was a thing. Google it. Witnessing some of the greatest players of a generation grace the turf of Valley Parade...

Beckham, Scholes, Giggs, Owen, Shearer, Henry, Bergkamp, Vieira, Cole, Zola et al. all rocking up to play football only a stone's throw from your house.

Was it worth the ten years of pain that followed relegation in 2001? Maybe it's the rose-tinted spectacles of nostalgia playing their part but for 11-year-old me... yeah, it was worth it.

* Ashley Ward again still one of the most relegated players see list

BRIGHTON & HOVE ALBION STATS

NUMBER OF SEASONS:

2

2017/18-2018/19

NUMBER OF MATCHES:

76

Wins 18 (Home 13 Away 5)
Draws 22 (Home 13 Away 9)
Losses 36 (Home 12 Away 24)

[Win ratio 24%]

Goals F 69
(Home 43 Away 26)

Goals A 114
(Home 53 Away 61)

Goal Difference: -45

TOTAL POINTS

76

(Home 52: 68%; Away 24: 32%)
Av per season: 38

BEST POSITION:

15th

2017/18

WORST POSITION:

17th

2018/19

BIGGEST WIN:

4-1

v Swansea
(24th Feb, 2018)

BIGGEST LOSS:

0-5

v Bournemouth
(13th Apr, 2019)

LONGEST UNBEATEN RUN:

5 matches (2)

(15th Oct, 2017–20th Nov, 2017
and 31st Jan, 2018–4th Mar, 2018)

LONGEST WITHOUT A WIN:

9 matches

(30th, Mar 2019-12th May, 2019)
*still ongoing

ALL TIME RANKING

43rd

MOST GOALS SCORED IN A SEASON:

60

(2018/19)

FEWEST GOALS SCORED IN A SEASON:

54

(2017/18)

FEWEST GOALS CONCEDED IN A SEASON:

36

(2018/19)

MOST GOALS CONCEDED IN A SEASON:

40

(2017/18)

TOP GOALSCORER:

25

Glenn Murray

MOST APPEARANCES:

74

Lewis Dunk

OWN GOALS:

5

RED CARDS:

6

LOWEST ATTENDANCE:

29,323

v Burnley
(9th Feb, 2019)

HIGHEST ATTENDANCE:

30,682

v Liverpool
(12th Jan, 2019)

All statistics and records supplied by  gracenote.
A NIELSEN COMPANY

BRIGHTON & HOVE ALBION

FIRST PREMIER LEAGUE MATCH: 12TH AUGUST, 2017
BRIGHTON 0
MANCHESTER CITY 2 (AGUERO, DUNK OG)

AMEX STADIUM 30,415

Mat Ryan, Bruno, Shane Duffy, Lewis Dunk, Markus Kuttner, Dale Stephens, Solly March (Anthony Knockaert), Davy Propper, Isaiah Brown (Jamie Murphy), Pascal Gross, Tomer Hemed (Glenn Murray), Manager: Chris Hughton

The range of attendances at the AmEx Stadium is remarkably consistent, with only 1,359 between the highest against Liverpool in January 2019 and the lowest only a month later when they lost to Burnley. That gap represents a differential of less than 5%, among the lowest of any club. Like another South Coast club Bournemouth, Brighton's rise to the sunny uplands of the Premier League was quite a journey, coming back from the brink of relegation from the old Division Four. Brighton's nadir came when they only salvaged their league status on the last day of the 1996/97 season with a draw at Hereford which consigned the Bulls to non-League football instead of the Seagulls.

Brighton had to endure a nomadic existence after the Goldstone Ground was sold for property development. They played games at Gillingham's Priestfield stadium, a 150-mile round trip, and also made a temporary home of a dilapidated athletics venue, the Withdean. After owner Tony Bloom took over in 2009, the club opened their new ground in nearby Falmer in 2011. This marked a turning point for the club and the American Express Community stadium is now a shining example of the change in fortunes for the club as Bloom's gamble has borne fruit.

Brighton survived their first season with a fair degree of comfort, finishing seven points above the drop zone, mostly based on solid home form where they picked up 29 of their 40 points (or 72%) and ensured survival with a memorable 2-1 win over Manchester United, having previously beaten Arsenal and drawn with Tottenham at the Amex. Their only two away victories came in successive matches at West Ham and Swansea.

Brighton ended the 2018/19 season with their worst run of results of their two-season spell and their nine-match winless run since beating arch rivals Crystal Palace in March dragged them into the relegation battle, which ultimately they survived. However, Chris Hughton did not and he was dismissed the day after the season's final match when Manchester City were duly crowned champions after their 4-1 win at the AmEx. Brighton's 3-1 win over Palace on the 4th December was their only victory of more than one goal.

When Alireza Jahanbakhsh arrived at the AmEx in the summer of 2018 he came with a reputation for goals and assists. He was the top scorer in the Eredivisie with 21 goals and also weighed in with 12 assists so expectations were high that he could make an impact. However, the Iranian midfielder certainly did not set the world alight after joining the Seagulls. In his 25 appearances in his first season he did not manage to contribute to either the goals column or even the assists one.

ONE HIT WONDER

Uwe Hünemeier had the misfortune of being brought in to act as back-up to one of the most reliable centre-back partnerships in the Premier League. Dunk was an ever present in the 2017/18 season while Shane Duffy missed one match through suspension. Hünemeier's only opportunity came when he was brought on during the 1-1 home draw with Everton on 15th October, 2017 to replace the injured Duffy in the 73rd minute. It could be said that Hünemeier's career hit the Brighton rocks of Dunk and Duffy.

In May 2018 Hünemeier decided to cut his losses and returned to SC Paderborn from whom he had joined the South Coast outfit in 2015.

FOOTNOTE

DUNK IN A FUNK

Lewis Dunk's own goal in Brighton's first-ever Premier League match against Manchester City set the tone for his season as he managed to add three more of his own, which matches the record of Martin Skrtel's for an individual player in 2013/14. Dunk's quadruple contributed to the Seagulls' tally of five, which is the joint highest for a club in single season. By contrast in the following season neither Dunk nor any Brighton player scored an own goal.

Four players have scored own goals on their club's PL debut and oddly all of them were playing at home.

Jacob Laursen	Derby vs Leeds 1996
Richard Johnson	Watford vs Wimbledon 1999
Stephen Jordan	Burnley vs Stoke 2009
Lewis Dunk	Brighton vs Man City 2017

A VIEW FROM THE STANDS

David Hartrick

What was your club's 'Sliding Doors' moment, that seemingly inconsequential action, which actually became a turning point in their fortunes, for either good or bad?

Sliding Doors moments come along all the time but no one ever tells you they are happening. Losing to Middlesbrough on the final day of the 2015/16 season it didn't feel much like things were going to be alright. I mean in reality the game was a draw but we very much finished as losers on the wrong side of a winner-takes-all game: win/draw for Boro meant they went up, win for us meant we went up. We limped into the Play-Offs with a half-fit first XI with nothing left to give and inevitably lost again. If someone had thought to mention this was a Sliding Doors moment, things might have felt better. As it was I was off to drown my sorrows for a summer.

What followed was a season of triumph opening with an 18-game unbeaten run and ending with a second-place finish which would seen us top the table if our defence hadn't been on the ale from the minute promotion was secured. The title's just a trophy, promotion was everything, and with a better squad than the previous season, a battle-hardened attitude, and a real desire to get over the line, we were up. Pain in the north-east that sharpened minds on the south coast paid off in full. Joyous.

That attitude served us well in our first season and a lack of fear took us to what ended up being a comfortable 15th place finish. Our sophomore season has been tougher and approaches need to change going forward, but that defeat at Boro started everything. Remember next time you find yourself pounding the ground in frustration or calling Aitor Karanka a very rude word, you might be at a crossroads.

BURNLEY STATS

NUMBER OF SEASONS:

5 (3 spells)

2009/10, 2014/15, 2016/17-2018/19

NUMBER OF MATCHES:

190

Wins 51(Home 35 Away 16)
Draws 44 (Home 22 Away 22)
Losses 95 (Home 38 Away 57)

[Win ratio 27%]

Goals F 190
(Home 105 Away 85)

Goals A 297
(Home 120 Away 177)

Goal Difference -107

TOTAL POINTS

197

(Home 127: 64%; Away 70: 36%)
Av per season: 39

BEST POSITION:

7th

2017/18

WORST POSITION:

19th

2014/15 (RELEGATED)

BIGGEST WIN:

4-0

v Burnley
(22nd Sep, 2018)

BIGGEST LOSS:

1-6

v Manchester City
(3rd Apr, 2010)

LONGEST UNBEATEN RUN:

8 matches

(30th Dec, 2018-23rd Feb, 2019)

LONGEST WITHOUT A WIN:

12 matches

(7th Nov, 2009-30th Jan, 2010)

ALL TIME RANKING

43rd

MOST GOALS SCORED IN A SEASON:

45

(2018/19)

FEWEST GOALS SCORED IN A SEASON:

28

(2014/15)

FEWEST GOALS CONCEDED IN A SEASON:

39

(2017/18)

MOST GOALS CONCEDED IN A SEASON:

82

(2009/10)

TOP GOALSCORER:

32

Ashley Barnes

MOST APPEARANCES:

136

Ashley Barnes

OWN GOALS:

11

RED CARDS:

7

LOWEST ATTENDANCE:

16,904

v West Bromwich Albion
(8th Feb, 2015)

HIGHEST ATTENDANCE:

21,870

v Manchester United
(23rd Apr, 2017)

BURNLEY

FIRST PREMIER LEAGUE MATCH: 15TH AUGUST, 2009
STOKE CITY 2 (SHAWCROSS, JORDAN OG)
BURNLEY 0

BRITANNIA STADIUM 27,385

Brian Jensen, Graham Alexander (Steven Thompson), Christian Kalvenes, Clarke Carlisle, Tyrone Mears, Stephen Jordan, Chris McCann, Wade Elliott, Steven Fletcher, Martin Paterson (Fernando Guerrero), Robbie Blake (Chris Eagles), Manager Owen Coyle

Burnley are rightly lauded for their level-headed approach to Premier League status, in that they do not panic when getting either promoted or relegated. Their model equanimity is underlined by the fact that there is no great exodus following relegation or any massive influx of new players when going up. As a result, Sean Dyche is the second longest-serving manager in the Premier League, only 17 days behind Eddie Howe. Howe and Dyche are third and fourth in the list for all 92 English league clubs, just behind Jim Bentley of Morecambe and Garth Ainsworth of Wycombe Wanderers.

Having been appointed in October 2012 he has overseen two promotions and one relegation and is one of only a few managers who has stayed in their job following relegation and has done so for a further four years, which is the longest of any relegated club in recent years. Rafa Benitez is the only manager still in office having suffered Premier League relegation before this season. The Spaniard was brought in to save Newcastle in 2015/16 and failed, but somehow he lasted through all the Mike Ashley shenanigans to get Newcastle back up in 2016/17. However, Benitez's commendable patience ran out in the summer of 2019 and his statement even brought the odd tear to those with no affiliation with Newcastle: "Dear NUFC fans, Thank you for three fantastic, exciting and, at times, challenging years."

Burnley have been rewarded for such rectitude as they now face the prospect of their fourth consecutive season, having been relegated after a single season twice beforehand. In qualifying for Europe in 2017/18 they did so for the only the third time in their 137-year history and for the first time in 51 years. Speaking of history they are one of only four founder clubs of the Football League to be playing in the Premier League in 2019/20 alongside Everton, Wolves and newly-promoted Villa.

They do not score many goals, having the average of exactly one per game as pointed out above, which means they are one of only three clubs with a ratio not above one per game. Hull have the lowest ratio with 181 scored in 190 matches - 0.95 and Barnsley 37 in 38 - 0.97. This goal shyness is reflected in their top individual scorers for each season ranging from eleven by Danny Ings in 2014/15 and Chris Wood in 2017/18 through to Steven Fletcher in 2009/10, Sam Vokes in 2016/17 and Ashley Barnes in 2018/19 with a dozen each. It has certainly not been raining goals at Turf Moor over the years.

Burnley held the spotless record for going 68 games without being awarded a penalty until they were finally given one in the 94th minute against Southampton in February 2019. That penalty was awarded for a foul on Peter Crouch who had just come one as a substitute against one of his former clubs. Crouch set the record for number of appearances as a sub back in November 2017 when he overtook Shola Ameobi's mark of 142. During the 2018/19 season Crouch made half a dozen appearances for the Clarets all from the bench as he extended his record to 159. Unlike with his other six Premier League clubs Crouch did not get on to the scoresheet.

And then very much in the tradition of London buses, they did not have to wait too long before the next one, which came in the very next game against Brighton. Ashley Barnes slotted home both those spot kicks and in his time at Turf Moor he has collected a unique quadruple. For not only is he the top goalscorer for the Clarets with 32 but also he has made the record number of appearances with 136.

Added to which he has the most red cards with two, while also playing in the most wins of any player (38) he has a clean sweep of accolades. And finally he is the only Burnley player or indeed any player to be booked for kissing an opponent as he did with Cardiff's Joe Bennett on April 13th 2019. As Gary Lineker tweeted "Ashley Barnes has received a yellow card after coming face-to-face with Joe Bennett. Barnes kissed Bennett on the nose (honestly), not once but twice. Lucky perhaps not to get 2 yellows." Naturally the referee was none other than Mike Dean. Barnes truly is Burnley's Everyman.

ONE HIT WONDER

Burnley have been blessed with some excellent keepers in recent times with three full England internationals in Tom Heaton, Nick Pope and Joe Hart all vying for a place between the sticks in 2018/19. But before this strong triumvirate were in situ at Turf Moor Brian Jensen was the No.1 and they signed Diego Penny as back-up to the Great Dane in 2008 from Peruvian side Coronel Bolognesi. Penny did play once in the Championship as the Clarets won promotion via the Play-Offs in 2009.

On October 24 2009 Penny got his chance when in the 11th minute of the match Jensen slipped and allowed Hugo Rodallega to roll the ball into an empty net to equalise for Wigan after Steven Fletcher's early goal. Having bruised his pride in the incident Jensen also injured his ankle and was soon replaced by Penny. Alas Penny was not able to keep Roberto Martinez's team out as they ran out 3-1 winners, inflicting Burnley's first defeat at home since February 2009.

Penny was then dropped and never returned. He went back to Peru and his last port of call was Lima-based Universidad San Martin.

FOOTNOTE

22 GO MAD IN EUROPE
When Burnley qualified for Europe courtesy of their 7th place
in the 2017/18 season they became the 21st Premier League club
to claim a European spot through their league position.
European club representation, excluding the Intertoto Cup
and via UEFA Fair Play.

CLUB WITH FIRST SEASON QUALIFYING VIA PREMIER LEAGUE

CLUB	YEAR
Manchester United	1992/93
Aston Villa	1992/93
Norwich City	1992/93
Blackburn Rovers	1993/94
Newcastle United	1993/94
Nottingham Forest	1994/95
Liverpool	1994/95
Leeds United	1994/95
Arsenal	1995/96
Chelsea	1998/99
Ipswich Town	2000/01
Everton	2004/05
Bolton Wanderers	2004/05
Middlesbrough	2004/05
Tottenham Hotspur	2005/06
Fulham	2008/09
Manchester City	2009/10
Southampton	2014/15
Leicester City	2015/16
West Ham United	2015/16
Burnley	2017/18
Wolves	2018/19

A VIEW FROM THE STANDS

Matt Moss, from the No Nay Never podcast

What was your club's 'Sliding Doors' moment, that seemingly inconsequential action, which actually became a turning point in their fortunes, for either good or bad?

Burnley had finished the six seasons prior to 2008-09 in the bottom half of the Championship and were experiencing deepening financial difficulties, thanks in no part to the failure of ITV Digital. In November 2004 the board had sold off the club's historic ground, Turf Moor, along with the training facilities at Gawthorpe Hall on a leaseback deal in order to clear debts that were threatening to send one of the founder members of the Football League into administration.

However, 2008-09 brought better times on the pitch with manager Owen Coyle in his first full season in charge leading Burnley to the semi-finals of the League Cup at the expense of Fulham, Arsenal and Chelsea. Only an extra-time winner stopped them from beating Spurs and heading to Wembley. This proved to be the incentive the Clarets needed to push on to the end of the season. They lost just three of their remaining 18 games to finish fifth and reach the play-offs.

Two commanding victories over Reading sent Burnley to Wembley to face Sheffield United for a place in the Premier League. The 10th anniversary of this historic day occurred recently and both players and staff recall the confidence in the dressing room and belief that there was no way they were going to lose that match. Win it they did, albeit thanks to a nervy 1-0 victory, and the Clarets were promoted and received an estimated £60m, more than enough to rescue the club, buy back the ground (which they did in the summer of 2013) and protect the club financially for the future.

Even now as we enter a fourth consecutive Premier League season with all the riches it brings, the club still maintain a sensible financial plan, supported by Dyche, in the knowledge that should the unthinkable occur and the club is relegated, it would not free-fall into the kinds of financial catastrophes that we have witnessed other great clubs suffer over recent years.

The appointment and retention of Sean Dyche has been a huge part of Burnley's success over the last six years, but there may not have been a club for him to lead had that squad of 2008-09 not achieved the unthinkable and taken us all to the PL (promised land).

CARDIFF CITY STATS

NUMBER OF SEASONS:

2 (2 spells)

014/15, 2018/19

NUMBER OF MATCHES:

76

Wins 17 (Home 11 Away 6)
Draws 13 (Home 7 Away 6)
Losses 46 (Home 20 Away 26)

[Win ratio 22%]

Goals F 66
(Home 41 Away 25)

Goals A 143
(Home 73 Away 70)

Goal Difference: -77

TOTAL POINTS

64

(Home 40: 62%; Away 24: 38%)
Av per season: 32

BEST POSITION:

18th

2018/19 (RELEGATED)

WORST POSITION:

20th

2013/14 (RELEGATED)

BIGGEST WIN:

4-2

v Fulham
(20th Oct, 2018)

BIGGEST LOSS:

0-5

v Manchester City
(22nd Sep, 2018)

LONGEST UNBEATEN RUN:

3 matches

(25th Aug, 2013–14th Sep, 2013)

LONGEST WITHOUT A WIN:

12 matches

(19th Apr, 2014–6th Oct, 2018)

ALL TIME RANKING

44th

MOST GOALS SCORED IN A SEASON:

40

(2013/14)

FEWEST GOALS SCORED IN A SEASON:

34

(2018/19)

FEWEST GOALS CONCEDED IN A SEASON:

69

(2018/19)

MOST GOALS CONCEDED IN A SEASON:

74

(2013/14)

TOP GOALSCORER:

7

Jordon Mutch

MOST APPEARANCES:

51

Aron Gunnarsson

OWN GOALS:

0

RED CARDS:

2

LOWEST ATTENDANCE:

26,167

v Hull City
(22nd Feb, 2014)

HIGHEST ATTENDANCE:

30,419

v Liverpool
(21st Apr, 2019)

All statistics and records supplied by

CARDIFF CITY

DID YOU KNOW?

Of their 17 wins over two seasons only six have been by more than a one goal margin of which two were against Fulham—4-2 in October 2018 and 3-1 in March 2014. Considering Cardiff only scored more than two goals in a match five times in 76 fixtures, Fulham were clearly their most favoured opposition. Added to this they also beat Fulham 2-1 away in 2013/14, which was their only double of that season. So nine of their 64 points have been at Fulham's expense or 14% of their total.

FIRST PREMIER LEAGUE MATCH: 27TH AUGUST, 2013
WEST HAM UNITED 2 (J.COLE, NOLAN)
CARDIFF CITY 0

UPTON PARK 34,977

*David Marshall, Steven Caulker, Ben Turner, Declan Jones,
Matthew Connolly, Peter Whittingham, Gary Medel,
Kim Bo-Kyung (Nicky Maynard), Aron Gunnarsson,
Craig Bellamy (Rudy Gestede), Fraizer Campbell (Jordon Mutch),
Manager: Malky Mackay*

Cardiff were first promoted to the Premier League two seasons after their South Wales rivals, Swansea who made it to the top flight in 2011/12. Unfortunately for the Bluebirds fans they did not linger long, finishing rock bottom in 2013/14. By the time they had returned Swansea had been relegated so there has only been one single season with two Welsh clubs in the Premier League. Cardiff's second relegation in 2018/19 was an improvement on their first effort and they became the first club since Bolton in 2010/11 to record ten wins but still be relegated.

Neil Warnock had performed a minor miracle getting Cardiff automatic promotion in 2017/18 with a limited squad and a similarly small budget, but as Warnock's wont he then saw them relegated. Having experienced the pain of Sheffield United's relegation in 2006/07, keeping Cardiff up proved too much for him. The tragic death of their record signing Emiliano Sala in January 2019 in a plane crash was a devastating blow to the club both emotionally and psychologically and one from which they did not recover.

One thing that the Bluebirds have achieved in their brief sojourns is that they are the only club to have played more than one season and not conceded an own goal. The fact that their top scorer over those two seasons was a midfield player who only played in the first season and managed a mere seven goals is an indication of where their problems lay. And that Jordon Mutch was that man says a fair bit about their so-called strikers.

Their last game of 2018/19 season was a 2-0 win at Old Trafford inflicting a defeat on their old manager Ole Gunnar Solksjaer while their very first Premier League win was a 3-2 victory over Manchester City in August 2013. Their only other double in their two spells aside from against Fulham, was over Brighton in the 2018/19 season, whom they were vying with to escape the clutches of relegation. The Seagulls ultimately prevailed over the Bluebirds by two points.

ONE HIT WONDER

Jo Inge Berget arrived at Cardiff as one of Gunnar Solksjaer's first signings in January 2014, having been with his fellow Norwegian at Molde. He was one of three Norwegians to play for The Bluebirds, which is the highest number of players from one country outside the British Isles for the Welsh club. Berget found it difficult to break into the struggling Cardiff team, who were looking increasingly doomed as each game passed. He came on as a replacement for Fraizer Campbell in the 79th minute of a pretty disastrous 4-0 defeat to fellow relegation candidates, Hull City, which pretty much sealed their fate.

After Cardiff were duly relegated in 20th place Berget moved on loan to Celtic and eventually departed these shores. He moved to Malmo FF then spent a season with New York City FC before returning to Malmo where he is currently under contract until 2022.

FOOTNOTE

DOUBLE-FIGURE TROUBLE

All three clubs relegated in the very first Premier League season managed to get into double figures for wins albeit in a 42-game season. Palace and Middlesbrough have twice got into double figures and gone down.

HIGHEST NUMBER OF WINS FOR RELEGATED CLUBS

WINS	CLUB	SEASON
11	Crystal Palace	1992/93* & 1994/95*
11	Middlesbrough	1992/93*
10	Nottingham Forest	1992/93*
10	Norwich City	1994/95*
10	Middlesbrough	1996/97
10	Sunderland	1996/97
10	Barnsley	1997/98
10	West Ham	2002/03
10	Sheffield United	2006/07
10	Reading	2007/08
10	Blackpool	2010/11
10	Bolton Wanderers	2011/12
10	Cardiff City	2018/19

* 42-game season

A VIEW FROM THE STANDS

Scott Salter, View From The Ninian

Your club's spell in the Premier League was brief and while there was the odd glorious moment ultimately it was short-lived. Looking back now, one question remains - Was it really worth it?

It was short but sweet, but on the whole the 2018/19 season was an enjoyable experience for Cardiff City in the Premier League. Certainly far more enjoyable than our last stint in the top flight!

I actually don't think I'd do anything differently, which may sound strange considering we were relegated. While our fellow promoted sides spent big, Cardiff were more conservative and brought in players for modest fees and wages.

We learnt our lesson from 2013/14 and stability and building for the future were the most important aspects for the club. Would Neil Warnock have been sacked by another club at some point in the season? Probably. For Cardiff though, context is key. Warnock has transformed the club on and off the pitch. When he joined the relationship between the club and fans was fragmented. Now we are united.

Was it worth it? That's certainly a more difficult question to answer. For the club, yes. Our long-awaited new training ground has now finally got the green light and the club is now better off financially. However, two men, Emiliano Sala and pilot David Ibbotson, lost their lives as a result of Cardiff City being a Premier League club, which puts everything into perspective.

CHARLTON ATHLETIC STATS

NUMBER OF SEASONS:

8 (2 spells)

1998/99; 2000/1-2006/07

NUMBER OF MATCHES:

304

Wins 93 (Home 58 Away 35)
Draws 82 (Home 40 Away 42)
Losses 129 (Home 54 Away 75)

[Win ratio 30%]

Goals F 342
(Home 199 Away 143)

Goals A 442
(Home 198 Away 244)

Goal Difference: -100

TOTAL POINTS

361

(Home 214: 59% ; Away 147: 41%)
Av per season: -45

BEST POSITION:

7th

2003/04

WORST POSITION:

19th

2006/07 (RELEGATED)

BIGGEST WIN:

5-0

v Southampton
(22nd Aug, 1998)

BIGGEST LOSS:

1-6

v Leeds
(5th Apr, 2003)

LONGEST UNBEATEN RUN:

9 matches

(30th Dec, 2000–3rd Mar, 2001)

LONGEST WITHOUT A WIN:

13 matches

(2nd Nov, 1998–31st Jan, 1999)

ALL TIME RANKING

25th

MOST GOALS SCORED IN A SEASON:

51

(2003/04)

FEWEST GOALS SCORED IN A SEASON:

34

(2006/07)

FEWEST GOALS CONCEDED IN A SEASON:

49

(2001/02)

MOST GOALS CONCEDED IN A SEASON:

60

(2006/07)

TOP GOALSCORER:

34

Jason Euell

MOST APPEARANCES:

187

Chris Powell

OWN GOALS:

12

RED CARDS:

24

LOWEST ATTENDANCE:

16,488

v Southampton
(16th Aug, 1998)

HIGHEST ATTENDANCE:

27,111

v Chelsea
(17th Sep, 2005)

CHARLTON ATHLETIC

FIRST PREMIER LEAGUE MATCH: 15TH AUGUST, 1998
NEWCASTLE UNITED 0
CHARLTON ATHLETIC 0

ST JAMES' PARK 36,719

Sasa Ilic, Danny Mills, Chris Powell, Neil Redfearn, Richard Rufus, Eddie Youds, Shaun Newton, Mark Kinsella, Andy Hunt (Steve Brown), Clive Mendonca (Steve Jones), John Robinson (Paul Mortimer), Manager: Alan Curbishley

Having won promotion through one of the most dramatic Play-Offs Finals ever, against Sunderland, Charlton's first match was by coincidence away against their opponents' North East rivals, Newcastle United. After the thrills and spills of their 4-4 draw in May at Wembley their goalless draw was something of an anti-climax. One of the heroes from the Play-Offs had a bad, truncated day as one-club man Richard Rufus, who had scored his first-ever Charlton goal in that final, was sent off in the 24th minute and in so doing became the quickest Premier League debutant to be sent off and one of only three players to be dismissed in their club's opening Premier League match (see Birmingham Footnote).

On a more positive note Neil Redfearn played in that game and is the only player to have featured in three different clubs' first-ever Premier League games as he also appeared in the opening games for Barnsley in 1997 and Bradford in 1999, neatly completing the feat in three consecutive seasons. Chris Powell also played in Charlton's debut match and went on to play in every game that season with only a couple of late substitutions denying him the rare achievement of playing every minute of a club's campaign. In that first season he scored his only goal in a 4-2 win over West Ham, who were clearly impressed as they bought him a few years later. He featured in six of Charlton's eight Premier League seasons, racking up almost 200 appearances, which represents over 60% of their matches.

Their Play-Offs hat-trick hero Clive Mendonca was at it again in the Valiants' first home match when he scored three in a 5-0 win against Southampton. It turned out to be Charlton's biggest-ever Premier League win in their 304 matches but ironically was in front of their lowest-ever attendance at the Valley of 16,488. That win saw Charlton move to the top of the table and alongside Bolton in 2011/12 and Hull in 2016/17 this trio are the only clubs to have been top of the table and then get relegated in the same season. Mendonca went on to become their top scorer in that first season, but with only eight goals their lack of firepower was evident and the main reason why they finished 18th and like so many clubs Charlton were relegated immediately after gaining promotion to the Premier League. However, they did bounce back the following year and spent the next seven years in the top flight.

Charlton's best season was in 2003/04 when they reached a highly creditable seventh under Alan Curbishley finishing as the third highest-placed London side with Tottenham way down in 14th. For the only time in their eight seasons they won more games (14) than they lost (13). They also finished that season with a neutral goal difference, one of only five teams to achieve this peculiar feat, the others being Leicester in 1999/2000, Middlesbrough 2000/01, Tottenham 2008/09 & Swansea 2013/14.

Scoring goals had been a perennial problem for Charlton and even in their best season their overall top scorer Jason Euell only got ten goals. The paucity of goals left Charlton with a measly average of only 1.3 scored per game, which is among the lowest ratios of any club. This shyness in front of goal is also illustrated by the fact that only twice in eight seasons did their leading scorer get more than 11 goals and both times that was Darren Bent, with 18 in 2005/06 and 13 in 2006/07, when ironically they were relegated. Rather neatly for those fond of round numbers their overall goal difference is -100. If that is rather pleasing for those of a neat inclination, they almost reached a state of fastidiousness as they scored 199 goals at home and 198 away. So nearly the ultimate in neatness, so near yet so far, but a Valiant effort all the same.

ONE HIT WONDER

Darren Randolph has had plenty of Premier League experience with West Ham and has become a full international with the Republic of Ireland. However, during his six years at Charlton, his first club, he only made one appearance at the highest level and bizarrely it was the very last game that Charlton played in the Premier League when they drew 2-2 with Liverpool at Anfield in May 2007. Randolph stayed at Charlton for a few more years but they failed to recapture their top-flight status before he moved to Motherwell and Birmingham before finally getting regular Premier League action at West Ham.

Randolph started the 2018/19 season at Middlesbrough

FOOTNOTE

Charlton are one of only five clubs to register a zero goal difference, Charlton's 7th place in 2003/04 is the highest achieved by this group.

SEASON	CLUB	POSITION
1999/2000	Leicester City	8th
2000/2001	Middlesbrough	14th
2003/2004	Charlton	7th
2008/2009	Tottenham	8th
2013/2014	Swansea	12th

A VIEW FROM THE STANDS

Sam Spong, Charlton Soul

What was your club's 'Sliding Doors' moment, that seemingly inconsequential action, which actually became a turning point in their fortunes, for either good or bad?

Friday 30th January, 2004. Scott Parker stands in a typically Noughties, combination of blazer and jeans on the Stamford Bridge turf, grinning from ear to ear at joining the club he had humiliated a matter of weeks earlier on Boxing Day. A man who embodied everything we loved about Charlton, gone, and for a pitiful £10m.

Charlton's 2003/04 season had been nothing short of breathtaking. They had spent almost the entire campaign in fourth place, and deservedly so. A genuine, hardened belief had replaced the pleasant summer surprise at a good start. It was actually going to happen. Liverpool, Tottenham, Everton. Occasions that should've been seen as once-in-a-lifetime, 'wish you were there' victories, for better or worse, were now expected results. And at the middle of it all shone Scott Parker. A new breed from the old school. A South London-born, firebrand academy product terrorising Premier League sides up and down the country from St Mary's to St James'. The grit of a pit bull, the flair of Gazza and the grace of Best. A player who made every single Charlton fan burst with pride. The paradoxical spectacle of radical commitment appearing so effortless. But forget what it looked like, the local lad with global talent was dragging his modest, respectable, overlooked club to the brink of the Champions League. Nothing felt beyond us. Club, owners and fans playing an equal role in the unflinching defiance of hierarchy. Charlton Athletic were heading to Europe.

And just like that, it was over. A firm kick to the stomach that felt personally delivered by Abramovich himself. That 4-2 defeat at The Valley on Boxing Day in 2004 had been the first humiliation of Chelsea's new money Galacticos. A cold, hard South London wake-up call he felt compelled to avenge. One deceitful, bad-blooded transfer saga later and Charlton's talisman was Chelsea's toy. Never truly welcomed or integrated, Parker would go on to play a peripheral role in West London and quietly depart for Newcastle just a few years later. Despite glimpses here and there, neither the Premier League nor England would ever fully feel the glory of a player who made the Saturday afternoons and cold Wednesday nights of so many, so special.

The new age of the billionaire had reached British football. A click of one man's fingers had commodified the dreams of an entire community. Charlton would never fully recover from the ominous sense of loss that Parker's departure had left. It confirmed the nagging realism that the ethically run, family club had reached terminal velocity. Our Truman Show boat had hit the wall. The message from the top was clear: clubs like yours go no further, please turn back. And we did.

CHELSEA STATS

NUMBER OF SEASONS:

27

1992/93-2018/19

TOTAL POINTS

1,931

(Home 1,102: 57%; Away 829: 43%)
Av per season: 72

NUMBER OF MATCHES:

1,038

Wins 558 (Home 325 Away 233)
Draws 257 (Home 127 Away 130)
Losses 223 (Home 67 Away 156)

[Win ratio 54%]

Goals F 1,770
(Home 1,023 Away 747)

Goals A 1,002
(Home 429 Away 573)

Goal Difference: +768

BEST POSITION:

1st (5)

2004/05; 2005/06; 2009/10;
2014/15; 2016/17 (CHAMPIONS)

WORST POSITION:

14th

1993/94

BIGGEST WIN:

8-0 (2)

v Wigan (9th May, 2010)
v Aston Villa (23rd Dec, 2012)

BIGGEST LOSS:

6-0

v Manchester City
(10th Feb, 2019)

LONGEST UNBEATEN RUN:

40 matches

(23rd Oct, 2004–29th Oct, 2005)

LONGEST WITHOUT A WIN:

12 matches

(11th Dec, 1992–21st Feb, 1993)

ALL TIME RANKING

3rd

MOST GOALS SCORED IN A SEASON:

103

(2009/10)

FEWEST GOALS SCORED IN A SEASON:

46

(1995/96)

FEWEST GOALS CONCEDED IN A SEASON:

15

(2004/05)

MOST GOALS CONCEDED IN A SEASON:

55 (2)

(1994/95 & 1996/97)

TOP GOALSCORER:

147

Frank Lampard

MOST APPEARANCES:

492

John Terry

OWN GOALS:

34

RED CARDS:

78

LOWEST ATTENDANCE:

8,923

v Coventry
(4th May, 1994)

HIGHEST ATTENDANCE:

43,417

v West Bromwich Albion
(26th Dec, 2008)

CHELSEA

FIRST PREMIER LEAGUE MATCH: 15TH AUGUST, 1992
CHELSEA 1 (HARFORD)
OLDHAM ATHLETIC 1 (HENRY)

STAMFORD BRIDGE 20,699

Dave Beasant, Gareth Hall, Mal Donaghy, Paul Elliott, Steve Clarke, Graham Stuart, Damien Matthew (Eddie Newton), Andy Townsend, Vinnie Jones, Robert Fleck, Mick Harford, Manager: Ian Porterfield

Chelsea have won more Premier League titles (five) than any club apart from Manchester United and were the last club to successfully defend the trophy in 2005/06 before Manchester City did so in 2018/19. They also became the first club in Premier League history to dismiss their manager. We have grown accustomed to the dizzying pace of the managerial merry-go-round when the first casualty is announced before the clocks go back and the winter ball is unveiled but in 1992/93 there was just the one managerial casualty throughout the entire season.

The first, and only, dismissal of the opening year was Chelsea's Ian Porterfield. In the very next season six managers lost their jobs, so in the space of a year there had already been a radical change in the attitude to the role of the manager that has continued ever since, with an average of seven managers leaving their posts over the last ten years. In that inaugural season Chelsea achieved a balanced record that was matched by Coventry in the following season as they won 14 games, drew 14 and lost 14; something that is impossible in a 38-match season. It is worth remembering that Chelsea were not the dominant force they are today and in the first four seasons they could not break into the top ten but since 1996/97 they have only finished outside the top six once, in 2015/16 when the Mourinho meltdown saw them slip to a lowly tenth.

Chelsea had held the record for the fewest number of draws in a season for more than 20 years, having twice drawn only three games throughout an entire season, in 1997/98 and 2016/17 until Tottenham broke the Blues' grip on the record by drawing only two in 2018/19, including one on the very last day of the season against Everton.

In 2004/05, Jose Mourinho's first season at Stamford Bridge and following the arrival of Petr Cech from French club Rennes, Chelsea conceded just 15 goals, including going a record ten games without conceding between beating Norwich 4-0 on 18th December, 2004 to 5th March, 2005 when they also beat Norwich 3-1. Only twice throughout the entire season did they let in more than one goal, against Bolton and Arsenal in 2-2 draws and Cech kept a record 24 clean sheets. Cech made a total of 89 appearances during this three-year period and would have featured more heavily if he had not suffered a serious skull injury against Reading, which forced him to miss 15 consecutive games from October 2006 until January 2007.

Mourinho may have been heavily criticised for his negative approach at times but Chelsea's defensive resilience should be recognised. Over his first three full seasons, from 2004/05 to 2006/07, Chelsea let in only 61 goals in 114 league matches, which amounts to slightly more than a goal every two games. Only once did they concede more than two goals during that entire period in a 3-0 loss at Middlesbrough on 11th February 2006 when they had pretty much wrapped up the title already. On only a dozen occasions did they let in two goals in a game and significantly Cech missed six of those games, mostly because of his enforced absence in 2006/07. Of those twelve games they lost only three, drawing five and winning four.

The next time Cech conceded more than two goals was in a 4-4 draw with Aston Villa on Boxing Day 2007, which meant that he went 113 games with only once letting in more than two goals. He played in 280 league wins throughout his career, more than Barnsley (10), Blackpool (10), Bradford (14), Cardiff (17), Huddersfield (12), Hull (41), Ipswich (57), Oldham (22), Reading (32), Sheffield United (32) and Swindon (5) (252) combined.

Chelsea remained undefeated at Stamford Bridge in Mourinho's first spell, an impressive total of 60 league games that came in the middle of the record unbeaten home run, which stretched for over four and a half years from February 2004 when they lost 2-1 to Arsenal all the way to October 2008 when they lost 1-0 to Liverpool. In all, Chelsea's impressive home form amounted to 86 matches unbeaten and up to the most recent season the closest to this had been Manchester City who went 37 games unbeaten at the Etihad between December 2010 and December 2012, when they lost painfully to a last minute Robin van Persie winner in the Manchester derby. But now Liverpool have gone for over two years and 40 Premier League matches at Anfield without suffering a defeat since a 2-1 loss to Crystal Palace in April 2017.

Not only have Chelsea proven to be pretty formidable at home but they also are pretty good at starting as they hold the record for the most consecutive victories in their opening fixtures. Nine wins on the trot between 2002/03 and 2011/12 were at the heart of an 18-match unbeaten opening game run that stretched from 1999 to 2017 when the champions were shocked by Burnley's 3-2 win at Stamford Bridge. They also recorded the biggest win in the first game of the season when as champions they crushed newly promoted West Brom 6-0 on 14th August, 2010 led by a Didier Drogba hat-trick.

Drogba had also scored a hat-trick on the last day of the previous season when Chelsea beat Wigan 8-0 to secure the Premier League title in style, making him one of the few players to score successive trebles. In the game before that Wigan match, fellow Ivorian Salomon Kalou scored in Chelsea's 7-0 win over Stoke. This run was the only time three successive hat-tricks have been scored by non-English players. Drogba's hat-trick against West Brom was the last one scored in an opening fixture, there have been five other hat-tricks in the first round of games, starting with Mick Quinn's for Coventry in 1993 when they beat Arsenal 3-0 at Highbury.

In all, Drogba scored three hat-tricks, a feat matched for the Blues by Jimmy Floyd Hasselbaink between 2000 and 2004. Probably his most well-known was his 'perfect hat-trick' against none other than Tottenham. His other notable hat-trick came on 27th March, 2004, when Hasselbaink came on as a 60th-minute substitute for Geremi when a struggling Wolves were 2-1 up at Stamford Bridge. After Frank Lampard equalised the Dutchman took over, scoring in the 77th, 88th and 93rd minutes to secure victory. Hasselbaink's timing could not have been better as this just happened to be his 32nd birthday. The only other player to score a Premier League hat-trick on his birthday was Carlos Tevez who scored all three goals in Manchester City's win over West Brom on 5th February, 2011, the Argentinian's 27th birthday.

ONE HIT WONDER

A Brazilian international with 24 caps who was an ever-present in the triumphant Copa America team in 2007, Mineiro arrived at Stamford Bridge from Hertha Berlin in September 2008, fully expecting to become a regular member of the team. But he was behind Michael Essien and Jon Obi Mikel in the pecking order and had to make do with a single substitute appearance. At least that one game was a comfortable win. Mineiro's cameo lasted 15 minutes after he came on for Nicolas Anelka, who had already scored a hat-trick, against Sunderland on 1st November. By the end of the season he was considered surplus to requirements and went back to Germany joining Schalke 04 in August 2009.

He ended up playing in the fourth tier of German football with FC Koblenz before retiring in 2012.

FOOTNOTE

FEWEST GOALS CONCEDED IN A SEASON
Chelsea feature four times, more than any other club.

CLUB	SEASON	CONCEDED
Chelsea	2004/05	15
Arsenal	1998/99	17
Chelsea	2005/06	22
Man United	2007/08	22
Liverpool	2018/19	22
Man City	2018/19	23
Man United	2008/09	24
Chelsea	2006/07	24
Chelsea	2008/09	24
Liverpool	2004/05	25

A VIEW FROM THE STANDS

James Evans

As one of the select clubs that is an ever-present throughout Premier League history your club has enjoyed prolonged success so what is your favourite moment from the last 27 years?

Chelsea could finally claim to be one of the big European clubs with THAT Champions League victory against Bayern Munich on the 19th May, 2012 in the Allianz Arena. However, even though that is one of the club's highest points, for me personally the title victory in 2004/05 was my favourite moment. It set us on the path to becoming one of the most successful clubs in English football over the next 15 or so years. It gave us an identity and an attacking style of play that was at times breathtaking to watch with Damien Duff and Arjen Robben on the break. But the team was equally stubborn and resilient at the back, led by "captain – leader – legend" John Terry.

That season the stars aligned. Terry, Petr Čech and Frank Lampard formed the spine of the team which would stay in place for many years to come; a brash, young, manager created a fortress-like mentality and the fact it was 50 years since our last title win. It all culminated in an away trip to the Bolton. A nervous looking team on the brink of glory was led by a heroic Lampard performance. His two goals secured the title as Jose sat in the dugout, smile on his face, calmly talking to his wife on the mobile letting her know that Chelsea FC were indeed champions of England!

COVENTRY CITY STATS

NUMBER OF SEASONS:

9

1992/93 – 2000/01

NUMBER OF MATCHES:

354

Wins 99 (Home 65 Away 34)
Draws 112 (Home 56 Away 56)
Losses 143 (Home 56 Away 87)

[Win ratio 28%]

Goals F 387
(Home 219 Away 168)

Goals A 490
(Home 199 Away 291)

Goal Difference: -103

TOTAL POINTS

409

(Home 251: 61%; Away 158: 39%)
Av per season: -45

BEST POSITION:

11th

(1993/94 & 1997/98)

WORST POSITION:

19th

2001/02 (RELEGATED)

BIGGEST WIN:

5-0

v Blackburn
(9th Dec, 1995)

BIGGEST LOSS:

6-1

v Chelsea
(21st Oct, 2000)

LONGEST UNBEATEN RUN:

9 matches (3)

(8th May, 1993-18th Sep, 1993;
25th Jan, 1995-14th Mar, 1995;
17th Jan, 1998-4th Apr, 1998)

LONGEST WITHOUT A WIN:

14 matches

(26th Aug, 1995-4th Dec, 1995)

ALL TIME RANKING

22rd

MOST GOALS SCORED IN A SEASON:

52

(1992/93)

FEWEST GOALS SCORED IN A SEASON:

36

(2000/01)

FEWEST GOALS CONCEDED IN A SEASON:

44

(1997/98)

MOST GOALS CONCEDED IN A SEASON:

63

(2000/01)

TOP GOALSCORER:

61

Dion Dublin

MOST APPEARANCES:

191

Steve Ogrizovic
Paul Telfer 191

OWN GOALS:

10

RED CARDS:

24

LOWEST ATTENDANCE:

9,509

v Ipswich
(10th Oct, 1994)

HIGHEST ATTENDANCE:

24,429

v Manchester United
(12th Apr, 1993)

All statistics and records supplied by

COVENTRY CITY

FIRST PREMIER LEAGUE MATCH: 15TH AUGUST, 1992
COVENTRY CITY 2 (WILLIAMS, SMITH)
MIDDLESBROUGH 1 (WILKINSON)

HIGHFIELD ROAD 12,681

Steve Ogrizovic, Terry Fleming, Kenny Sansom, Stewart Robson, Andy Pearce, Peter Atherton, Micky Gynn, Lee Hurst (Phil Babb), Robert Rosario, John Williams, David Smith (Sean Flynn), Manager: Bobby Gould

Coventry were an established top flight club when the Premier League started, having been a First Division outfit since 1967/68. Indeed Coventry fans may have grown too used to seeing their club in the top division as they attracted just under 13,000 to their opening game, which was the lowest crowd of that first weekend. They scored 52 goals in that first season, the most productive of all of the nine seasons they played in the Premier League. Although they only finished 15th they secured arguably their greatest Premier League victory when they thrashed Graeme Souness' Liverpool 5-1 in December 1992 with both Brian Borrows and Mick Quinn notching doubles while the Reds' Jamie Redknapp had a mixed day giving away a penalty, scoring Liverpool's goal with a beautiful free-kick before being dismissed for a second yellow.

Jonathan Gould was in goal for Coventry, one of the 26 appearances he made for the Sky Blues, and became one of the group of players who played under their father as manager. The Goulds were not the only father-son pairing at Coventry with Gavin Strachan playing 16 times under his father Gordon between 1997 and 2001, when both left the club.

Coventry are one of only two of the original 22 Premier League clubs to have fallen all the way down to the lowest division (Wimbledon are not included for obvious reasons). Since relegation in 2000/01 they scuttled down the divisions, beset by ownership problems and complications with their ground. They spent a single year in League Two in 2017/18 before being promoted via the Play-Offs, swapping positions with Oldham who then became the second club from that original season's Premier League line-up to slide all the way down to the lowest tier.

Before Coventry were eventually relegated from the Premier League, they did manage one of the more unlikely escapes from the trapdoor when they secured their safety by winning at White Hart Lane on the last day of the 1996/97 season to send both Middlesbrough and Sunderland down instead. They benefited directly from Middlesbrough's three-point deduction for not fielding team earlier in the season as they survived by two points. They were also helped by the fact that their match with Spurs kicked off 15 minutes late because of traffic problems so they had the advantage of knowing what their rivals from the North East had done—Sunderland lost and Boro drew—so for the latter stages of the match Coventry knew a win would keep them up.

That win over Spurs was almost inevitably set up by their record Premier League goal-scorer Dion Dublin's opening header and Dublin also provided the assist for City's second after 39 minutes. Although Spurs got one back before half-time Coventry resisted the home side's pressure in the second half to stay above the dreaded dotted line. Dublin was the club's top scorer for four seasons on the trot and he became the joint highest scorer in the league in 1997/98 alongside Michael Owen and Chris Sutton. Dublin's achievement in that season was all the more impressive as Coventry finished 11th, which is the only time the league's top scorer has come from a club outside the top 10.

Unusually two players share Coventry's appearance record with Steve Ogrizovic and Paul Telfer both racking up 191. Ogrizovic had been at Highfield Road since 1984 so had already played more than 300 games when the Premier League started and he was the regular keeper for the first six seasons before being replaced by Magnus Hedman. Telfer joined from Luton in 1995 and was a regular over his six seasons with the club until he departed to Southampton after relegation in 2001. Ogrizovic is one of the few goalkeepers who has scored a goal in the top flight but his effort against Sheffield Wednesday was achieved before the Premier League was formed, in 1986.

Coventry made quite an impact on the opening games of the season in the early days of the Premier League, being involved in half of the games that featured hat-tricks. Micky Quinn became the first player to score a hat-trick in a season's opener when Coventry shocked Arsenal in a 3-0 win at Highbury on the 14th August, 1993.

The Sky Blues were also involved in two of the other five hat-tricks scored in the first games of the season when in 1996 Kevin Campbell scored three for Forest in a 3-0 win at Highfield Road. Then a year later top goalscorer Dion Dublin did so against Chelsea in a 3-2 victory, with two of his goals coming in the last ten minutes. One of Dublin's other two hat-tricks was scored when Coventry lost 4-3 at Sheffield Wednesday in December 1995 and he is one of only four players to have scored a hat-trick but end up on the losing side (see Footnote).

Like Wimbledon, Coventry have tantalisingly notched up 99 Premier League wins, although it took Coventry one more season than The Dons to accumulate that many wins and with 409 points they are just outside the top 20 for all-time points. Having dropped down to League Two by 2017/18 they have started to climb back up the league ladder, winning the play-offs to return to the third tier but it will require some blue sky thinking before they can hope to gain that 100th victory.

ONE HIT WONDER

Mick Harford was well-known for his rumbustious style, having made his name playing for Luton and before seeing out his career at Wimbledon but it may have escaped most people's attention that he spent a season at Highfield Road in 1993/94. In their first home match of the season Harford came on as a substitute in the 73rd minute against one of his former clubs, Newcastle. The visitors had held out for almost an hour after keeper Pavel Srnicek had been sent off but Harford scored the winning goal with five minutes remaining. This was not however the start of a glorious career for Coventry as Harford was denied any further action with the Sky Blues when he sustained a serious back injury that put him on the sidelines for the rest of the season. A small consolation was that he became a member of that elite band of players who have scored on their one and only Premier League appearance for a club.

Harford took over as interim Luton manager when Nathan Jones left to join Stoke in January 2019 and led them to promotion to the Championship.

FOOTNOTE

HAT-TRICKS ON LOSING SIDE

Matthew Le Tissier	**Oldham 4 Southampton 3 - May 1993**
Matthew Le Tissier	Southampton 3 Nottingham Forest 4 - August 1995
Dion Dublin	Sheffield Wednesday 4 Coventry 3 - December 1995
Dwight Yorke	Newcastle 4 Aston Villa 3 - September 1996
Roque Santa Cruz	Wigan 5 Blackburn 3 - December 2007

A VIEW FROM THE STANDS

Mick Quinn became the first player to score a hat-trick on the opening weekend of a Premier League season on 14th August, 1993. Things were different back then. His goals came in an unlikely 3-0 for Coventry City against Arsenal. Quinn scored a penalty past David Seaman in the first half before adding a couple more goals around the hour mark. The big striker said he was the league's "fastest player over a yard and he had a knack of starting quickly. He scored in his first six Premier League games in 1992, a feat that has still not been matched.

Coventry City have not played in the Premier League for 18 years, but they remain the only side to have provided two opening day hat-tricks. Dion Dublin emulated Mick Quinn's achievement in August 1997, scoring all three goals as Coventry came from behind twice to beat Chelsea 3-2 at Highfield Road. His first was a header from a throw-in, his second was a header from a corner and his third was a lovely half-volley that he sliced into the far corner of Ed de Goey's net.

CRYSTAL PALACE STATS

NUMBER OF SEASONS:

10 (5 spells)

1992/93; 1994/95; 1997/98;
2004/05, 2013/14 - 2018/19

NUMBER OF MATCHES:

388

Wins 111 (Home 58 Away 53)
Draws 96 (Home 46 Away 50)
Losses 181 (Home 90 Away 91)

[Win ratio 29%]

Goals F 425
(Home 209 Away 216)

Goals A 564
(Home 254 Away 310)

Goal Difference: -139

TOTAL POINTS

429

(Home 220: 51%; Away 209: 49%)
Av per season: 43

BEST POSITION:

10th

(2014/15)

WORST POSITION:

20th

1997/98 (RELEGATED)

BIGGEST WIN:

5-0

v Leicester
(28th Apr, 2018)

BIGGEST LOSS:

6-1

v Liverpool
(20th Aug, 1994)

LONGEST UNBEATEN RUN:

8 matches

(18th Nov, 2017–23rd Dec, 2017)

LONGEST WITHOUT A WIN:

15 matches

(29th Nov, 1997–14th Mar, 1998)

ALL TIME RANKING

21st

MOST GOALS SCORED IN A SEASON:

51

(2018/19)

FEWEST GOALS SCORED IN A SEASON:

33

(2013/14)

FEWEST GOALS CONCEDED IN A SEASON:

48

(2013/14)

MOST GOALS CONCEDED IN A SEASON:

71

(1997/98)

TOP GOALSCORER:

32

Wilfried Zaha

MOST APPEARANCES:

167

Joel Ward

OWN GOALS:

15

RED CARDS:

20

LOWEST ATTENDANCE:

10,964

v Sheffield Wednesday
(14th Mar, 1995)

HIGHEST ATTENDANCE:

30,115

v Manchester United
(21st Apr, 1993)

CRYSTAL PALACE

FIRST PREMIER LEAGUE MATCH: 15TH AUGUST, 1992
CRYSTAL PALACE 3 (BRIGHT, SOUTHGATE, OSBORN)
BLACKBURN ROVERS 3 (RIPLEY, SHEARER 2)

SELHURST PARK 17,086

Nigel Martyn, John Humphrey, Richard Shaw, Eric Young, Andy Thorn, Chris Coleman (Simon Osborn), Gareth Southgate, John Salako (Simon Rodger), Geoff Thomas, Eddie McGoldrick, Mark Bright , Manager: Steve Coppell

It is fair to say that Palace encountered some teething problems in their early Premier League days with their first four spells each lasting just one season: 1992/93, 1994/95, 1997/98 and 2004/05. During those four successive relegations a player who became a 'specialist in failure' featured. Hermann Hreidarsson was in the 1997/98 team that finished bottom of the table and then he followed this up with also getting relegated with neighbours and tenants Wimbledon in 1999/2000, Ipswich in 2001/02, Charlton in 2006/07 and Portsmouth in 2009/10. The Icelander is one of only two players to endure the pain of relegation from the Premier League on five occasions (see Portsmouth Footnote).

During their record-setting fourth successive relegation in 2004/05 Palace managed to have the privilege of containing the leading English scorer in the Premier League in their ranks. Just behind top scorer Thierry Henry's 25 goals, Andy Johnson weighed in with 21, which was one more than the rest of the team achieved put together. This was one of the few times that an individual player has bagged more than 50% of his club's goals.

Johnson's feat was achieved in large part thanks to 11 penalties, which remains the most notched by any player in a single season. Palace's penchant for penalties was confirmed in the 2018/19 season when captain Luka Milivojevic went mightily close to matching Johnson's exploits. Despite missing his first spot kick at Everton in October, Milivojevic converted ten in the rest of the season to join some illustrious names (see Footnote below).

Relegation is always a bitter experience and often a very painful one with Palace seeming to specialise in excruciating failure, having notched up the two largest points totals of any relegated club (albeit during the early 42-match seasons) but the 2004/05 contained a little too much cruelty for even the more hardened soul to bear. West Brom's miraculous rise off the canvas, when they became the first club to be bottom at Christmas and survive, meant it all went down to the wire. Unfortunately for the Eagles a late Charlton equaliser condemned them to the drop.

The Charlton fans took sadistic pleasure in their rivals' misfortune and turned their ground into the Valley of Death as they tortured the away fans with endless renditions of that god-awful Amarillo song, popularised by Peter Kay. Palace fans will never forget the harsh treatment that day and when Iain Dowie who had masterminded the club's own miracle in getting the club promoted through the play-offs the previous season, left to join Charlton the whiff of betrayal scorched the nostrils of many Eagles. The club's then chairman, Simon Jordan, sued Dowie for breach of contract and the whiff of cordite has hung over the relationship between the two clubs ever since.

Palace finally managed to break that unhealthy sequence of relegation when they survived in the 2013/14 season against all the odds. Having earned only three points from their first ten matches, with some justification everybody wrote them off and consigned them to a fifth successive one-season stay. The recovery was masterminded by Tony Pulis, who took over from Ian Holloway in October 2013, and after steering them to the safety of 11th place he won the Manager of the Year, one of only four managers to win the accolade but not win the title.

Only once in their current six-season stay in the Premier League—in 2013/14—were they higher in the home form table than the away one. In the most recent season, 2018/19, the difference was stark. Huddersfield were the only club that had a worse home record, their paltry nine points from two wins and three draws. Palace only accumulated 20 points at home with five wins and five draws, scoring 19 goals, including five on the final day against Bournemouth. Seven of those 19 goals were scored by Milivojevic, a tally which included five penalties.

By contrast Palace were a heady sixth in the away form table, having been the only team to take anything from Man City at The Etihad when they beat them 3-2. Furthermore they were the only club to grab a League win at The Emirates apart from Manchester City, and were the only club to score more than two goals at Anfield. Manchester City, Liverpool and Arsenal were the top three teams in the home form table and Palace grabbed three goals against each of them. In so doing they were responsible for just under a quarter of all the goals conceded by those clubs at home, with nine out of 38.

Palace developed an odd affinity of conceding extraordinary goals in London derbies in their latest spell in the Premier League. I believe these goals are called 'Worldies' by the youth of today and indeed some of these were not just out of this world but on another planet altogether. These have included Kasami's swivel and shot in October 2013 for Fulham, a thunderbolt from QPR's Matt Phillips in March 2016, Dele Alli's over-the-shoulder volley in January 2016 and Olivier Giroud's scorpion kick in January 2017. The pattern was well and truly established and any suspicion that this was all a bit freaky was totally confirmed a few weeks after Giroud's effort was followed by Andy Carroll's outrageous, athletic bicycle kick. Think about that sentence for a while; Bicycle kick. Outrageous. Andy Carroll. Athletic. The gods were clearly conspiring against the Eagles with a wilful malevolence.

ONE HIT WONDER

The late Ray Wilkins arrived at Selhurst Park towards the end of his playing career. In 1994/95 he was bought in by Alan Smith to provide some experience to the young side that had bounced back from relegation in 1992/93. Wilkins started in the opening game against Liverpool at Selhurst Park and it proved a harsh reality check as the visitors romped past poor Palace 6-1. At least Wilkins did not have to suffer the indignity of being on the pitch at the sorry finish, having broken his foot he was substituted eight minutes before the end.

Wilkins never recovered from that injury and did not appear again for the Eagles and returned to QPR at the end of that curtailed season. Wilkins went on to become assistant manager at various clubs including Chelsea and QPR before sadly dying in April 2018 aged 61 after suffering a heart attack.

FOOTNOTE

LEADING PREMIER LEAGUE PENALTY SCORERS IN A SEASON (ALL TIME)

PLAYER	CLUB	SEASON	GLS
Andy Johnson	Crystal Palace	2004/05	11
Alan Shearer	Blackburn Rovers	1994/95	10
Frank Lampard	Chelsea	2009/10	10
Steven Gerrard	Liverpool	2013/14	10
Luka Milivojevic	Crystal Palace	2018/19	10

A VIEW FROM THE STANDS

Kevin Day

What was your club's 'Sliding Doors' moment, that seemingly inconsequential action, which actually became a turning point in their fortunes, for either good or bad?

Many football clubs can pinpoint the day they refused to sign Lionel Messi as the beginning of a long, sad decline into obscurity. But for many Crystal Palace fans, the day they refused to sign Tim Cahill was the day our relegation from the Premier League was sealed—and that's a big claim since the day in question was six weeks before the season started.

Managed by Iain Dowie, Palace had been promoted to the Premier League in 2004 after a glorious day out in Cardiff where Neil Shipperley scored the play-off final winner against West Ham (from anywhere between five and 25 yards, depending on how many pints he's had) and I was told off by a policeman for over-vigorously suggesting where Hammers' fans could stick their bubbles.

Our previous two visits to the Premier League had lasted one season each, and, with the team we had, after the euphoria of Cardiff had worn off, it looked to most of us as though that would be the case again. And, let's be fair, with the team we had, the euphoria of Cardiff had worn off by the time the train reached Swindon.

So, we had to sign players, big players. Not Tim Cahill. But, for some reason, the announcement that we were going to give Millwall £2m for him was met with astonishment and joy by a lot of Palace fans. And mild bemusement by many of us who wouldn't give Millwall £2m to disappear, let alone for Tim Cahill.

But he represented potential, and he represented annoying 'wall fans and for many, that was enough.

You remember Tim Cahill? Of course you do, he was the young Australian midfielder famous for pretending to fight the corner flag when he scored a goal (did I mention he played for Millwall?)

He was a decent player but the fact that, at the time, he was more famous for flag-fighting than for football-kicking tells you all you need to know.

Our chairman was a show-pony called Simon Jordan, now a pundit on TalkSport (although his punditry rarely mentions that the club went into administration under his leadership).

You could smell him before you could see him, wafted along on a cloud of expensive scent. He was a middle-class wannabe ducker and diver who referred to us as 'customers'. I don't like him, can you tell?

However, to his credit, he acknowledged that we needed investment and for us, £2m was a big transfer. Except it never happened. Two days after it was announced, it was unannounced again.

And the cause of the unannouncement was Jordan's claim that Cahill's agent had demanded a fee of £125,000, presumably for handing Cahill the pen to sign with.

The agent of course firmly denied this, but Jordan was clever enough to know that a lot of Palace fans who may have been disappointed that the deal had fallen through would be delighted that their previously die-hard Thatcherite chairman was now sticking it to the agents.

Because as we all know, for football fans, agents are up there alongside referees and Robbie Savage as everything that is wrong with modern football.

So why did it matter so much? Because for every Palace fan who thought Jordan was right, and for every Palace fan who wasn't fussed by Cahill (me) there were ten who thought the lack of a deal illustrated the sort of club we had become. A run-of-the-mill outfit incapable of making a simple deal for a run-of-the-mill player who may have been just the spark we needed to make a fist of staying up.

We went down. By a point. Tim Cahill went to an Everton team who presumably didn't flinch at the agent's demands. An Everton team who scored seven goals against us. The 'run-of-the-mill' Tim Cahill scored two of those goals and became one of the best midfield players in the Premier League as well as winning 108 caps for Australia.

Chances are, of course, that but for that £125,000 Cahill would have joined Palace, got injured in his first game and never played again. Or, he could have scored the goal that got us the one point that kept us up, meaning the administration would never have happened and we would now be winning our third Champions' League in a row. Small margins my friend.

DERBY COUNTY STATS

NUMBER OF SEASONS:

7 (2 spells)

1996/97-2001/02; 2007/08

TOTAL POINTS

274

(Home 179: 65%; Away 95: 35%)
Average per season - 39

BEST POSITION:

8th

1998/99

BIGGEST WIN:

4-0 (2)

v Southampton (27th Sep, 1997)
v Wimbledon (4th Mar, 2000)

LONGEST UNBEATEN RUN:

8 matches

(2nd May, 1998-19th Sep, 1998)

NUMBER OF MATCHES:

266

Wins 68 (Home 48 Away 20)
Draws 70 (Home 35 Away 35)
Losses 128 (Home 50 Away 78)

[Win ratio 26%]

Goals F 271
(Home 157 Away 114)

Goals A 420
(Home 177 Away 243)

Goal Difference: -149

WORST POSITION:

20th

2007/08 (RELEGATED)

BIGGEST LOSS:

6-0 (2)

v Liverpool (1st Sep, 2007)
v Aston Villa (12th Apr, 2008)

LONGEST WITHOUT A WIN:

32 matches

(22nd Sep 2007-11th May, 2008)
*still ongoing

ALL TIME RANKING

32nd

MOST GOALS SCORED IN A SEASON:

52

(1997/98)

FEWEST GOALS SCORED IN A SEASON:

20

(2007/08)

FEWEST GOALS CONCEDED IN A SEASON:

45

(1998/99)

MOST GOALS CONCEDED IN A SEASON:

89

(2007/08)

TOP GOALSCORER:

32

Dean Sturridge

MOST APPEARANCES:

170

Darryl Powel

OWN GOALS:

13

RED CARDS:

17

LOWEST ATTENDANCE:

17,022

v Wimbledon
(28th Sep, 1996)

HIGHEST ATTENDANCE:

33,378

v Liverpool
(18th Mar, 2000)

All statistics and records supplied by  gracenote.
A NIELSEN COMPANY

DERBY COUNTY

FIRST PREMIER LEAGUE MATCH: 17TH AUGUST, 1996
DERBY 3 (STURRIDGE 2, SIMPSON)
LEEDS UNITED 3 (LAURSEN OG, HARTE, BOWYER)

BASEBALL GROUND 17,927

Russell Hoult, Paul Parker, Chris Powell, Jacob Laursen (Sean Flynn), Dean Yates, Gary Rowett, Aljosa Asanovic, Dean Sturridge, Darryl Powell (Paul Simpson), Marco Gabbiadini (Ron Willems), Christian Dailly, Manager: Jim Smith

Derby's Premier League life certainly started with a bang as they drew 3-3 with Leeds United, scoring all three goals in the space of ten frantic minutes late in the second half. Derby jointly hold the record for the highest scoring draw in their opening match along with Crystal Palace and Blackburn, who also shared six goals in the inaugural season. Russell Hoult was in goal for Derby that day and six years later he also played in West Brom's first match—a rare double. The Rams' Danish defender, Jacob Laursen marked this opening game in his own way with an own goal in 19th minute and became the first player to put into his own net in his club's debut match. He is joined a group of three other unfortunates to do so (see Brighton Footnote). To cap his afternoon off he was substituted in the 76th minute.

Derby's return to the Premier League after their play-off win in 2007 was pretty much doomed from the start as manager Billy Davies was uncertain of his position because of a mooted change of ownership. So, despite their triumph at Wembley he was not allowed any significant funds to improve the squad. But that pessimism was briefly lifted when they took the lead in their opening game at home to Portsmouth thanks to a Matt Oakley goal after just four minutes. Briefly they were, as their fans chanted, 'top of the league', with the earliest goal on that opening day. But in the end they drew 2-2 and that was pretty much as good as it got.

Their dismal 2007/08 season set a host of records including fewest wins with just a single victory, in their sixth match at home to Newcastle in mid-September. They also drew with at St James' Park, so the Magpies provided the Rams with 36% of their points. After that win against Newcastle, Derby played 32 more League games without victory. After drawing 2-2 with Fulham on 29th March, they were relegated with six games remaining, the earliest a club has been relegated. The 29 losses Derby endured were the most by any team even including the 42-match seasons. To put it into further context the top five clubs that season—Manchester United, Chelsea, Arsenal, Liverpool and Everton—collectively lost three games fewer than the wretched Rams. Inevitably their sorry total of 11 points is the lowest tally of any club in the Premier League, the next lowest points total is 15 by Sunderland in 2005/06. And in 2018/19, Derby were joined by Huddersfield as the only clubs to be relegated in March.

The Rams' notched a meagre tally of 20 goals all season, averaging just over one goal every two matches, and they only managed to score more than once on six occasions. Cristiano Ronaldo scored 11 more goals than Derby and he wasn't the only individual to outscore the entire Derby team that season, as both Fernando Torres and Emmanuel Adebayor did so with 24 each. In only three seasons has the leading individual goalscorer scored fewer than Derby that season—in 1997/98 when Dion Dublin, Michael Owen and Chris Sutton all scored 18; 1998/99 when Owen again, Jimmy Floyd Hasselbaink and Dwight Yorke each scored 18 each, and; 2008/09 when Nicholas Anelka scored 19. Meanwhile Derby's top scorer in 2007/08 season was Kenny Miller with four and only three other players scored more than one goal with Matt Oakley, the scorer of that first goal that gave rise to fleeting optimism, and Emanuel Villa getting three each and Jay McElevey getting two. Dismal, dreadful and downright disastrous.

There were even worse problems at the other end as Derby conceded an eye-watering 89 goals, and on six occasions shipped at least five, reaching a nadir in a season of lows with their last three home matches. After racking up their joint record worse defeat in losing 6-0 to Aston Villa, they then suffered a 6-2 drubbing at the hands of Arsenal before succumbing 4-0 to Reading in their last match. An aggregate of 2-16 was a fitting epitaph to a team that had tanked so badly. They have not returned since, which may be a blessing in disguise. Unsurprisingly their goal difference of -69 has never been challenged, as an illustration of how poor they were compared to others, the team above them in the table Birmingham City had a goal difference of -16. Only Ipswich in 1994/95 came anywhere close with -57 and that was in a 42-game season. Derby also managed to concede two hat-tricks by the same player with Arsenal's Emmanuel Adebayor getting his first in a 5-0 home win on 22nd September, 2007, and then on 28th April, 2008 he repeated the trick in a 6-2 win in the reverse fixture. This was the first time a player had scored two trebles against the same club in a season and it will take something to see this repeated.

If 2007/08 was all doom and gloom, Derby did at least enjoy some success in their other spell that lasted for six seasons and was punctuated with two top ten finishes under Jim Smith—9th in 1997/98 and 8th in 1998/99. Their aggregate goal difference over those six seasons was -80, only 11 worse than that single horror season. The highlight of the first season and probably their Premier League history was the 3-2 win at Old Trafford when Costa Rican Paulo Wanchope burst onto the scene on his full debut in April 1997. Not content with setting up the first goal via a deft header he then announced his arrival in style with a goal that shook Old Trafford to its very core. Wanchope picked up the ball from a loose Roy Keane pass on the halfway line, scythed through a retreating United defense with that characteristic long-legged style, bamboozling Phil Neville and Gary Pallister along the way and then calmly stroking the ball past Peter Schmeichel.

If that rare win at United was justifiably considered their finest performance then Derby's joint largest wins bear striking similarities as in both games they scored all four goals in the last 25 minutes. Their 4-0 win over Wimbledon in 2000 included two goals scored after the 90th minute while they scored four in less than ten minutes when blitzing Southampton between the 76th and 83rd minutes in 1997. Both cases of Ram raiding at its very finest.

ONE HIT WONDER

Marino Rahmberg is another in the surprisingly long line of players who have played less than 10 minutes in the Premier League. The Swede arrived on loan from Swedish second tier club Degerfors and came on as a substitute in 82nd minute during a 4-2 defeat to Leicester in February 1997. He was soon on his way back to Degerfors with just those eight minutes of Premier League action as a memory of his time in English football.

FOOTNOTE

FEWEST WINS IN A SEASON - FIVE OR FEWER

CLUB	SEASON	NO. OF WINS
Derby	2007/08	1
Sunderland	2005/06	3
Aston Villa	2015/16	3
Huddersfield	2018/19	3
Sunderland	2002/03	4
QPR	2012/13	4
Swindon	1993/94	5*
Bradford	2000/01	5
Leicester	2001/02	5
Watford	2006/07	5
Wolves	2011/12	5
Middlesbrough	2016/17	5

*in a 42-match season

A VIEW FROM THE STANDS

Tom Rodger

What was the club's 'Sliding Doors' moment, that seemingly inconsequential action, which actually became a turning point in their fortunes, for either good or bad?

Derby County are best known for being the worst Premier League team of all time after finishing with only 11 points in the 2007/08 season. It could be hard to pick out one particular moment from that season, as everything that could have possibly gone wrong, did. For me, the 'sliding door' moment was the appointment of Paul Jewell, Derby could not have hired a more uninspirational manager if they had tried. Derby had not had the greatest of starts but had shown some signs of recovery by picking up a few draws and also a win at home to Newcastle.

Billy Davies left the club to be replaced by Jewell, who was warned at the time not to take the Derby job by David Moyes who believed: "Derby wouldn't win another game all season." This turned out to be true. Along with the poor football on show, Jewell's January transfer window included some questionable signings such as Robbie Savage and the Rangers' third choice keeper at the time, Roy Carroll. Jewell did nothing to improve the side's fortunes and if anything, they were worse than before his appointment going on to lose 6-0 at home to Aston Villa, 6-1 away at Chelsea and 6-2 at home to Arsenal. Derby became the first side relegated in March (a 'feat' not matched until 2019 by Huddersfield) and would only record one win all season, going on to truly be the worst Premier League side of all time.

EVERTON STATS

NUMBER OF SEASONS:

27

1992/93-2018/19

NUMBER OF MATCHES:

1,038

Wins 377 (Home 244 Away 133)
Draws 296 (Home 141 Away 155)
Losses 365 (Home 134 Away 231)

[Win ratio 36%]

Goals F 1,357
(Home 806 Away 551)

Goals A 1,311
(Home 566 Away 745)

Goal Difference: +46

TOTAL POINTS

1,427

(Home 873: 61%; Away 554: 39%)
Average per season: 53

BEST POSITION:

4th

(2004/05)

WORST POSITION:

17th (3)

(1993/94, 1997/98, 2003/04)

BIGGEST WIN:

7-1 (2)

v Southampton (16th Nov, 1996)
v Sunderland (24th Nov, 2007)

BIGGEST LOSS:

7-0

v Arsenal
(11th May, 2005)

LONGEST UNBEATEN RUN:

11 matches (2)

(7th Mar, 2010-9th May, 2010 & 24th
Mar, 2012-25th Aug, 2012)

LONGEST WITHOUT A WIN:

12 matches

(20th Aug, 1994-29th Oct, 1994)

ALL TIME RANKING

6th

MOST GOALS SCORED IN A SEASON:

64

(1995/96)

FEWEST GOALS SCORED IN A SEASON:

34

(2005/06)

FEWEST GOALS CONCEDED IN A SEASON:

33

(2007/08)

MOST GOALS CONCEDED IN A SEASON:

63

(1993/94)

TOP GOALSCORER:

68

Romelu Lukaku

MOST APPEARANCES:

354

Tim Howard

OWN GOALS:

50

RED CARDS:

93

LOWEST ATTENDANCE:

13,265

v Southampton
(4th Dec, 1993)

HIGHEST ATTENDANCE:

40,552

v Liverpool
(11th Dec, 2004)

All statistics and records supplied by

EVERTON

FIRST PREMIER LEAGUE MATCH: 15TH AUGUST, 1992
EVERTON 1 (HORNE)
SHEFFIELD WEDNESDAY 1 (PEARSON)

GOODISON PARK 27,687

Neville Southall, Gary Ablett, Mark Ward, Matt Jackson, Dave Watson, Andy Hinchcliffe, Peter Beagrie, Barry Horne (Robert Warzycha), John Ebbrell, Peter Beardsley, Paul Rideout, Manager: Howard Kendall

Everton are now entering their 66th consecutive season in the top flight of English football, the second longest run behind Arsenal, and they are one of only six ever-presents throughout the 27 seasons of the Premier League, but that does lead to a few unwanted records as a corollary. They have lost the most amount of games—365—which is one more than West Ham.

As the only one of the ever-presents to have been embroiled in the lower reaches of the table on several occasions and never having finished higher than the 4th place they achieved in 2004/05 they unsurprisingly have recorded the most draws with 296. *The Guardian Football Weekly* podcast refers to the Everton Cup—the battle to be the next best team outside the pre-ordained Top Six—although this moniker has only really been true in the last dozen years. Since 2007/08 the Toffees have only been outside the top half twice when they were 11th in consecutive seasons in

2015/16 and 2016/17. This contrasts with the first 15 seasons when they only reached the top half three times—6th in 1996/97, 7th in 2003/04 and 4th in 2005/06.

There was a certain near-synchronicity about their record goals for and against - the most goals they conceded was 63 in 1992/93 season and three years later they scored the most with just one more. Then the fewest goals they scored was 34 in 2005/06 followed two years later by the fewest they let in which was, inevitably, one less. Of all the six ever-present clubs Everton have been closest to falling out of the Premier League, finishing just above the trap door three times and the closest they came to going down came in 1993/94.

THE GREAT GOODISON ESCAPE

SATURDAY 7 MAY 1994

EVERTON 3 (1) STUART 24' (PEN), 81' HORNE 67'
WIMBLEDON 2 (2) HOLDSWORTH 4' (PEN), ABLETT (OG) 20'

GOODISON PARK (31,297)

Everton's brush with relegation led to one of the most dramatic last-day escapes as they started in the drop zone, just a single point behind the three teams above them—Ipswich, Southampton and Sheffield United. The start of the match against Wimbledon could not have been more calamitous as Anders Limpar gave away an inexplicable penalty when he handled under no pressure. Holdsworth converted and this was followed by a horrendous mix-up between two defenders that allowed Andy Clarke to hook the ball over Neville Southall. The keeper's attempt to stop the goal-bound shot merely flicked the ball into Gary Ablett's path and in his desperate attempt to scramble it away, the defender only succeeded in pushing the ball almost apologetically into the net.

With the minimum requirement being a draw, Everton started to claw their way back just four minutes after they went 2-0 behind. The errant Limpar went down under minimal contact winning a highly dubious penalty and Graham Stuart scored. That revival could have been throttled at birth had Dean Holdsworth not contrived to miss three clear headers from less than six yards out. Midway through the second half Barry Horne unleashed a 30-yard rocket to drag Everton level before Stuart popped up with a scruffy finish to seal unlikely salvation.

A relieved Everton manager Mike Walker said: "People questioned whether we had the guts to stay up and when it came down to it we proved we had it. Graham Stuart in particular epitomised that, by taking that penalty at 2-0. That was a high-pressure situation and it was fitting that as a result he scored the winner. Barry Horne, too, has had his critics this season, but when it came down to it, in the games that mattered at the back end of the season he produced the goods."

Everton's two largest victories both came in late November when they beat two clubs beginning with 'S' 7-1, Southampton on 16th November. 1996 and Sunderland on 24th November, 2007. Their goal difference of -1 when finishing fourth in 2004/05 is only the second time a team in the top six has conceded more than it has scored, following Norwich's -4 when they reached the giddy heights of third in the very first Premier League season.

Following a goalless draw against Liverpool at Goodison Park in March 2019, Everton's winless run against their neighbours stretched to 17 matches, their last win coming almost a decade previously in October 2010. Furthermore, a worrying pattern continued for The Toffees as they have yet to win any of the second league meetings of the Mersey derby in the 27 years of the Premier League era. Their fans will be desperate for them to break this Mersey mare.

By dint of their longevity Everton have conceded the most goals in Premier League history shipping 1,311 in their 27 seasons, but only five behind are another ever-present Tottenham with 1,306, swiftly followed by West Ham (1,269), Newcastle (1,235), Aston Villa (1,186) and Southampton (1,087). Manchester United are the only ever-present to have not conceded more than 1,000 goals, with just 929, an average of 35 per season.

ONE HIT WONDER

Blink and you may well have missed Anderson de Silva's Everton career. The Brazilian midfield endured a false start to his time at Goodison Park when he arrived from Uruguayan club Montevideo in late 2005. Unfortunately, there was a hiccup with his immigration papers and he was packed off to Malaga before returning to Goodison in January 2007, the proud owner of a European passport, which smoothed his passage back to England. On the 15th April, 2007 he came on for the last two minutes of the home game against Charlton. It must have been a mighty impressive couple of minutes as his contract was extended for another year. However, with no more first-team action he was considered surplus to requirements and left for Barnsley in January 2008.

After a couple of years sampling the delights of South Yorkshire he went back to Uruguayan football before retiring in February 2018, his last club was the exotically-named El Tanque Sisley.

FOOTNOTE

IF YOU'RE GOOD ENOUGH, YOU'RE OLD ENOUGH

On 10 April 2005 James Vaughan came on as a substitute with Everton cursing to victory and then became the youngest player to score in the Premier League, aged 16 years 270 days, grabbing Everton's fourth goal in 87th minute. There are only two other 16 year-olds who have done so, another James, Milner and another Everton player, Wayne Rooney. Like Vaughan, Rooney came on as a late substitute and curled in a 30-yarder to end Arsenal's 30-match unbeaten run. Michael Owen was also a young scoring substitute.

Youngest goal-scorers

PLAYER	AGE	MATCH
James Vaughan 16y 270d10th Apr, 2005	16y 270d	Everton 4 Crystal Palace 0
James Milner 26th Dec, 2002	16y 356d	Leeds 2 Sunderland 1
Wayne Rooney 19th Oct, 2002	16y 360d	Everton 2 Arsenal 1
Cesc Fabregas 26th Nov, 2005	17y 114d	Arsenal 3 Blackburn 0
Michael Owen 6th May, 1997	17y 144d	Wimbledon 2 Liverpool 1

A VIEW FROM THE STANDS

Jim Keoghan

What was your club's 'Sliding Doors' moment, that seemingly inconsequential action, which actually became a turning point in their fortunes, for either good or bad?

Everton's sliding doors moment was a non-goal that saved the club's fortunes. In early September 1997, the Toffees played Bolton at the Reebok Stadium. About half-way through the second half the home side thought they had gone ahead through Nathan Blake. But the goal wasn't given. Although the ball had crossed the line by some distance, Terry Phelan's clearance, and the poor positioning of the officials contrived to deny Bolton a deserved lead. The game would end 0-0, giving Everton an unwarranted point and Bolton the loss of two.

Fast forward to the end of the season, and the final table would illustrate just how important the mistake was. Although both clubs finished on 40 points, it would be Bolton who would occupy the last relegation position, due to their inferior goal difference.

That final-day escape represented a nadir for Everton, a low not repeated since and one from which the club has slowly, stutteringly, recovered from. But it could all have been so different. Blake's non-goal, unrecognised for its significance at the time, was the moment that could have doomed Everton to a very different future.

FULHAM STATS

NUMBER OF SEASONS:

14 (2 spells)

2001/02-2013/14, 2018/19

NUMBER OF MATCHES:

532

Wins 157 (Home 118 Away 39)
Draws 141 (Home 59 Away 82)
Losses 234 (Home 89 Away 145)

[Win ratio 30%]

Goals F 604
(Home 371 Away 233)

Goals A 778
(Home 335 Away 443)

Goal Difference: -174

TOTAL POINTS

612

(Home 413 Away 199)
Average per season: 44

BEST POSITION:

7th

2008/09

WORST POSITION:

19th

2013/14 & 2018/19 (RELEGATED)

BIGGEST WIN:

6-0 (2)

v QPR (2nd Oct, 2011)
v Norwich (15th May, 2005)

BIGGEST LOSS:

6-0

v Hull
(28th Dec, 2013)

LONGEST UNBEATEN RUN:

9 matches

(9th Nov, 2008-28th Dec, 2008)

LONGEST WITHOUT A WIN:

12 matches

(10th Nov, 2007-29th Jan, 2008)

ALL TIME RANKING

16th

MOST GOALS SCORED IN A SEASON:

52 (2)

(2003/04 & 2004/05)

FEWEST GOALS SCORED IN A SEASON:

34

(2018/19)

FEWEST GOALS CONCEDED IN A SEASON:

34

(2008/09)

MOST GOALS CONCEDED IN A SEASON:

85

(2013/14)

TOP GOALSCORER:

50

Clint Dempsey

MOST APPEARANCES:

217

Brede Hangeland

OWN GOALS:

38

RED CARDS:

38

LOWEST ATTENDANCE:

13,981

v Blackburn
(12th Apr, 2004)

HIGHEST ATTENDANCE:

25,700

v Arsenal
(26th Sept, 2009)

All statistics and records supplied by

FULHAM

FIRST PREMIER LEAGUE MATCH: 19TH AUGUST, 2001
MANCHESTER UNITED 3 (BECKHAM, VAN NISTELROOY 2)
FULHAM 2 (SAHA)

OLD TRAFFORD 67,534

Edwin van der Saar, Andy Melville, Jon Harley, Steve Finnan, Alain Goma, Bjarne Goldbaek (Andrejs Stolcers), Steed Malbranque (Abdeslam Ouaddou), Sean Davis, John Collins, Louis Saha, Barry Hayles (Kevin Betsy), Manager: Jean Tigana

Fulham's tough baptism away at Old Trafford was noteworthy because of Luis Saha's brace, which put the visitors ahead twice and made Ferguson's team sweat a tad before they ended up winning 3-2. Saha is one of only a few players to score two goals on their club's Premier League debut. Four players—Lee Chapman, Brian Deane, Mark Robins and Alan Shearer—did so on the opening day of the first season, as did Dean Sturridge for Derby in 1996, Marlon Harewood for Blackpool in 2010 and Steve Mounie for Huddersfield in 2017.

Qualifying for the Europa League, having finished 7th in 2008/09 under Roy Hodgson, was an outstanding achievement for Fulham. It was embellished by when they reached the final the following season, losing 2-1 to Atletico Madrid. Along the way they beat the mighty Juventus on a quite incredible night at Craven Cottage when they handed the Old Lady a 4-1 thrashing, in the process overturned a 3-1 deficit from the first leg. Fulham are only the second club from outside the Premier League top six to qualify for a European final after Middlesbrough in 2006. They became the sixth Premier League side to reach a European final and did so before either Manchester City or Tottenham managed it.

It takes some going to be quite as porous as Fulham's defence was in

2018/19, even the calamitous centurions of Swindon team or the disastrous Derby of the 2007/08 vintage did not plumb the depths reached by the Cottagers in the first few months of 2019. When they allowed Harry Winks to score a 93rd minute winner on 30 January they became the fastest club to concede 50 goals. Fulham did not enjoy much capital comfort as they became the first London club to lose every single derby, ten in all, with a aggregate score of 6-27 and they conceded at least two goals in each of those derbies.

From 1st January to 13th April they went on a run of 13 matches in which they conceded at least two goals per game and that is something which no other Premier League team has ever done. In that leaky period they let in 33 goals. With five games remaining they had fielded more goalkeepers (three) than kept clean sheets (two) but the rot was finally ended when they kept a rare clean sheet against Everton in a 2-0 win. That they then followed that with another two shut outs away at Bournemouth and home to Cardiff meant they drew level with Swindon (although in a 42-game season) and just one more than that dismal Derby team of 2007/08. It was all a little too late to save them and their final goals against total of 81 was still at a ratio of 2.1 goals per match which at one stage of the season, before their late resurgence, was uncomfortably close to that of Swindon's record-breaking 2.4 from 1993/94.

That they used three different goalkeepers—the Spaniards Fabri and Sergio Rico plus Marcus Bettinelli—in their first ten games suggested that they had not quite settled on their last line of defence. The indecision over who was their best No.1/No.25/No.31 sowed seeds of doubt and how it showed, during those opening ten games, as they conceded 28 goals, recorded no clean sheets and only once restricting the opposition to a single goal.

Having brought in Claudio Ranieri to halt their slide back to the Championship they jettisoned the Italian at the end of February after just 106 days and 16 matches. It was one of the shortest managerial reigns alongside Tony Adams who lasted the same length of time at Portsmouth in 2008/09, slightly longer than Frank de Boer's 77 days at Crystal Palace in 2017/18 and that of another Fulham misfit, Rene Meulensteen who spent just 75 days in charge at Craven Cottage in 2013/14. And of course there is dear old Les Reed's 40 days and 40 nights at Charlton in 2006, which is still the briefest stay in the managerial hot seat.

When Harvey Elliott came on as a substitute in the 88th minute of Fulham's game at Molineux on 4th May, 2019 he became the youngest ever Premier League player. Aged just 16 years and 30 days, he broke the record previously set by another Fulham youngster Matthew Briggs, who also came on as a substitute, against Middlesbrough on 13th May, 2007, by 38 days. Coincidentally, on the same day Elliott gained his place in the record books, Bournemouth's 19-year-old Mark Travers became the youngest goalkeeper to appear in the Premier League since Joe Hart in October 2006 when he kept a clean sheet against Tottenham. Meanwhile on the same day in Cardiff when Palace's win relegated the home team the combined ages of their battle-hardened bosses, Roy Hodgson and Neil Warnock, was just over 142 years.

ONE HIT WONDER

Mesca, or Buomesca Tue Na Banga, to give him his full resplendent name arrived at Fulham from neighbours Chelsea in 2011. With a neat twist of fate he made his Premier League debut against the Blues when replacing Swede Alexander Kacaniklic in the 72nd minute during the 2-0 defeat at Stamford Bridge. Within a few months he was shipped out on loan to Crewe and eventually moved to Cypriot club AEL Limassol in 2015. Although he was born in Guinea-Bissau he represented Portugal at youth level.

For the 2018/19 season Mesca moved to Bulgaria, playing for the exotically named top division club, Beroe Stara Zagora.

FOOTNOTE

In 2018/19 Fulham and Huddersfield were vying for last place from very early on and in their flight to the bottom they managed to accumulate the fewest points gained by the bottom two clubs.

SEASON	CLUBS	COMBINED POINTS TOTAL
2018/19	Fulham/Huddersfield	42
2002/03	West Brom/Sunderland	45
2005/06	West Brom/Sunderland	45
2007/08	Birmingham/Derby	46
2009/10	Hull/Portsmouth	49

A VIEW FROM THE STANDS

Farrell Monk, @Fulhamishpod

What was your club's 'Sliding Doors' moment, that seemingly inconsequential action, which actually became a turning point in their fortunes, for either good or bad?

"I think he was probably the only one in the stadium who really thought it was a red card," lamented Martin Jol about Lee Probert's decision in November 2012.

Fulham had gone into their home game against Sunderland sitting very pretty in eighth place, unbeaten in five. Sixteen points from 11 games is a solid start for an 'established' Premier League side, if you can believe a team of Fulham's stature could ever be described as such.

Hangeland's dismissal—an untidy challenge on an untidy Lee Cattermole (exemplary shorts wearing aside), following full debutant Giorgos Karagounis' woefully short back pass—led to a 3-1 defeat that day, and was actually Fulham's first red card in 50 games.

Such was the Norwegian's form and importance, the subsequent three-match absence triggered a down-turn in fortunes; one win in eight followed. Confidence stricken, the season ended with a whimper. That continued into 2013/14 and Jol was dismissed almost exactly a year later.

A multitude of questionable managerial and player acquisitions to plug the leaks in the sinking ship failed and culminated in our departure from the top flight after a 13-year stay.

HUDDERSFIELD TOWN STATS

NUMBER OF SEASONS:

2

2017/18-2018/19

NUMBER OF MATCHES:

76

Wins 12 (Home 8 Away 4)
Draws 17 (Home 8 Away 9)
Losses 47 (Home 22 Away 25)

[Win ratio 16%]

Goals F 50
(Home 26 Away 24)

Goals A 134
(Home 56 Away 78)

Goal Difference: -84

TOTAL POINTS

53

(Home 32: 60%; Away 21: 40%)
Average per season: 26

BEST POSITION:

17th

2017/18

WORST POSITION:

20th

2018/1 (RELEGATED)

BIGGEST WIN:

1-4

v Watford
(16th Dec, 2017)

BIGGEST LOSS:

6-1

v Manchester City
(19th Aug, 2018)

LONGEST UNBEATEN RUN:

4 matches

(16th Dec, 2017–30th Dec, 2017)

LONGEST WITHOUT A WIN:

14 matches (2)

(28th Apr, 2018–27th Oct, 2018) &
(1st Dec, 2018–23rd Feb, 2019)

ALL TIME RANKING

46th

MOST GOALS SCORED IN A SEASON:

28

(2017/18)

FEWEST GOALS SCORED IN A SEASON:

22

(2018/19)

FEWEST GOALS CONCEDED IN A SEASON:

58

(2017/18)

MOST GOALS CONCEDED IN A SEASON:

76

(2018/19)

TOP GOALSCORER:

9

Steve Mounie

MOST APPEARANCES:

74

Christopher Schindler

OWN GOALS:

38

RED CARDS:

38

LOWEST ATTENDANCE:

17,082

v Fulham
(5th Nov, 2018)

HIGHEST ATTENDANCE:

24,426

v Manchester United
(21st Oct, 2017)

All statistics and records supplied by

HUDDERSFIELD TOWN

FIRST PREMIER LEAGUE MATCH: 12TH AUGUST, 2017
CRYSTAL PALACE 0
HUDDERSFIELD TOWN 3 (WARD OG, MOUNIE 2)

SELHURST PARK 25,448

*Jonas Lossl, Tommy Smith (Danny Williams), Chris Lowe, Zanka,
Christopher Schindler, Philip Billing, Elias Kachunga,
Aaron Mooy, Tom Ince, Kasey Palmer (Colin Quaner),
Steve Mounie (Rajiv van La Parra), Manager: David Wagner*

A little like Blackpool in 2010/11, Huddersfield announced their arrival
in the Premier League with a bang thanks to a comfortable 3-0 victory
away at Selhurst Park on the opening day of the 2017/18 season. But unlike
Blackpool, The Terriers, under David Wagner, proved to be of sterner
stuff and against all the odds they survived their debut campaign, sealing
safety with a memorable draw at Stamford Bridge in their penultimate
match. They only scored more than twice another three times in the next
75 games, against Watford and Bournemouth in 2017/18 and West Ham

in 2018/19. Oddly the Bournemouth game was the only one out of the four when they achieved the feat at home.

The next season did not go so well with Wagner departing in January when Huddersfield already looked doomed. Fellow German Jan Siewert could do nothing to reverse the trend and the team collected a mere four points from his 17 games in charge with a solitary win against Wolves, which remarkably completed the double over the club which finished 7th. They only won one other match all season and that was against fellow strugglers, Fulham.

Their paltry total of 22 goals scored was only marginally ahead of Derby's pitiful 20 goals in 2007/08. In fact the ten Huddersfield scored at home was even fewer than Derby's 12 in 2007/08 and is the joint lowest home goals tally, a record they share with none other than Manchester City in 2006/07.

The Terriers have completed a dubious double in that over their two seasons they have the worst average goals per game of 0.66 (50 in 76 matches). Alongside that they also have the worst points per game average ever with 0.70, marginally behind Swindon's 0.71. They only managed to score more than one goal twice, against Wolves and at West Ham, where despite being 3-1 up they lost the game.

One other thing that the 2018/19 Huddersfield vintage share with that desperate Derby team was that this terrible two are the only Premier League clubs to be relegated in March. Neither of them had the gumption to even make it to April Fool's Day. Derby's relegation was confirmed on 29th March, 2008 with six games remaining and Huddersfield similarly had a half a dozen matches left when the trap door was firmly shut on their Premier League existence on 30th March, 2019 after losing 2-0 at Selhurst Park. Fulham followed a few days later but at least managed to stave off relegation until April.

Huddersfield's shyness in front of goal is best illustrated by the number of games in which they failed to score across their two seasons. Out of their 76 games they drew a blank in 40, or 54%. That is the highest proportion in Premier League history with Cardiff 48% (36/78) Bradford's 43% (33/76) and Hull's 41% (77/190), the closest challengers in the ranks of arid sterility.

ONE HIT WONDER

Demeaco Duhaney had a dozen years at Manchester City before joining Huddersfield in 2018. He played in the first half of the match of the 1-0 win against Wolves on 26th February in 2019 before being substituted at half-time because of injury. That must have been disappointing for the Mancunian but at least he can boast a 100% record and will be the only Huddersfield player to do so. Duhaney is under contract with Huddersfield until 2020.

FOOTNOTE

EARLY EXIT

CLUB	DATE	GAMES REMAINING
Derby County	29th March, 2008	6
Huddersfield Town	30th March, 2019	6
Fulham	2nd April, 2019	5
Leicester City	6th April, 2002	4
Portsmouth	10th April, 2010	5*

*9 points deducted

A VIEW FROM THE STANDS

Gavin Hutchinson

Your club's spell in the Premier League was brief and while there was the odd glorious moment ultimately it was short-lived. Looking back now, one question remains - Was it really worth it?

Worth it? Absolutely. Despite this season's dip, the Wagner era has provided the best Town teams and moments of my lifetime by a country mile. Our attendances, finances and profile would have been unthinkable during administration in the 2000s. My old school was visited by our World Cup-winning fullback for heaven's sake.

And, while no board is perfect, responsible management has prevailed. We've not Ridsdale-ed our money up the wall ahead of our return to the Championship (though I suspect next season will be tough). Even Wagner's departure seems to have been handled with decency on all sides.

What would I have done differently? Hugely speculative here, but maybe Stuart Webber, our Head of Football Operations who left in April 2017 for Norwich the club that ultimately replaced us in the Premier

League, could have been persuaded to stay. The limited inside info I have from his time there painted a very positive picture. Recruitment since has been less successful.

In our last Premier League season I was surprised by our early team selections. We didn't start with the spine of Jonas Lössl, Christopher Schindler, Aaron Mooy, and Steve Michel Mounié until September, at which point we immediately got a point away at Everton. After that Mounié quickly fell out of favour. I suspect it's no coincidence that our only decent run came through November when they all started. Improved attacking coaching might also have been useful, as defensively and in midfield we held our own, but predictable crossing towards a single striker is not going to worry PL defences overly.

All in all though, it's been a remarkable achievement, by a group of thoroughly likeable people, and we're in the best shape since... about 1927..

HULL CITY STATS

NUMBER OF SEASONS:

5 (3 spells)

2008/09-2009/10, 2013/14-
2014/15; 2016/17

TOTAL POINTS

171

(Home 111: 65%; Away 60: 35%)
Average per season: 34

NUMBER OF MATCHES:

190

Wins 41 (Home 29 Away 12)
Draws 48 (Home 24 Away 24)
Losses 101 (Home 42 Away 59)

[Win ratio 22%]

Goals F 181
(Home 107 Away 74)

Goals A 323
(Home 145 Away 178)

Goal Difference: -142

BEST POSITION:

16th

2013/14

WORST POSITION:

19th

2009/10 (RELEGATED)

BIGGEST WIN:

6-0

v Fulham
(28th Dec, 2013)

BIGGEST LOSS:

1-7

v Tottenham
(21st May, 2017)

LONGEST UNBEATEN RUN:

6 matches

(13th Sept 2008–25th Oct, 2008)

LONGEST WITHOUT A WIN:

10 matches

(14th Mar, 2009–19th Aug, 2009)

ALL TIME RANKING

39th

MOST GOALS SCORED IN A SEASON:

39

(2008/09)

FEWEST GOALS SCORED IN A SEASON:

33

(2014/15)

FEWEST GOALS CONCEDED IN A SEASON:

51

(2014/15)

MOST GOALS CONCEDED IN A SEASON:

80

(2016/17)

TOP GOALSCORER:

12

Jelavic

MOST APPEARANCES:

109

El Mohamady

OWN GOALS:

16

RED CARDS:

24

LOWEST ATTENDANCE:

17,403

v Crystal Palace
(10th Dec, 2016)

HIGHEST ATTENDANCE:

25,030

v Liverpool
(9th May, 2010)

All statistics and records supplied by  gracenote.
A NIELSEN COMPANY

HULL CITY

FIRST PREMIER LEAGUE MATCH: 16TH AUGUST, 2008
HULL CITY 2 (GEOVANNI, FOLAN)
FULHAM 1 (SEOL)

KC STADIUM 24,525

Boaz Myhill, Sam Ricketts, Andy Dawson, Michael Turner , Anthony Gardner, Ian Ashbee, Richard Garcia (Craig Fagan), George Boateng, Marlon King (Caleb Folan), Geovanni, Nick Barmby (Peter Halmosi), Manager: Phil Brown

Hull made one of the more impressive starts to life in the top division as was highlighted by their form in the first nine matches, after which they were sitting pretty in third place, bolstered by a string of fine away performances. Having drawn at Blackburn and then won at Newcastle they secured a North London double by winning at Arsenal and Tottenham in successive weekends. Not content with this they beat West Brom 3-0 at the Hawthorns thus completing the rare feat of winning four successive away games before suffering their first away defeat, a narrow 4-3 reverse at Old Trafford.

Undeterred, their next three away games were draws so their first nine away games yielded four wins, four draws and one solitary loss. However, in the remainder of the season they added one more victory on the road to total five in all, two more than they recorded at home. Unusually for a newly promoted club they gathered 21 points away and only 14 at home. Gaining 60% of their points on the road puts them third in the table for clubs achieving the highest proportion of their points away. By contrast the next season Hull did not win a single game away from the KCOM stadium collecting a measly six points away from home. Indeed in their other four seasons they only won seven matches overall on the road, so clearly overperformed in their debut season.

Having had three spells in the last ten years Hull can lay claim to being the yo-yo club of the last decade. No other club has been up and down so many times since 2008. They also have never reached a higher position than 16th, which is the lowest for any club spending at least three seasons in the Premier League. During that topsy-turvy existence they did top the league briefly after the first game in August 2016 under Mike Phelan albeit only for a few hours but ended up being relegated at the end of the season with Marco Silva then in charge. Their last match ended in a humbling 7-1 defeat at home to Spurs, which was also the biggest loss of all their 190 Premier League matches so far and acts as a somewhat cruel epitaph to their story. But at least they scored for the first time on the final day, having been scoreless in their four previous last-day games all of which have been at home.

Hull have certainly been consistent in the amount of goals they have scored, the least was 33, the most was 39, a variance of six over five seasons is the smallest of any club with more than two seasons' experience. Their top scorer Nikika Jelavic has a mere dozen goals to his name, which is the lowest total for a club's top goalscorer of at least three seasons. During their opening win against Fulham in August 2008, Geovanni became the first Brazilian to score in a club's debut Premier League game with a delicious curler from outside the box.

At the other end of the pitch, Hull's ratio of 3.2 own goals per season is the worst of any club that has spent at least three seasons in the Premier League. The lead culprit of this tally of 16 own goals in five seasons was Kamil Zayatte who weighed in with four. That is one more than the Guinean managed to score at the right end in just over 70 matches with the Tigers between 2008 and 2011. Zayatte could be considered to be one tiger who did not earn his stripes.

ONE HIT WONDER

Aaron McLean joined Hull in January 2011 with a growing reputation built over a couple of successful years at Peterborough. Hull were then a

Championship club so McLean had to wait for more than two and a half years before making his Premier League debut. On 27th October, 2013 he came on as a substitute against Tottenham in the 84th minute. A few weeks after this fleeting appearance McLean was sent on loan to Birmingham and eventually signed for Bradford. He is currently coach at Ebbsfleet United.

FOOTNOTE

In the 2016/17 season Hull gave away the most penalties in a single season, with a particularly unlucky 13 conceded and of those 11 were scored, which did not help their chances of survival.

CLUB	SEASON	CONCEDED
Hull City	2016/17	13
Blackburn	2006/07	11
Norwich	2015/16	10
Arsenal	2016/17	10
Brighton	2018/19	10

A VIEW FROM THE STANDS

Rick Skelton

What was your club's 'Sliding Doors' moment, that seemingly inconsequential action, which actually became a turning point in their fortunes, for either good or bad?

City made a miraculous start to life in the Premier League in 2008/09 continuing the momentum from a strong finish to the previous season which culminated in a play-off final win at Wembley. The whole year of 2008 was a dream come true. Winning at Wembley, Emirates, White Hart Lane, St. James Park—all moments that required a pinch of yourself. We jointly topped the Premier League momentarily and occupied the top half going into Christmas. Behind the scenes our Chairman Paul Duffen and Manager Phil Brown started to believe the hype.

Both made noises about qualifying for Europe while Brown appeared on Sky TV infamously wearing a light pink jumper draped over his shoulders. They loved the spotlight far more than the fans and players. That came to a head on Boxing Day when City trailed Man City 4-0 at Eastlands and Brown bollocked the players on the pitch in front of the travelling hoards—of which I was one. It was unnecessary given it was the first poor performance since August for a group who'd been playing out of their skin.

The players responded with a solid performance against Aston Villa a couple of days later but there was a feeling of humiliation that overwhelmed the squad for the rest of the season and we slid down the league and only survived thanks to the ineptitude of Newcastle United. Brown never really recovered either and the next 13 months were a slog until he was finally placed on "gardening leave" with relegation inevitable in 2010.

IPSWICH TOWN STATS

NUMBER OF SEASONS:

5 (2 spells)

1992/93-1994/95;
2000/01-2001/02

NUMBER OF MATCHES:

202

Wins 57 (Home 35 Away 22)
Draws 53 (Home 29 Away 24)
Losses 92 (Home 37 Away 55)

[Win ratio 28%]

Goals F 219
(Home 125 Away 94)

Goals A 312
(Home 127 Away 185)

Goal Difference: -93

TOTAL POINTS

224

(Home 134: 60%; Away 90: 40%)
Average per season: 45

BEST POSITION:

5th

2000/01

WORST POSITION:

22nd

1994/95 (RELEGATED)

BIGGEST WIN:

5-0

v Sunderland
(29th Dec, 2001)

BIGGEST LOSS:

9-0

v Manchester United
(4th Mar, 1995)

LONGEST UNBEATEN RUN:

10 matches

(24th Oct, 1992-28th Dec, 1992)

LONGEST WITHOUT A WIN:

15 matches

(25th Aug, 2001-17th Dec, 2001)

ALL TIME RANKING

35th

MOST GOALS SCORED IN A SEASON:

57

(2000/01)

FEWEST GOALS SCORED IN A SEASON:

35

(1993/94)

FEWEST GOALS CONCEDED IN A SEASON:

42

(2000/01)

MOST GOALS CONCEDED IN A SEASON:

93

(1994/95)

TOP GOALSCORER:

25

Marcus Stewart

MOST APPEARANCES:

112

David Linighan

OWN GOALS:

10

RED CARDS:

6

LOWEST ATTENDANCE:

11,282

v Wimbledon
(16th Dec, 1994)

HIGHEST ATTENDANCE:

28,433

v Manchester United
(27th Apr, 2002)

All statistics and records supplied by

IPSWICH TOWN

FIRST PREMIER LEAGUE MATCH: 15TH AUGUST, 1992
IPSWICH TOWN 1 (JOHNSON)
ASTON VILLA 1 (ATKINSON)

PORTMAN ROAD 16,977

Craig Forrest, Phil Whelan, Neil Thompson, Mick Stockwell (Simon Milton), John Wark, David Linighan, Geraint Williams, Paul Goddard, Gavin Johnson, Jason Dozzell (Eddie Youds), Chris Kiwomya, Manager: John Lyall

Burley's achievement was recognised when he was named as Manager of the Season, one of only five bosses to earn that accolade when not in charge of the champions (see Footnote). Qualifying for Europe was a great achievement for Ipswich but with a small squad it became a burden, which they could not overcome and they were relegated the following season.

Ipswich also hold the record for the longest run without scoring a goal, an unwanted feat achieved in the 1994/95 season. After Lee Chapman scored their second goal in a 2-1 win against Southampton in the 77th minute on the 25th February, The Tractor Boys had to wait another 49 days until the 15th April for their next goal. It may have only been a consolation by Ian Marshall in a 4-1 thrashing at Arsenal but at least the drought was broken in the 71st minute. The goal difference during that dismal run was 0-23 and in total Chapman's and Marshall's goals were separated by 724 minutes (excluding added time), so they played out over 12 barren hours.

Amongst the rubble of those seven scoreless games was the infamous 9-0 defeat at Old Trafford, which remains the Premier League record winning margin. In their previous two fixtures away to United Ipswich had come away with creditable draws so there was no historical reason why they should have expected quite such a thumping. Roy Keane, who would later go on to manage the Suffolk side, started the rout in the 15th minute and then it turned into the Andy Cole show as the recent purchase from Newcastle scored a hat-trick in less than 30 minutes before adding a couple more for good measure. A Mark Hughes double and an impudent Paul Ince chip rounded things off. Old Trafford was not a happy hunting ground for the unfortunate goalkeeper Craig Forrest as the Canadian's next visit to Old Trafford in April 2000, for West Ham, ended in him conceding a further seven goals.

Since their last relegation from the Premier League in 2001/02 Ipswich have spent 17 consecutive seasons in the second tier. It was the longest current spell in that division until it was ended by their dismal showing in 2018/19 when they were finally relegated from the Championship. Ipswich finished bottom with a meagre 31 points, 63 behind the champions, who much to their chagrin were Norwich. It is a long way from qualifying for Europe in the early 2000s.

On a more positive note Ipswich can claim to be among the cleanest teams to have ever played in the Premier League, a badge of honour that serves as a fitting tribute to the legacy and principles of Sir Bobby Robson. Over five seasons and a total of 202 matches they only received six red cards, at an average of one every 34 games—the lowest of any club. By contrast Sunderland in 2009/10 and QPR in 2011/12 received nine cards in a single season. Ipswich's six red cards were shared between six different players—Craig Forrest, John McGreal, Matteo Sereni, Marcus Stewart, John Wark and Phil Whelan—so not one Ipswich player has been sent off twice while Richard Dunne, Duncan Ferguson and Patrick Vieira have all notched up eight dismissals each, more than Ipswich altogether.

One of Ipswich's most cherished victories came in the very first Premier League season when they beat their East Anglian neighbours Norwich 2-0 at Carrow Road on 21st December, 1992. At the time the Canaries were unbeaten at home and were sitting pretty five points clear at the top of the table. Second-half goals from Chris Kiwomya and Neil Thompson took the wind out of the Canaries' sails and they did not win until late January, by which time Manchester United had overtaken them. Ipswich finished a lowly 16th but the Tractor Boys could at least derive great pleasure from halting Norwich in their tracks.

ONE HIT WONDER

Having started as a youth player at the age of 11 Darren Ambrose finally made the first team squad in 2001/02. His solitary appearance for Ipswich in the Premier League was against Arsenal on 21st April, 2002 when he came on for the last five minutes of a 2-0 defeat. Ipswich were relegated at the end of the season and Ambrose then spent a year in the Championship before he moved to Newcastle. He went on to make 91 Premier League appearances for both Newcastle and Charlton however, the remainder of Ambrose's career was spent outside the Premier League. He played more than 100 times for Palace in the Championship before he ended up at Colchester in 2015/16 and he retired after their relegation to League Two. Ambrose co-owns a barber's shop in Ipswich.

FOOTNOTE

MANAGERS OF THE SEASON WHO WERE NOT CHAMPIONS

SEASON	MANAGER	CLUB	POS
1992/92	Dave Bassett	Sheffield United	14th
2000/01	George Burley	Ipswich Town	5th
2009/10	Harry Redknapp	Tottenham	4th
2011/12	Alan Pardew	Newcastle United	5th
2013/14	Tony Pulis	Crystal Palace	11th

A VIEW FROM THE STANDS

Gavin Barber

What was the club's 'Sliding Doors' moment, that seemingly inconsequential action, which actually became a turning point in their fortunes, for either good or bad?

Ipswich's most recent seasons in the Premier League—2000/01 and 2001/02—were, to say the least, contrasting. The first was stellar, the second an embarrassment. The most decisive moment between them was the sale of goalkeeper Richard Wright to Arsenal in the summer of 2001. Wright, a local boy, was only 23 at the time of the transfer, but had been a fixture in the Ipswich team since his teenage years, and his development as a player epitomised the team's growth under George Burley.

With Wright gone, and a UEFA Cup campaign to prepare for, Burley went on a bizarre spending spree, signing not one but two keepers to replace him, neither of whom was up to the task. The coherence and stability that had characterised Burley's Ipswich was sacrificed for a bloated, unbalanced squad, unrecognisable from previous seasons, and relegation inevitably followed. Even more gallingly, we learned from Tom Bower's 2003 book Broken Dreams that Arsène Wenger didn't actually want Wright: he was trying to sign Jerzy Dudek, but was scuppered by power-games between agents. The sale of Wright was pivotal in Ipswich losing a Premier League status which hasn't been regained since.

LEEDS UNITED STATS

NUMBER OF SEASONS:

12

1992/93-2003/04

NUMBER OF MATCHES:

468

Wins 189 (Home 118 Away 71)
Draws 125 (Home 60 Away 65)
Losses 154 (Home 56 Away 98)

[Win ratio 40%]

Goals F 641
(Home 357 Away 284)

Goals A 573
(Home 231 Away 342)

Goal Difference: +68

TOTAL POINTS

692

(Home 414: 60%; Away 278: 40%)
Average per season - 58

BEST POSITION:

3rd

1999/2000

WORST POSITION:

19th

2003/04 (RELEGATED)

BIGGEST WIN:

6-1 (2)

v Bradford (13th May, 2001)
v Charlton (5th Apr, 2003)

BIGGEST LOSS:

6-1

v Portsmouth
(8th Nov, 2003)

LONGEST UNBEATEN RUN:

14 matches

(30th Aug, 1993–8th Dec, 1993)

LONGEST WITHOUT A WIN:

10 matches

(12th Mar, 1997–9th Aug, 1997)

ALL TIME RANKING

13th

MOST GOALS SCORED IN A SEASON:

65

(1993/94)

FEWEST GOALS SCORED IN A SEASON:

28

(1996/97)

FEWEST GOALS CONCEDED IN A SEASON:

34

(1998/99)

MOST GOALS CONCEDED IN A SEASON:

79

(2003/04)

TOP GOALSCORER:

59

Gary Kelly

MOST APPEARANCES:

325

Cyril Chapuis

OWN GOALS:

14

RED CARDS:

28

LOWEST ATTENDANCE:

25,795

v Wimbledon
(15th Aug, 1992)

HIGHEST ATTENDANCE:

41,127

v Manchester United
(27th Apr, 1994)

LEEDS UNITED

FIRST PREMIER LEAGUE MATCH: 15TH AUGUST, 1992
LEEDS 2 (CHAPMAN 2)
WIMBLEDON 1 (BARTON)

ELLAND ROAD 25,795

John Lukic, Jon Newsome (Gordon Strachan), Tony Dorigo, David Batty (Steve Hodge), Chris Fairclough, Chris Whyte, Eric Cantona, Rod Wallace, Lee Chapman, Gary McAllister, Gary Speed, Manager: Howard Wilkinson

Having now spent 15 years outside the top flight there will be a raft of younger fans who have never seen Leeds in the Premier League. After a series of financial mishaps that have undermined the club and a succession of flakey owners which contributed to their slide to the third tier by 2007, it is worth reminding ourselves that Leeds were once a well-established Premier League side.

Having won the last pre-Premier League Division One title in 1992 under Howard Wilkinson, the last British manager to take the title, Leeds achieved seven top five finishes in the first ten Premier League seasons—three more than Chelsea. By contrast in that same period Tottenham did not finish higher than 7th and Manchester City's highest position was 8th while they were also relegated twice. Leeds' relegation in 2004 was something of a shock to the system as a team that had reached the semi-finals of the Champions League three years before were cast adrift and have not returned since.

In the first Premier League season, the loss of their talisman Eric Cantona after a few months was a blow from which they never truly recovered and eventually they limped home in a distant 17th, only two points outside the relegation places. Or that should be limped 'away' as they did not win single fixture away from Elland Road—the only Premier League club to not be able to win away over 21 matches. They drew seven games and compared to their home haul of 44 points, which was the third best in the division, the difference of 37 points remains the largest ever between home and away records. With only 14% of their points total gained away this is the lowest proportion of any Premier League club.

Cantona started the season with a bang, already signaling his intent with a hat-trick against Liverpool in the Charity Shield. Almost inevitably, he followed this up with the first-ever Premier League hat-trick in the space of 20 minutes during Leeds' 5-0 demolition of Tottenham on 25th August. But he was soon jettisoned by Wilkinson and joined Manchester United in November for what now seems the almost derisory figure of just over £1m after a swap deal with Denis Irwin broke down.

In the inaugural season, 36-year-old Gordon Strachan became the only player who was born before 1960 to have scored a Premier League hattrick when he notched three goals in a 5-2 win against Blackburn on 10th April, 1993, which included two penalties. Despite their years in the wilderness Leeds have the seventh highest win ratio of 40% and are also seventh on the list of goal difference with a healthy +68. They are one of only ten teams with a positive goal difference and by some margin have the best record of clubs no longer in the Premier League.

Their relegation in 2004 was the only time in Premier League history that all three clubs that went down were on exactly the same points, as alongside Leicester and Wolves, Leeds amassed 33. In fact Leeds and Wolves also ended up with an identical goal difference of -39, Leeds managing to stay off the bottom of the table by dint of scoring two more goals.

Mark Viduka may be Leeds' top goalscorer but Tony Yeboah is probably more fondly remembered because of his penchant for spectacular strikes and none more impressive than his extraordinary goal against Wimbledon in 1995/96. After chesting the ball down, the Ghanian nudged it forward with his thigh then wriggled past a couple of defenders before unleashing a shot that flew in off the bar with such ferocity that it induced an involuntary yelp from Martin Tyler in his commentary. Tyler summed it up perfectly: "Even by his standards, breathtakingly brilliant."

Leeds managed to escape relegation in the following season when they scored a mere 28 goals, the lowest number of goals by a side to not go down and somehow managed to finish a fairly giddy 11th. It is worth noting that they scored three in the opening match so notched just 25 from the remaining 37 matches at anaemic ratio of 0.67.

As superb as Yeboah's goals were, the most successful Premier League Leeds team were a little more functional. Marshalled by David O'Leary, who took over from George Graham, himself the master of functionality, they finished third behind Manchester United and Arsenal in 1999/2000 and qualified for the Champions League. Under O'Leary they managed fourth and fifth in the following two seasons, and reached the Champions League semi-final in 2001 but after O'Leary departed they slipped to 15th before relegation in 2004. Within three years they were languishing in League One, completing one of the steeper declines with the accompanying financial crises adding to their fall from grace.

During their 12-season tenure in the Premier League Leeds can lay claim to being the best starters as they never lost their opening match, winning five and drawing seven between 1992/93 and 2003/04. They hold the only unbeaten opening game record for a club that has spent at least ten seasons in the Premier League. Drawing 58% of those opening fixtures is the highest proportion of any club with a minimum of ten seasons. Leeds were not bad finishers either as they had an unbeaten record for the final day right up to their 12th season—winning four and drawing seven but, in what proved to be their last match in the top-flight to date, they lost 1-0 at Chelsea, blotting The Peacocks' proud opening day/last day copybook.

ONE HIT WONDERS

Frenchman Cyril Chapuis arrived on loan at Elland Road from Marseille in August 2003 and came on as a half-time substitute with Leeds trailing 2-0 to Bolton on 22nd November. Chapuis could not rescue United on that occasion nor could they do it without him as Chapuis left for Strasbourg in January 2004 and Leeds were duly relegated.

FOOTNOTE

Only four clubs outside the Big Six have an overall
positive goal difference.

CLUB	GOAL DIFF
Leeds United	+ 68
Everton	+ 46
Blackburn Rovers	+ 20
Newcastle United	+ 14

A VIEW FROM THE STANDS

Robert Endeacott, author of The Gigante

What was your club's 'Sliding Doors' moment, that seemingly inconsequential action, which actually became a turning point in their fortunes, for either good or bad?

The Championship, or to give it its proper name, 'Division Two', has always been a pig of a division to get out of. We Leeds supporters are experiencing the hellish Pork Life as I write this, and I well remember the last time we actually succeeded in promotion to the top flight.

After trying Leeds legends Billy Bremner and Eddie Gray before him, but not backing them anywhere near enough (and binning them off like ancient clapped out Vauxhall Vivas) the Leeds board finally showed some wisdom, foresight and yes, courage in hiring Howard Wilkinson as new Leeds manager. Even then though they nearly loused it up, Wilko wasn't their first choice; he wasn't even their second!

Anyway, before Wilko, I actually did think Bremner would take us back to the top. I was wrong, obviously, but I just KNEW it would happen under Wilkinson, there was a dourness and a pragmatism to him that the club needed, and it was of course clear that he wouldn't accept anything less than 100% commitment from the players. Just as importantly, he had plans which the directors agreed with, such as investing in a much-improved youth system; a wider network of talent scouting and, crucially for the long-term future of the club; a dedicated and technically excellent training and development academy. Wilkinson, in what some wrongly saw as disrespectful, demanded that the club and fans forgot about the glory years under Don Revie and looked to the future. And yet, for all this apparent desire, his ideas were very similar indeed to those of Revie and chairman Harry Reynolds back in 1961 when Revie began his managerial career at Elland Road.

Despite an alarming 5-2 defeat at Newcastle on the opening day of The Big Season, Wilkinson's Leeds were crowned champions of the Second Division in 1990, with Sheffield United as runners-up. In the top division, Leeds succeeded 'too early' according to legend, but no one was complaining!

LEICESTER CITY STATS

NUMBER OF SEASONS:

13 (4 spells)

1994/95, 1996/97-2001/02,
2003/04, 2014/15-2018/19

NUMBER OF MATCHES:

498

Wins 157 (Home 95 Away 62)
Draws 136 (Home 75 Away 61)
Losses 205 (Home 79 Away 126)

[Win ratio 32%]

Goals F 623
(Home 332 Away 291)

Goals A 718
(Home 319 Away 399)

Goal Difference: -95

TOTAL POINTS

607

(Home 360: 59%; Away 247: 41%)
Average per season: 47

BEST POSITION:

1st

2015/16 (CHAMPIONS)

WORST POSITION:

20th

2001/02 (RELEGATED)

BIGGEST WIN:

5-1

v QPR
(24th May, 2015)

BIGGEST LOSS:

6-1 (2)

v Leicester (26th Dec, 2000)
v Tottenham (18th May, 2017)

**LONGEST
UNBEATEN RUN:**

12 matches

(27th Feb, 2016-15th May, 2016)

**LONGEST
WITHOUT A WIN:**

16 matches

(8th Dec, 2001-23rd Mar, 2002)

ALL TIME RANKING

17th

MOST GOALS SCORED IN A SEASON:

68

(2015/16)

FEWEST GOALS SCORED IN A SEASON:

30

(2001/02)

FEWEST GOALS CONCEDED IN A SEASON:

36

(2015/16)

MOST GOALS CONCEDED IN A SEASON:

80

(1994/5)

TOP GOALSCORER:

80

Jamie Vardy

MOST APPEARANCES:

222

Muzzy Izzet

OWN GOALS:

26

RED CARDS:

47

LOWEST ATTENDANCE:

15,248

v Ipswich Town
(29th Apr, 1995)

HIGHEST ATTENDANCE:

32,242

v Sunderland
(8th Aug, 2015)

All statistics and records supplied by

LEICESTER CITY

DID YOU KNOW?

On 16th March, 2019 Wes Morgan, the redoubtable captain who had been one of the stalwarts of the 2016 title-winning side, broke a Premier League record that had stood for 23 years. Morgan can thank Harry Maguire for creating the opportunity after his fellow centre half was sent off in the 4th minute of their match with Burnley, leading to Morgan being brought on. It wasn't the quickest red card in Premier League history (that dubious honour goes to Tim Flowers who was dismissed after 72 seconds against Leeds in Blackburn's title-winning season) but when Morgan scored the winning goal in added time, 84 minutes after joining the action, it was the longest time between a player coming on as a substitute and subsequently scoring.

The previous proud holder of this record had been Jim Magilton of Southampton who, in December 1996, came on as a sub for Richard Dryden in the 9th minute of the home game against Derby County and stepped up to score a penalty in the 90th minute to wrap up a 3-1 win.

With that victory against Burnley Leicester also gained the record for the longest a side had played with ten men and still won. To embellish his goal-scoring prowess further, Morgan popped up two weeks later with a cheeky backheel to open the scoring against Bournemouth.

FIRST PREMIER LEAGUE MATCH: 21ST AUGUST, 1994
LEICESTER CITY 1(JOACHIM)
NEWCASTLE UNITED 3 (COLE, BEARDSLEY, ELLIOTT)

FILBERT STREET 20,048

Gavin Ward, Colin Hill, Nicky Mohan, Steve Walsh, Mike Whitlow, Simon Grayson (Steve Thompson), Richard Smith, Mark Draper, Mark Blake (Iwan Roberts), Steve Agnew, Julian Joachim, Manager: Brian Little

In recent years Leicester have managed to become quite the surprise package. In 2014/15 they became the club that had spent most time at the bottom of the table, 140 days in total, but not been relegated. They were as good as written off when losing 4-3 to Tottenham in late March courtesy of a Harry Kane hat-trick and Jeffrey Schlupp's own goal. That left them seven points adrift with only nine games remaining and it seemed as if the Foxes were on their way back from whence they came having been promoted the season before.

But a remarkable renaissance followed and seven wins, one draw and a solitary loss catapulted them up the table and they finished the season in some style, thrashing QPR 5-1 in their last game and reaching the dizzy heights of 14th, three points above the relegation zone. If the football world thought that was extraordinary then Nigel Pearson was in no doubt where the media's attentions were directed: "If you don't know the answer to that question, then I think you are an ostrich." Pearson told a journalist. "Your head must be in the sand. Is your head in the sand? Are you flexible enough to get your head in the sand? My suspicion would be no. I can, you can't"

Not to be outdone they then performed the sort of miracle that only comes around once every couple of thousand years. If Blackburn's unexpected ascent to the summit in 1994/95 caused a fair few ripples in English football then Leicester's triumph in 2015/16 sent shockwaves of seismic proportions across the world. This unlikeliest of titles was secured by Claudio Ranieri's team with a swashbuckling counter-attacking approach that took their opponents by storm and left the so-called Top Six gasping in their wake. By breaking the grip of the Manchester clubs and the London pair of Chelsea and Arsenal the Foxes were the first club to win the Premier League outside those four since Blackburn's success 21 years beforehand.

Although everybody assumed they were going to blow up at the next hurdle The Foxes ended up cantering home with Arsenal a distant second by the considerable margin of ten points. Only five other title-winning teams have had such a large points difference over the runners-up - Manchester United in 1999/2000 and 2012/13, the Invincibles of Arsenal in 2003/04, Chelsea in 2004/05 and the record-breaking Manchester City in 2017/18. The more curmudgeonly observers might point to their lack of possession, they ranked 18th in the league with just shy of 45% on average but the fact is they lost just three games all season, the fourth fewest after Arsenal in 2003/04 (0) Chelsea in 2004/05 (1), Manchester City in 2017/18 (2) and Liverpool in 2018/19 (1).

The goals of Jamie Vardy and Riyad Mahrez led them to the title. Vardy breaking the record of scoring in 11 consecutive games when he appropriately enough scored against Manchester United as he overtook

Ruud van Nistelrooy's ten consecutive games in 2003. Vardy scored 24 goals in total, missing out on the Golden Boot to Harry Kane by one goal, while Mahrez got 17, so between them they scored 65% of the Champions' goals. Leicester only failed to score on three occasions and strangely they were in consecutive matches from a 1-0 Boxing Day defeat at Liverpool, followed by a couple of goalless draws at home to Bournemouth and Manchester City. All the naysayers were then claiming that the Leicester fairytale was well and truly over, little did they know. The following season Leicester could not maintain their astonishing rise and in finishing twelfth they broke another record in becoming the lowest placed Champions.

Another interesting aspect of Leicester's triumph which may have slipped under the radar because of the general astonishment of their 5,000-1 shot was their propensity to be awarded penalties with 13 in total, of which they scored ten. Only four clubs have been awarded more than ten penalties in a season with Chelsea having done so three times - twice they have been awarded 11 in 2008/09 and 2012/13 and in 2009/10 they got 12 while Liverpool were also awarded a dozen in 2013/14. Crystal Palace have twice been awarded 11 in 2004/05 and in 2018/19 (see Footnote below).

ONE HIT WONDER

Joseph Dodoo made his Premier League bow as a substitute in 72nd minute on 29th August, 2015 for Marc Albrighton in a 1-1 draw at Bournemouth. Despite Dodoo scoring in his next game, a League Cup tie against West Ham, he could not convince manager Claudio Ranieri that he was part of his plans so he went on loan to Bury and then transferred to Rangers in July 2016. Since his move to Glasgow he has been on loan at Charlton and Blackpool.

FOOTNOTE

FOXES IN THE BOX

Leicester's remarkable title win in 2015/16 was helped by collecting the most penalties ever awarded in a single season, of which ten were scored (five by Vardy, four by Riyad Mahrez and a solitary one by Leonardo Ulloa).

CLUB	SEASON	NO. OF PENS AWARDED
Leicester City	2015/16	13
Chelsea	2009/10	12
Liverpool	2013/14	12
Crystal Palace	2004/05 & 2018/19	11
Chelsea	2008/09 & 2012/13	11

A VIEW FROM THE STANDS

Roger Domeneghetti, author of From the Back Page to the Front Room: Football's Journey Through the English Media

What was your club's 'Sliding Doors' moment, that seemingly inconsequential action, which actually became a turning point in their fortunes, for either good or bad?

It's May 12th, 2013. We are deep in stoppage time in the Championship play-off semi-final second leg. The score is level at two apiece. Leicester's Anthony Knockaert stands with his hands on his hips ready to take a penalty that will send his team to Wembley. It's saved, and 28 seconds later, Watford have scored. That sliding doors moment kick started a rollercoaster three years for The Foxes.

Of course, had Leicester won there would have been the small matter of a play-off final against eventual winners Crystal Palace to negotiate. But truth be told, Leicester simply weren't equipped for the Premier League. Had we gone up, we almost certainly would have come straight back down. That would have meant no record-breaking Championship title in 2014, no miraculous escape from relegation in 2015 and no even-more miraculous Premier League title in 2016. Numerous factors fed into that 5,000-1 triumph but the journey began at Vicarage Road and the first step was that penalty miss. Anthony Knockaert, we salute you.

LIVERPOOL STATS

NUMBER OF SEASONS:

27

1992/93 - 2018/19

NUMBER OF MATCHES:

1,038

Wins 529 (Home 320 Away 209)
Draws 262 (Home 129 Away 133)
Losses 247 (Home 70 Away 177)

[Win ratio 51%]

Goals F 1,774
(Home 1,026 Away 748)

Goals A 1,046
(Home 413 Away 633)

Goal Difference: +728

TOTAL POINTS

1,849

(Home 1,089: 59%; Away 760: 41%)
Average per season: 68

BEST POSITION:

2nd (4)

2001/02, 2008/09, 2013/14
& 2018/19

WORST POSITION:

8th (3)

1993/94, 2011/12 & 2015/16

BIGGEST WIN:

7-1

v Southampton
(16th Jan, 1999)

BIGGEST LOSS:

6-1

v Stoke City
(24th May, 2015)

LONGEST UNBEATEN RUN:

21 matches

(13th May, 2018–29th Dec, 2018)

LONGEST WITHOUT A WIN:

11 matches

(9th Nov 2002–11th Jan 2003)

ALL TIME RANKING

4th

MOST GOALS SCORED IN A SEASON:

101

(2013/14)

FEWEST GOALS SCORED IN A SEASON:

47

(2011/2012)

FEWEST GOALS CONCEDED IN A SEASON:

22

(2018/19)

MOST GOALS CONCEDED IN A SEASON:

55 (2)

(1992/93 & 1993/94)

TOP GOALSCORER:

128

Robbie Fowler

MOST APPEARANCES:

508

Jamie Carragher

OWN GOALS:

39

RED CARDS:

58

LOWEST ATTENDANCE:

24,561

v QPR
(8th Dec, 1993)

HIGHEST ATTENDANCE:

53,373

v Cardiff City
(27th Oct, 2018)

All statistics and records supplied by  gracenote.
A NIELSEN COMPANY

LIVERPOOL

FIRST PREMIER LEAGUE MATCH: 16TH AUGUST, 1992
NOTTINGHAM FOREST 1 (SHERINGHAM)
LIVERPOOL 0

CITY GROUND 20,038

David James, David Burrows, Nicky Tanner, Mark Wright, Steve Nicol, Mark Walters (Ronnie Rosenthal), Michael Thomas, Ronnie Whelan, Dean Saunders, Ian Rush (Steve McManaman), Paul Stewart, Manager: Graeme Souness

Liverpool fans need no reminding that the Premier League has remained as elusive as the Holy Grail was to the medieval knights of the 13th century. Since they were crowned champions of the old Division One 11 times between 1973 and their last title in 1990, the wait for a Premier League title that is now stretching into its third decade is becoming a serious thorn in the side of the Red Men.

The fact that that another red team from the North West have carried off the Premier League on 13 occasions in the meantime is unlucky for those associated with Anfield but no doubt a source of pride for Manchester United fans. As Alex Ferguson once gleefully pointed out: "My greatest challenge is not what is happening at the moment, my greatest challenge was knocking Liverpool right off their fucking perch. And you can print that."

Liverpool can point to the fact that they have never been lower than 8th and their average position is between 4th and 5th. No team other than Manchester United can come close to such consistency in the Premier League, but it's just that falling short which is so frustrating. However hard they have tried, however tantalisingly near to the main prize they have been, it still eludes them and over those barren seasons there is a litany of 'if onlys' be it Steven Gerrard losing his grip or the 11 millimetres that separated them from a crucial own goal at The Etihad in January.

They have been runners-up four times and on each occasion they have been getting closer and closer but never quite chugging away on the cigar. In 2001/02 they were seven points behind Arsenal; in 2008/09 they were four points behind Manchester United; in 2013/14 they finished two points behind Manchester City. But of course the latest instalment in their runners-up quadrilogy is the most hurtful as it just seems infeasible that a team that loses just one game all season can possibly end up not winning the title. Being the greatest runners-up ever, not just in the Premier League, but in top flight history is a consolation prize that Liverpool do not want.

The 97 points they accrued in 2018/19 is by far and away the most for a team that has not won the top flight, even after adjustments for clubs playing in the days before three points for a win. The next closest are Leeds, who in 1970/71 were second behind Arsenal with 64 points, which would have been 91 points if three points had been awarded for a win. As a result of Liverpool's almost imperious form, new arrival Naby Keita has made more Premier League appearances without defeat than any other player— a record that stands at 25 matches.

During that 2018/19 title race the lead changed hands a record 32 times before City eventually came out on top. It may have been an artificial barometer of the fluctuating fortunes as the staggered kick-off times meant that the two clubs rarely played simultaneously, especially during the run-in, but the previous record which stood at 28 in the 2001/02 season involved many more clubs with Arsenal eventually being crowned champions after trading blows with both their traditional rivals Manchester United, who were runners-up, and also Liverpool, Newcastle and Leeds.

Steven Gerrard holds many records, including the second most appearances with 504 just behind Jamie Carragher's 508 and the second most goals with 120 nestling in between Robbie Fowler's 128 and Michael Owen's 118. But Gerrard does lead one chart for his only club, he has the most red cards with six and there is one dismissal which stands out. On 22nd March, 2015 he was sent off a mere 38 seconds after coming on as a substitute against Manchester United having decided the best way to make his mark on the game was to stamp on Anders Herrera. This was an interesting way for Gerrard to begin the run-in during his farewell season.

In fact Gerrard's last few games did not prove to be quite the tribute they should have been. For his last game at Anfield the Crystal Palace players formed a guard of honour as he came on to the pitch and then former Liverpool player Martin Kelly gifted Adam Lallana the chance to take the lead midway through the first half but that was where the charity stopped and Palace went on to win 3-1, completing their first ever double over Liverpool. In a post-match interview with Gary Lineker for Match of the Day Gerrard admitted things did not go according to plan: "Credit to Crystal Palace today, they were fantastic and they spoiled the party if you like but I couldn't ask for any more off the supporters they have been brilliant again."

GOODBYE STEVIE G

SUNDAY 24TH MAY 2015

STOKE CITY 6 (5) DIOUF 22', 26', WALTERS 30',
ADAMS 41', NZONZI 45', CROUCH 86'
LIVERPOOL 1 (0) GERRARD 70'

Then it was off to the Britannia Stadium on 24 May for his 504th and last Liverpool game but that one ended even more disastrously for Gerrard as the Potters were merciless in racing into a 5-0 half-time lead. Mame Biram Diouf bagged a brace, before Jonathan Walters and Charlie Adam joined in the fun and Steven Nzonzi made Jurgen Klopp's half-time talk more of a damage limitation exercise than a tactical masterplan.

Maybe Stoke did then ease off as Gerrard scored his 120th, and possibly most pointless, Premier League goal. But even then ex-Red Peter Crouch followed Charlie Adam in sticking the knife into their former club by finishing it all off with an 86th-minute goal and in so doing handed out Liverpool's biggest ever Premier League defeat. It was the first time they had conceded six goals in a league match for more than 50 years. As shellackings go, 6-1 in your final game is one that must have hurt Gerrard.

ONE HIT WONDER

If things had gone the way he hoped Conor Coady would have become a stalwart at the heart of the Liverpool defence. Coady was born in Liverpool, supported them as a boy and joined the academy at the age of

12 before graduating to the seniors where he popped up now and again in the first team squad. On the penultimate day of the 2012/13 season Coady finally got his chance as he managed to make his Premier League debut at Craven Cottage when replacing Philippe Coutinho, but it was not until the 89th minute of a comfortable 3-1 win.

In the close season Coady was loaned out to League One outfit Sheffield United before moving to Huddersfield and scored his first goal for the club at Molineux, which was his ultimate destination and he was an ever-present in Wolves' golden return in 2018/19 season.

FOOTNOTE

Liverpool and Arsenal share the record for the most hat-tricks in Premier League history with 39 each. With eight each Henry and Fowler lead the way for their respective clubs, while Luis Suarez notched six in the space of just over three seasons with Norwich as his favourite victims against whom he scored half of those. His first two were recorded at Carrow Road, on 28th April, 2012 in a 3-0 win, swiftly followed by another in a 5-2 away win on 29th September, 2012. Suarez then waited for over a year before inflicting more damage against the Canaries when he scored four in a 5-1 win at Anfield on 4th December, 2013. No other club has been on the receiving end of as many hat-tricks by a single player.

LEADING INDIVIDUAL HAT-TRICKS

ARSENAL	LIVERPOOL
Henry 8	Fowler 8
Wright 5	Owen 7
Adebayor 3	Suarez 6
Walcott 3	

A VIEW FROM THE STANDS

Seb Patrick

As one of the select clubs that is an ever-present throughout Premier League history your club has enjoyed prolonged success so what is your favourite moment from the last 27 years?.

Liverpool have come painfully close to winning the title three times in the Premier League area, but on only one of those occasions did I actually feel at the time like it was going to happen. The 3-2 win over Manchester City at Anfield in April 2014 really did seem like a proper title decider, and everything about the day was everything that it means to be a Liverpool fan wrapped up in one game. The emotion of the occasion, coming exactly on the 25th anniversary of Hillsborough, undoubtedly played a part. Liverpool fans get accused of being over-emotional, and at times that's true, but on other occasions it channels itself into Anfield being like nowhere else. That usually happens on Classic European Nights, but this was a rare example of a Premier League game being charged with that same feeling.

The ramshackle rollercoaster that was Liverpool's 2013/14 season, meanwhile, was in full effect. We accelerated into a two-goal lead before conspiring to seemingly throw it all away. Then there was a final twist courtesy of a wonderful late Philippe Coutinho goal to seal the win. You could have stopped football right there and I'd have been happy. Of course, the following weeks would render the effort futile. Futile, but never forgotten.

MANCHESTER CITY STATS

NUMBER OF SEASONS:

22 (3 spells)

1992/93-1995/96,
1997/98, 2002/03-2018/19

TOTAL POINTS

1,369

(Home 802: 59%; Away 567: 41%)
Average per season: 62

NUMBER OF MATCHES:

848

Wins 391 (Home 237 Away 154)
Draws 196 (Home 91 Away 105)
Losses 261 (Home 96 Away 165)

[Win ratio 46%]

Goals F 1,374
(Home 799 Away 575)

Goals A 975
(Home 413 Away 562)

Goal Difference: +399

BEST POSITION:

1st (4)

2011/12, 2013/14, 2017/18 &
2018/19 (CHAMPIONS)

WORST POSITION:

18th (2)

1995/96 & 2000/01
(RELEGATED)

BIGGEST WIN:

7-0

v Norwich City
(2nd Nov, 2013)

BIGGEST LOSS:

8-1

v Middlesbrough
(11th May, 2008)

LONGEST UNBEATEN RUN:

30 matches

(8th Apr, 2017-2nd Jan, 2018)

LONGEST WITHOUT A WIN:

15 matches

(29nd Apr, 1995-28th Oct, 1995)

ALL TIME RANKING

7th

MOST GOALS SCORED IN A SEASON:

106

(2017/18)

FEWEST GOALS SCORED IN A SEASON:

29

(2006/07)

FEWEST GOALS CONCEDED IN A SEASON:

23

(2018/19)

MOST GOALS CONCEDED IN A SEASON:

65

(2000/01)

TOP GOALSCORER:

164

Sergio Aguero

MOST APPEARANCES:

282

David Silva

OWN GOALS:

37

RED CARDS:

66

LOWEST ATTENDANCE:

19,150

v West Ham
(24th Aug, 1994)

HIGHEST ATTENDANCE:

54,693

v Leicester City
(6th Feb, 2016)

All statistics and records supplied by  gracenote.
A NIELSEN COMPANY

MANCHESTER CITY

FIRST PREMIER LEAGUE MATCH: 17TH AUGUST, 1992
MANCHESTER CITY 1 (WHITE)
QUEENS PARK RANGERS 1 (SINTON)

MAINE ROAD 24,471

Tony Coton, Michael Vonk, Keith Curle, Andy Hill, Ian Brightwell, Steve McMahon, Fitzroy Simpson, Paul Lake (Mike Sheron), Richard Holden, David White, Nial Quinn, Manager: Peter Reid

Although Manchester United are indisputably the most successful Premier League team, the last decade has seen City and Chelsea emerge as equals—City have won four titles in the last eight years and Chelsea have won three of the last ten with Leicester as the outliers. City justifiably can lay claim to the greatest Premier League season and probably the second to boot. The 2017/18 season was remarkable for many reasons as City broke record after record and smashed most people's preconceptions of what success looks like. It is difficult to do their supremacy full justice but then they did it again in 2018/19 and came within whisker of another century of points for the second time running.

Aside from the most wins (32), most consecutive wins (18), most goals (106), most away wins (16), the highest points total (106), the best goal difference (+79) and the greatest points margin over the runners-up (19) there are a few other lesser-recognised records worth highlighting. As the only club to amass 100 points there was some verisimilitude with a club who broke records at the other end of the table. Swindon conceded their 100th goal in the last minute of their final game against Leeds in 1993/94 while City's 100th point was secured when Gabriel Jesus scored the only goal of the game in the 94th minute at Southampton.

They had an even distribution of points home and away—no title-winning team has won as many points away as at home. In more than half their games (21/38) they scored at least three goals, which puts them way ahead of the next most prolific team. They only failed to score twice in the 38 games, which were both against struggling teams. Palace ended their opening 18-match consecutive win streak run by holding out for a 0-0 at Selhurst Park after starting the season with seven successive losses. Even more surprising was the goalless draw at home to Huddersfield who were still hovering above the relegation zone, but by then the title was already well and truly wrapped up. They beat all 19 other teams at least once, which had not happened before, but just to prove that was not a freak they repeated the trick the following season.

The next season yet again they only failed to score twice—in a 0-0 draw at Anfield and then in a 2-0 defeat at Stamford Bridge. Oddly, for such a successful season they lost four games, three of which were over a four-match blip in December. Following their defeat to Chelsea they were stunned by Andros Townsend's stupendous strike at the Etihad and slumped to a 3-2 defeat at home to Palace, the only points they dropped at home. In the very next game on Boxing Day Leicester beat them 2-1 by which point Liverpool had opened up a seven-point gap, which they extended to 11 in January before being hauled in by the relentless City juggernaut. Following the Leicester defeat City won 18 out of the next 19 games, only slipping up at St. James's Park at the end of January.

Not only can City lay claim to the biggest points margin of any champions but also the most slender when they pipped Manchester United on goal difference in 2011/12—the only time the Premier League has been decided in that manner. Sergio Aguero's winner in the 94th minute followed swiftly on from Dzeko's equaliser two minutes earlier providing the most dramatic finish to a Premier League season. By contrast the last day of the 2007/08 season brought City's most humbling experience as Sven Goran Eriksson's team were humiliated by Middlesbrough in their biggest defeat, 8-1. This was Eriksson's last game in charge and his unhappy epitaph was underlined by his own damning assessment of his team: "We were not even on the pitch—the team had totally gone and it was embarrassing for everyone." Within a few weeks he was also gone.

In 2006/07, the season before that horror show at Middlesbrough, City managed ten goals at home, the last of which was Georgios Samaras' second in a 2-1 win over Everton on New Year's Day, they then proceeded to go goalless at Eastlands until the end of the season. During that eight-match run of firing blanks City even conspired to miss two penalties.

City have racked up so many records in the last few years that it seems slightly over-indulgent that they also boast having the player with the highest shirt number. Spaniard Jose Angel Pozo may not conjure up too many memories for those outside the most ardent fans but when he came on to replace Samir Nasri in the 83rd minute of a 4-1 win at the Stadium of Light in December 2014 with the number 78 emblazoned on his back he made an indelible mark on Premier League history. He may have made only one other Premier League appearance for City, later that month, but he has held on to his record although he was almost toppled from his lofty perch a few years later by the enigmatic Renato Sanches (see Swansea City).

Niall Quinn was never anything but a classic number nine for all his City career and since retiring from playing he has established himself as a calm, authoritative figure in televised commentary but his personal landmark was slightly out of kilter with such a composed demeanour. In City's second game of the 1992/93 season away at Middlesbrough Quinn became the first Premier League player to be sent off. This was Quinn's only sending off in 250 appearances, and so his lashing out at Paul Wilkinson was as uncharacteristic as it was unfortunate. The sight of the talented but fragile Paul Lake being carried off with another injury had upset Quinn as Lake explains in his autobiography *I'm Not Really Here, a Life of Two Halves* : "Quinn shared my devastation admitting that seeing me flat out on the pitch had contributed to his sending-off three minutes later, after an anger-fuelled late challenge." For once in his illustrious career, Quinn was not so mighty.

ONE HIT WONDER

Of all the one hit wonders featured in this book Christian Negouai is the only one who can lay claim to having made a red mark in Premier League history. He arrived from Charleroi in 2001 with City in the First Division. Manager Kevin Keegan described Negouai as "the most exciting player" he had signed and he made a handful of appearances in Cup competitions, including scoring in a UEFA Cup qualifier against Welsh side The New Saints, as well as in the odd First Division game over the next few years.

Negoaui's big chance arrived on Boxing Day 2004 when he finally got on to the pitch as a substitute for Jonathan Macken in the 81st minute of City's game at Goodison Park. This was to be one of the more short-lived appearances as within three minutes Negouai decided to nullify Darren Bent's chances of adding to his earlier goal by wiping him out. He succeeded in his mission but alas also received a straight red card and departed the stage, never to return. Negouai qualifies as the shortest debut both in terms of minutes on the pitch and temper-wise.

Keegan was now willing to part with his most exciting acquisition and sent Negoaui to Coventry on loan before he returned to Belgium and retired from the game in 2007, with the three minutes of fame enshrined.

FOOTNOTE

When Sergio Aguero's scuffed shot against Burnley on 28th April, 2019 was adjudged to have crossed the line by the small matter of 29.5 mm it was a long way from being the Argentine marksman's most spectacular goal but its significance far outweighed its aesthetics. Not only did it ensure City won at Turf Moor and put them back on top of the table with two games remaining, in scoring that goal he also became only the second player, after Thierry Henry, to score at least 20 goals in five consecutive seasons. In those five seasons between 2001/02 and 2005/06 Henry scored 130 goals while Aguero managed 112 between 2014/15 and 2018/19.

HENRY		AGUERO	
SEASON	GOALS	SEASON	GOALS
2001/02	24	2014/15	26
2002/03	24	2015/16	24
2003/04	30	2016/17	20
2004/05	25	2017/18	21
2005/06	27	2018/19	21
TOTAL	130	TOTAL	112

A VIEW FROM THE STANDS

David Mooney

What was your club's 'Sliding Doors' moment, that seemingly inconsequential action, which actually became a turning point in their fortunes, for either good or bad?

It's not easy enduring your worst-ever season while your cross-town rivals are becoming the most successful club in the country and the most powerful team in world football. Manchester City don't do things by halves—and while the global stage will remember 1999 as the year a last-minute goal won Manchester United a historic treble, it was actually a last-minute goal in a third-tier playoff that changed the course of football history.

City, hampered by crippling finances after years of mismanagement at all levels, had sunk to the Second Division (now League 1), where they had lost games to the likes of York City, Lincoln City and Wycombe Wanderers. They dragged themselves into the playoffs, despite being 12th just before Christmas, and should have won promotion comfortably on form alone—after half a season of winning nearly every game.

With 90 minutes on the clock in the play-off final, City were 2-0 against Gillingham. Then Kevin Horlock scored in the 91st minute to offer hope and Paul Dickov equalised in the 95th to take the game into extra time before City won on penalties. It's fair to say that without those two goals, City's future wouldn't have been the same. They may have gone out of business, though the chairman at the time, David Bernstein, refutes that idea.

More likely, they may not have won promotion back to the second tier for some time—and ultimately may not have been in the right place at the right time when Sheikh Mansour was looking for somewhere to invest his funds.

City were back in the Premier League by 2000-01, all because they were riding the wave of that win at Wembley in 1999. It doesn't bear thinking about what would have happened if Dickov had hit the post or blazed his shot over.

MANCHESTER UNITED STATS

NUMBER OF SEASONS:

27

1992/93-2018/19

NUMBER OF MATCHES:

1,038

Wins 648 (Home 373 Away 275)
Draws 224 (Home 94 Away 130)
Losses 166 (Home 52 Away 114)

[Win ratio 62%]

Goals F 1,989
(Home 1,104 Away 885)

Goals A 929
(Home 361 Away 568)

Goal Difference: +1,060

TOTAL POINTS

2,168

(Home 1,213: 56%; Away 955: 44%)
Avg. per season: 80

BEST POSITION:

1st (13)

1992/93, 1993/94, 1995/96,
1996/97, 1998/99, 1999/2000,
2000/01, 2002/03, 2006/07,
2007/08, 2008/09, 2010/11 &
2012/13 (CHAMPIONS)

WORST POSITION:

7th

2013/14

BIGGEST LOSS:

1-6

v Manchester City
(3rd Oct, 2011)

BIGGEST WIN:

9-0

v Ipswich Town
(4th Mar, 1995)

LONGEST WITHOUT A WIN:

7 matches

(19th Sept, 1992-7th Nov, 1992)

LONGEST UNBEATEN RUN:

29 matches (2)

(26th Dec, 1998–25th Sep, 1999
& 11th Apr, 2010-1st Feb, 2011)

ALL TIME RANKING

1st

MOST GOALS SCORED IN A SEASON:

97

(1999/2000)

FEWEST GOALS SCORED IN A SEASON:

49

(2015/16)

FEWEST GOALS CONCEDED IN A SEASON:

22

(2007/08)

MOST GOALS CONCEDED IN A SEASON:

54

(2018/19)

TOP GOALSCORER:

183

Wayne Rooney

MOST APPEARANCES:

632

Ryan Giggs

OWN GOALS:

38

RED CARDS:

66

LOWEST ATTENDANCE:

29,736

v Crystal Palace
(2nd Sep, 1992)

HIGHEST ATTENDANCE:

76,098

v Blackburn
(31st Mar, 2007)

MANCHESTER UNITED

FIRST PREMIER LEAGUE MATCH: 15TH AUGUST, 1992
SHEFFIELD UNITED 2 (DEANE 2)
MANCHESTER UNITED 1 (HUGHES)

BRAMALL LANE 28,070

*Peter Schmeichel, Denis Irwin, Clayton Blackmore, Steve Bruce,
Darren Ferguson, Gary Pallister, Andrei Kanchelskis (Dion Dublin),
Paul Ince (Mike Phelan), Brian McClair, Mark Hughes, Ryan Giggs,
Manager: Alex Ferguson*

Four of the players who featured in Manchester United's first game—
Schmeichel, Bruce, Pallister and McClair—were ever-presents during
1992/93 season, while six of that initial line-up went on to become managers.
Even the most diehard Liverpool or Manchester City fan cannot deny that
Manchester United have the best record in the Premier League by a country
mile. Thirteen titles in the space of 27 years is not to be sniffed at and is
more than the collective tally of their closest rivals—Arsenal, Chelsea and
Manchester City—combined. Of course all those successes came under the
stewardship of Sir Alex Ferguson and none of his successors have come
close to emulating the Glaswegian's masterful leadership.

It should be remembered that Ferguson's initial Premier League steps
did nothing to suggest that this was going to be a trail of glory. After his
first game ended in defeat at Bramall Lane things did not get that much

better as their next two matches, both at Old Trafford, ended in a 3-0 defeat to Everton, which left United rock bottom of the table followed by a 1-1 draw with Ipswich. Things did improve with five successive wins, but between 19 September and 21 November they went seven games without a win, in what proved to be Ferguson's worst run in a Premier League managerial career that stretched over 20 years.

It was an inauspicious beginning compared to Ole Gunnar Solskjaer's electric start in 2018/19 season when he equalled the record for six successive wins from the start of a manager's reign—sharing the accolade with Carlo Ancelotti in 2009 and Pep Guardiola in 2016. It took the Norwegian nine games to reach 25 points whereas after 15 matches Ferguson's team were 10th having collected 24 points. Even compared to the three managers who succeeded him, Ferguson was only marginally better at this stage of the season, with two more than David Moyes' team who were 9th, the same as Jose Mourinho who were 6th and actually four less than Louis van Gaal whose side were 3rd. That trio lasted an aggregate of just over five years.

After this faltering start Ferguson's United only lost two more games in the remaining 27, somewhat surprisingly to Ipswich and Oldham, ensuring that they secured their first Premier League title. The arrival of one man in late November 1992 was transformational. The iconic Eric Cantona was surprisingly prised away from champions Leeds and quickly made his mark at Old Trafford, becoming the focal point for United's four titles in the next five years. Ferguson dubbed him "the can-opener" but there were others who were not so convinced, former Liverpool legend Emlyn Hughes dismissed him as "a flashy foreigner".

It was Ferguson's most astute signing as the long wait for another title was ended after a quarter of a century. The facts are that in 37 matches before Cantona's arrival they had spluttered to a total of 54 points and a meagre return of 38 goals. The 37 matches after the Frenchman's arrival yielded 88 points and more than double the number of goals, with 77. As Ferguson himself said: "The club is alive. It's as if the good old days were back and the major factor, as far as I'm concerned, is the Frenchman." That set the tone for the rest of Ferguson's time at the top and he inevitably ended his career as he had started it by winning the Premier League 20 years later in his last season in charge.

Under Ferguson, United recorded 528 victories in 810 matches, a win ratio of 65%, the highest of any manager who has managed a minimum of at least five full seasons by a long stretch. The only managers to have a better ratio having managed at least 20 games are Antonio Conte who achieved a 67% ratio in his two-season spell at Chelsea and Pep Guardiola who has just completed his third at Manchester City, with a none too shabby ratio of 76%.

Longevity is a hallmark of the truly great managers and during his time in charge, United averaged 83.5 Premier League points per season and never finished lower than third. The only manager to have come close to Ferguson for length of time served at one club is Arsene Wenger, of course. The Frenchman lasted 22 years at Arsenal and managed 18 more Premier League games then Ferguson. With 476 victories Wenger's win ratio was 57%. While United were formidable at Old Trafford it is worth noting that in the first nine Premier League seasons they collected more points away from home than at The Theatre of Dreams.

United's relentless consistency under Ferguson saw them win three titles in a row twice between 1999-2002 and 2007-2009 and they retained the Premier League on two other occasions in 1993-94 and 1996-97. So in total, there have been eight successful defences of the Premier League title - Chelsea in 2005/06, Manchester City in 2018/19 and then the six times by United. United are the only club to notch up more than 2,000 points, with 2,188 at the end of 2018/19 and they are the only team to have a goal difference of over 1,000, at +1,060. And they are close to reaching the landmark of 2,000 goals, with just another 11 required.

Since Ferguson retired in 2013 United have played 228 matches with 120 wins, a win ratio of 53%. In those six seasons they have lost 52 games and finished outside the top four on four occasions as a succession of managers have failed to recapture the Ferguson formula. The only time they have finished in the top three in the post-Ferguson era was under Jose Mourinho in 2017/18 when they were runners-up to Manchester City season by the margin of 19 points. Of the eight times under Ferguson that United did not top the table, they were runners-up five times and lost out by a single point three times, and in 2011/12 they lost out on goal difference to City. On only three occasions did they finish third and the largest margin behind the winners that Ferguson suffered was 18 points in 2004/05.

Ferguson's 13 titles are exceptional in England and also stand the test of comparison with other major European leagues such as Italy, Spain and Germany. Over the same period of 21 years between 1992/93 and 2012/13 – Juventus won six Scudettos as did AC Milan, in Spain Barcelona won nine La Liga titles with Real Madrid securing seven and even the all-conquering Bayern Munich only took 11 Bundesligas.

If Cantona sparked the revolution then the Class of '92 continued it and extended it with a group of players who became the nucleus of the Ferguson years. This group racked up an extraordinary number of appearances and include the Top 3 in United's Premier League history:

Ryan Giggs 632, Paul Scholes 499 and Gary Neville 400. Add the next three, Nicky Butt at No.10 with 270 appearances, David Beckham at No.11 with 265 and Phil Neville at No.12 with 263 and those six players they represented United 2,329 times and scored 309 goals.

Another man who should be recognised as a major contributor to United's unparalleled success is Eric Harrison. Harrison, who died aged 81 in February 2019, was the youth coach who nurtured all this talent so masterfully. As Gary Neville said in his glowing tribute: "We've lost our mentor. Our coach and the man who made us. He taught us how to play, how to never give up, how important it was to win your individual battles and what we needed to do to play for Manchester United Football Club. Eric we owe you everything."

It all started with the FA Youth Cup Final win when they beat Crystal Palace 6-3 on aggregate, which catapulted the players into the first team squad. Giggs was the first to make the starting XI, appearing in the United's Premier League debut in August 1992 and then he was slowly but surely joined by his peers who were introduced in stages and by 1994 they were regulars in the starting XI. The infamous words of Alan Hansen that "you don't win anything with kids" after they lost to Aston Villa in November 1995, have haunted him ever since but remain a testimony to his fellow Scot's managerial excellence. It is doubtful that any other manager of that or any era could have steered them to such heights.

Ashley Young became Mike Dean's 100th red card after collecting his second booking away at Wolves on the 2nd of April 2019 (see Footnote below). It was Young's second red card in his career and by coincidence his first one was also at the hands of Dean when he was dismissed for Aston Villa against Sunderland in January 2009, just over ten years earlier. Young joins Andy Cole, Richard Dunne (of course), Laurent Koscielny, Fernando Torres and Mike Williamson in being sent off twice by Dean.

ONE HIT WONDERS

Michael Keane forged his reputation at Burnley and earned a move to Everton in 2017 but he had learned his craft at Old Trafford as an academy player. Having spent five years as a professional at the club Keane got his chance to play in the Premier League in August 2014 when he replaced the injured Chris Smalling at the end of the first half against Sunderland. Within the space of a week Keane was sent out on loan to Burnley, whom he joined permanently in January 2015. Keane is now an England international, having made his debut in March 2017.

FOOTNOTE

RED 100

Mike Dean became the first Premier League referee to issue 100 red cards when he dismissed Ashley Young in the 57th minute of the game against Wolves on 2nd April, 2019. His first sending-off was Noberto Solano of Newcastle against Ipswich in 2001, his first year as a Premier League referee and that was the only one he issued that season.

A VIEW FROM THE STANDS

John Ludden, author of Once Upon a Time in Naples

As one of the select clubs that is an ever-present throughout Premier League history your club has enjoyed prolonged success so what is your favourite moment from the last 27 years?.

It was a late, sunlit Saturday afternoon, 10thApril 1993. Manchester United were at home to Sheffield Wednesday and a goal down to Stretford-born John Sheridan. The title race had become a straight shoot-out between United and Aston Villa, and as Sheridan, a United fan, stroked home a penalty past Peter Schmeichel, a 26-year wait looked set to become 27.

United huffed and puffed after the game restarted and with four minutes remaining they won a corner. Ryan Giggs, a Salford lad, sent in a cross which was met by Steve Bruce who thundered a header past Chris Woods from 12 yards out. Old Trafford erupted in sheer unadulterated relief.

The pressure for a late winner became relentless. Paul Ince found Giggs with a raking pass, and his low cross was almost turned in by exhausted defender Viv Anderson. Instead the balls went inches for yet another corner. The baying crowd were on their feet.

Again, Giggs raced to take it. This time the ball was cleared, only to fall back to the brilliant Welsh winger. His overhit effort cleared the area only to land at the feet of Gary Pallister. His cross was deflected back over the penalty area and landed in the path of an on-rushing Steve Bruce, who smashed another unstoppable header past Woods to send Old Trafford spinning wildly out of control!

No one was spared the delirium with even Alex Ferguson and Brian Kidd going momentarily crazy. Ferguson charged down from the stand dancing a manic Scottish victory jig, whilst Kidd ran even further onto the pitch sliding to his knees with arms raised. The final whistle 'finally' blew.

An angry Wednesday manager Trevor Francis muttered, "Fuckin' 'ell it's Sunday". Something special was in the air, United had gone top of the league and would stay there. It was a Mancunian Easter miracle, and Fergie time had been born.

MIDDLESBROUGH STATS

NUMBER OF SEASONS:

15 (4 spells)

1992/93, 1995/96-1996/97, 1997/98-2008/09, 2016/17

NUMBER OF MATCHES:

574

Wins 165 (Home 110 Away 55)
Draws 169 (Home 84 Away 85)
Losses 240 (Home 93 Away 147)

[Win ratio 29%]

Goals F 648
(Home 393 Away 255 Goals)

A 794
(Home 355 Away 439)

Goal Difference: -146

TOTAL POINTS

664

(Home 414: 62%; Away 250: 38%)
Average per season: 44

BEST POSITION:

7th

2004/05

WORST POSITION:

21st

1992/93 (RELEGATED)

BIGGEST WIN:

8-1

v Manchester City
(11th May, 2008)

BIGGEST LOSS:

7-0

v Arsenal
(14th Jan, 2006)

LONGEST UNBEATEN RUN:

11 matches

(29th Aug, 1998-19th Dec, 1998)

LONGEST WITHOUT A WIN:

16 matches

(26th Dec, 2016-22nd Apr, 2017)

ALL TIME RANKING

14th

MOST GOALS SCORED IN A SEASON:

54

(1992/93)

FEWEST GOALS SCORED IN A SEASON:

27

(2016/17)

FEWEST GOALS CONCEDED IN A SEASON:

44

(2000/01 & 2002/03)

MOST GOALS CONCEDED IN A SEASON:

75

(1992/93)

TOP GOALSCORER:

31

Hamilton Ricard

MOST APPEARANCES:

332

Mark Schwarzer

OWN GOALS:

29

RED CARDS:

45

LOWEST ATTENDANCE:

12,290

v Oldham
(22nd Mar, 1993)

HIGHEST ATTENDANCE:

34,836

v Norwich
(28th Dec, 2004)

All statistics and records supplied by  gracenote.
A NIELSEN COMPANY

MIDDLESBROUGH

DID YOU KNOW?

Middlesbrough started with seven teenagers in a 1-0 defeat at Fulham on 7th May, 2006. Their average age of 20 years and 181 days is the youngest starting line-up by any team in a Premier League match. The fact that they had a UEFA Cup final a few days later justified their choice of so many callow youths.

FIRST PREMIER LEAGUE MATCH: 15TH AUGUST, 1992
COVENTRY CITY 2 (WILLIAMS, SMITH)
MIDDLESBROUGH 1 (WILKINSON)

HIGHFIELD ROAD 12,345

*Steve Pears, Chris Morris, Jimmy Phillips, Alan Kernaghan,
Derek Whyte, Andy Peake, Tommy Wright,
Robbie Mustoe (Bernie Slaven), Paul Wilkinson,
John Hendrie, Willie Falconer, Manager: Lennie Lawrence*

Middlesbrough are one of only two Premier League clubs to have been deducted points, but unlike Portsmouth who would have been relegated in 2009/10 even without their nine point handicap, Middlesbrough would have survived in 1996/97 had they not had those three points taken away. The dreaded asterisk appeared against them when they failed to fulfil their fixture with Blackburn, pulling out of the 21st December match with only 24 hours' notice. It now seems inconceivable that this would happen in the top flight but Middlesbrough claimed that they were struck by a bout of influenza leaving them with 23 players unavailable through a combination of illness, injury and suspension and therefore unable to field a team.

The loss of those three points was crucial as they would have been a point clear of relegation and would have actually finished as high as 14th with Coventry going down instead. Eventually the Blackburn game was rescheduled for 8th May, three days before the final day of the season and it ended in a mildly ironic and anti-climatic goalless draw.

Middlesbrough drew their final fixture away at Leeds but it was not enough to rescue them as Coventry surprisingly won away at Tottenham. To add insult to injury (or maybe even illness) Middlesbrough scored 51 goals, which was more than any team in the bottom half of the table that season and four more goals than Aston Villa who finished fifth. It also makes this Boro the third highest highest scoring relegated team. Blackpool have the most with 55 in 2009/10 and Middlesbrough themselves scored 54 goals in the inaugural season, albeit in 42 matches.

The most memorable match of the 1996/97 season was lit up by one man: Fabrizio Ravanelli, whose excellent nickname was only bested by his goal celebration when he pulled his shirt over his head. The White Feather enjoyed doing that three times against Liverpool in the opening game of the 1996/97 season as Middlesbrough drew 3-3 after being behind three times. There are not many players who would leave Juventus to join Middlesbrough especially after scoring in the Champions League Final. Ravanelli was an incredible coup for Bryan Robson who somehow persuaded him to swap Turin for Teesside. Despite the Italian's 16 goals, Middlesbrough were relegated and he soon left but at least he gave the Riverside faithful some memories to cherish.

Ravanelli also scored a hat-trick against Derby later that season in March and he remains the only player to score two hat-tricks in one season for a club that went on to get relegated. That was one of their four relegations which matches the most by any club, alongside Palace, Norwich, Sunderland and West Brom but unlike the other not so fab four they and Norwich have never finished rock bottom. Indeed whenever Middlesborough have been relegated they have finished second bottom.

Under Steve McLaren Middlesbrough reached the dizzy heights of a European Final in May 2006, the same year as Arsenal lost out to Barcelona in the Champions League Final, which was the only time two Premier League clubs reached two different European finals in the same year until 2018/19 when all four European finalists were English. Like Arsenal, Middlesbrough lost out to Spanish opposition, being thrashed 4-0 by Sevilla, but in so doing they became only the fifth Premier League club to be a European finalist. In the aftermath McLaren left the club to become England manager, continuing a run of Middlesbrough managers who were also national supremos including his predecessor Terry Venables and his successors, Gareth Southgate and Gordon Strachan.

ONE HIT WONDER

Anthony Ormerod's one and only appearance for Middlesbrough was against none other than Manchester United on 29th January, 2000 at Old Trafford and it was quite a game. He replaced Hamilton Ricard at half-time in his customary right wing position but got switched to the unfamiliar role of left back after German international Christian Ziege was sent off following a second yellow card for a foul on David Beckham. This positional move pitted Ormerod against Beckham and although they were down to 10 men, Middlesbrough were awarded a penalty which infamously led to the United players jostling referee Andy D'Urso with Roy Keane at the head of the baying pack.

Juninho who had been brought down by Jaap Stam for the penalty then had his spot kick saved by Mark Bosnich and almost inevitably it was Beckham who scored the only goal of the game with an 87th minute winner which somehow squirmed through Mark Schwarzer's grasp.

However, this was not the only time Ormerod rubbed shoulders with an England star. He spent the majority of his three years at Middlesbrough in the reserves and had the pleasure of playing with Paul Gascoigne just after the mercurial Geordie had joined: "I played the game of my life and I'll be honest, the reason I played the game of my life was because I was playing with him."

Ormerod is now a primary school teacher.

FOOTNOTE

There have been seven hat-tricks on the opening day of the season.

PLAYER	MATCH	DATE
M. Quinn	Arsenal 0 Coventry 3	14 Aug 1993
M. Le Tissier	Southampton 3 Nottingham Forest 4	19 Aug 1995
F. Ravanelli	Middlesbrough 3 Liverpool 3	17 Aug 1996
K. Campbell	Coventry 0 Nottingham Forest 3	17 Aug 1996
D. Dublin	Coventry 3 Chelsea 2	9 Aug 1997
G. Agbonlahor	Aston Villa 4 Manchester City 2	17 Aug 2008
D. Drogba	Chelsea 6 West Brom 0	14 Aug 2010

A VIEW FROM THE STANDS

Simon Banoub

What was your club's 'Sliding Doors' moment, that seemingly inconsequential action, which actually became a turning point in their fortunes, for either good or bad?

For Boro, the sliding doors moment is a case of a game that didn't happen, rather than one that did.

With 23 players either ill or injured after a flu virus rampaged through the squad, Boro decided to not fulfil a fixture away at Blackburn. The FA weren't impressed and a three-point deduction was imposed. Typically, predictably and depressingly, Boro then went on the be relegated by two points, meaning that had they'd rocked up to Ewood with a team full of kids and lost 10-0 instead of bailing on the match, they'd have avoided the drop.

Had Boro not gone down that year, we'd have retained Juninho, one of the best players in the world at the time, probably kept Ravanelli, and maybe even persuaded Emerson's Mrs that Teesside wasn't that bad after all. There were strong rumours that Boro had also "agreed" deals to sign Roberto Carlos and Gabriel Batistuta to add to the squad had they stayed up too.

And although we got promoted back to the Premiership after signing Paul Merson to tear through the second tier, Boro's Riverside Revolution never quite reached the fever pitch that had gripped the area in 1996/97. Even the subsequent success of winning the League Cup and reaching the UEFA Cup didn't have the same buzz as our first brush with attracting top talent to our beloved northern wastelands had.

NEWCASTLE UNITED STATS

NUMBER OF SEASONS:

24 (3 spells)

1993/94-2008/09, 2010/11-2015/16
& 2017/18-2018/19

NUMBER OF MATCHES:

920

Wins 346 (Home 233 Away 113)
Draws 234 (Home 109 Away 125)
Losses 340 (Home 118 Away 222)

[Win ratio 38%]

Goals F 1,249
(Home 759 Away 490)

Goals A 1,235
(Home 510 Away 725)

Goal Difference: +14

TOTAL POINTS

1,272

(Home 808: 64%; Away: 464: 36%)
Average per season: 53

BEST POSITION:

2nd (2)

1995/96 & 1996/97

WORST POSITION:

18th (2)

2008/09 & 2015/16 (RELEGATED)

BIGGEST WIN:

8-0

v Sheffield
Wednesday 0 (19th Sep, 1999)

BIGGEST LOSS:

6-0 (2)

v Liverpool (27th Apr, 2013)
v Manchester United (12th Jan, 2008)

LONGEST UNBEATEN RUN:

14 matches

(19th Apr, 2011-5th Nov, 2011)

LONGEST WITHOUT A WIN:

14 matches

(5th Apr, 1999-11th Sep, 1999)

ALL TIME RANKING

8th

MOST GOALS SCORED IN A SEASON:

82

(1993/94)

FEWEST GOALS SCORED IN A SEASON:

35

(1997/98)

FEWEST GOALS CONCEDED IN A SEASON:

37

(1995/96)

MOST GOALS CONCEDED IN A SEASON:

68

(2012/13)

TOP GOALSCORER:

148

Alan Shearer

MOST APPEARANCES:

354

Shay Given

OWN GOALS:

29

RED CARDS:

82

LOWEST ATTENDANCE:

32,067

v Southampton
(22nd Jan, 1994)

HIGHEST ATTENDANCE:

52,389

v Manchester City
(6th May, 2012)

NEWCASTLE UNITED

FIRST PREMIER LEAGUE MATCH: 14TH AUGUST, 1993
NEWCASTLE UNITED 0
TOTTENHAM HOTSPUR 1 (SHERINGHAM)

ST. JAMES' PARK 35,216

Pavel Srnicek, Steve Howey, Barry Venison, Kevin Scott, John Beresford, Nicolas Papavasiliou (Liam O'Brien), Robert Lee, Paul Bracewell, Lee Clark, Malcolm Allen (Steve Watson), Andrew Cole, Manager: Kevin Keegan

Newcastle missed out on the inaugural season but started life in the Premier League with a flourish in their first season of 1993/94. Aided by Andy Cole's impressive individual total of 34, their tally of 82 goals scored is still the most they have achieved in their 24 seasons. Added to which they conceded exactly half the number of goals they had scored. There is nothing like starting on a high.

Having secured another season in the Premier League under Rafa Benitez in 2018/19 Newcastle were set to become the club to have played the most games outside the six ever-presents. However, Aston Villa's promotion means they will stand as the club with the 8th most games under their belt next season and considering they were not in the original 22 and have been relegated twice that is some achievement. They bounced back from relegation both times at the first time of asking in 2009/10 and 2016/17.

Newcastle have been Premier League runners-up twice, under Kevin Keegan 9n 1995/96 and the following season with Kenny Dalglish in charge. Newcastle have been second more often than any club outside Arsenal, Chelsea, both Manchester clubs and Liverpool, furthermore they have eight top six finishes, which is one more than ever-present Everton. Keegan's meltdown in a Sky Sports interview towards the back end of the title race in 1996 was seen as the point at which the dam was broken and the red flood went unchecked towards their title as Newcastle's 12-point lead was frittered away. Unfortunately for Keegan and all those on Tyneside, Manchester United did go and get something at Middlesbrough—a comfortable 3-0 victory—with ex-Newcastle legend Andy Cole inevitably scoring. That win assured the Magpies didn't beat United to the title, even though Keegan would have loved it. Loved it. What Keegan would have loved was arguably Newcastle's greatest victory in their 920 games, which happened to be against his nemesis.

KEEGAN'S REVENGE

SUNDAY 20 OCTOBER 1996

NEWCASTLE UNITED 5 (2) PEACOCK 12', GINOLA 30',
FERDINAND 63', SHEARER 74', ALBERT 83'
MANCHESTER UNITED 0 (0)

From the moment pony-tailed Darren Peacock's header somehow eluded both Peter Schmeichel and Dennis Irwin, who desperately tried to scramble the ball off the line, Newcastle must have known this was going to be their day. If Peacock's goal was on the scruffy side, David Ginola's on the half hour was sumptuous as he took one touch to get away from his marker and with the next curled the ball with unerring accuracy and some power into the far corner from the left hand edge of the area.

The second half continued in the same vein as Shearer turned provider, crossing for partner Les Ferdinand's header that cannoned in off the bar and bounced off the line and in. Naturally Shearer was not too far behind in punishing Schmeichel after he had made two close-range saves by knocking the second one back past him.

And then it was all about Phillipe Albert who in the words of the Sky commentator was being urged to shoot by the crowd but went for the chip instead. That chip could not have bettered by Tiger Woods as it sailed with a perfect parabola over a stranded Schmeichel. It was almost as though it was in slow motion. The incessant rain that had been hammering down throughout the match provided the perfect pathetic fallacy for this humbling of Ferguson's men and some redemption for Keegan who had the last laugh and a quote to match.

"I always remember standing at the top of the steps as the Manchester United players left the ground. The last one out was Eric Cantona and he shook my hand and said 'You've got a fucking good team'. His English was perfect. You've got to enjoy those moments." Newcastle went top after this and even though Manchester United followed this humbling with another as severe when losing 6-3 to Southampton the following Saturday to complete Ferguson's 'greyest' managerial week, it was a familiar tale at the top of the table as Newcastle finished seven points shy for their second consecutive runners-up spot.

For a club that has always prided itself in its penchant for legendary centre forwards it is apposite that Newcastle are the only club to have had the Premier League's leading scorer in their ranks three times but never won the title. From Jackie Milburn through Malcolm MacDonald and Les Ferdinand all the way to Alan Shearer, strikers have flourished at St. James' Park. Andy Cole set the pace in 1993/94 with 34 goals and then Shearer took over, having been top scorer at Blackburn in their title-winning season, he moved to Newcastle and topped the league's scoring charts in his first two seasons with 31 and 25 goals to his name. He was the club's top scorer for ten seasons on the trot and nobody else has come close to such an achievement.

Shearer scored five goals in the 8-0 demolition of Sheffield Wednesday on 19th September, 1999, which just happened to be Bobby Robson's first game at St. James Park since his return to the club at the grand old age of 66.

ONE HIT WONDER

Many would believe that James Coppinger is the archetypal one-club man but in fact despite making almost 550 appearances for Doncaster Rovers, Coppinger started his career with Darlington and was brought to St. James' Park in 1998 as a teenager by Kenny Dalglish. He spent four years with Newcastle, which included a couple of loan spells with Hartlepool but his only appearance for the Magpies was on 26th August, 2000 in the 79th minute when he replaced Argentinian Daniel Cordone who had scored Newcastle's second goal in their 2-0 victory over Tottenham.

Coppinger eventually moved to the other St. James Park when he joined Exeter City in 2002, playing more than 80 games in two seasons before moving to his final destination Doncaster in 2004. Fifteen years later he is still with Rovers and signed a one-year contract extension in May 2019.

FOOTNOTE

WISE HEADS

The oldest Premier League managers

The late Sir Bobby Robson was one of the most revered managers in international football. His longevity was underlined by his return to his hometown club at the grand old age of 66, an appropriate figure for somebody who did so much for English football. On 23 February Roy Hodgson became the oldest Premier League manager at 71 years and 198 days when Palace won 4-1 away at Leicester. The day before the 2019/20 season starts Hodgson will celebrate his 72nd birthday.

MANAGER	CLUB	AGE	DATE
Roy Hodgson	Crystal Palace	71y 198d	23/02/2019
Bobby Robson	Newcastle Utd	71y 192d	28/08/2004
Alex Ferguson	Manchester Utd	71y 139d	19/05/2013
Neil Warnock	Cardiff City	70y 84d	22/02/2019
Gus Hiddink	Chelsea	69y 189d	15/05/2016

As for the other end of the spectrum here are the youngest Premier League managers and Palace head that table as well thanks to Attilio Lombardo's short-lived managerial spell at Selhurst. Second on the list is a former Palace player Chris Coleman and then three Chelsea managers. Who says Chelsea do not give youth a chance?

MANAGER	CLUB	AGE	DATE
Attilio Lombardo	Crystal Palace	32y 37d	14/03/1998
Chris Coleman	Fulham	32y 313d	19/04/2003
Gianluca Vialli	Chelsea	33y 227d	21/02/1998
Andre Villas-Boas	Chelsea	33y 301d	14/08/2011
Ruud Gullit	Chelsea	33y 351d	18/08/1996

A VIEW FROM THE STANDS

What was the club's 'Sliding Doors' moment, that seemingly inconsequential action, which actually became a turning point in their fortunes, for either good or bad?

In late March 2009 Newcastle were in a hole. They had just lost at home to Arsenal and had dropped into the relegation zone. For the first time in their Premier League history they were facing relegation and drastic circumstances demanded dramatic action. With the club already having already been managed by the revered Kevin Keegan, the reviled Joe Kinnear and the respected Chris Hughton, Mike Ashley turned to a Geordie legend as salvation. Alan Shearer may have broken all sorts of records for his goal-scoring prowess but his managerial experience was limited to a few games as assistant to Glenn Roeder at the back end of the 2006/2007 season.

So, it was on April Fool's Day that Shearer was announced. He had eight games to save his beloved club from losing their top-flight status after 16 consecutive seasons. His first game ended in a 2-0 loss at home to Chelsea, followed by two further losses and a couple of draws. With three games left they were three points behind Hull. Their next game was a 'must win' and after conceding an early own goal to Middlesbrough they stormed back to a 3-1 victory. Coupled with Hull's loss to Stoke the Magpies poked their head above the relegation parapet, sneaking into 17th place on goal difference. But they lost at home to Fulham while Hull drew at Bolton and so the stage was set for the final match, with a draw at Villa the minimum requirement.

Things were looking up when Manchester United took the lead at Hull but disaster struck just before half-time when an unfortunate deflection off Damien Duff gave Villa the lead. Newcastle failed to get the equaliser and in the 94th minute David Edgar received his second yellow card as relegation beckoned. The lasting image of that day was Shearer looking distinctly uncomfortable in his grey suit and appropriately coloured black tie. His managerial career was over with just a solitary win, two draws and five defeats.

NORWICH CITY STATS

NUMBER OF SEASONS:

8 (4 spells)

1992/93-1994/95, 2004/05, 2011/12-2013/14, 2015/16

TOTAL POINTS

359

(Home 229: 64%; Away 130: 36%)
Average per season: 45

NUMBER OF MATCHES:

316

Wins 89 (Home 59 Away 30)
Draws 92 (Home 52 Away 40)
Losses 135 (Home 47 Away 88)

[Win ratio 28%]

Goals F 365
(Home 209 Away 156)

Goals A 510
(Home 199 Away 311)

Goal Difference: -145

BEST POSITION:

3rd

1992/93

WORST POSITION:

20th

1994/95 (RELEGATED)

BIGGEST WIN:

5-1

v Everton
(25th Sept, 1993)

BIGGEST LOSS:

7-0

v Manchester City
(2nd Nov, 2013)

LONGEST UNBEATEN RUN:

10 matches

(20th Oct, 2012-15th Dec, 2012)

LONGEST WITHOUT A WIN:

21 matches

(1st Apr, 1995-13th Nov, 2004)

ALL TIME RANKING

8th

MOST GOALS SCORED IN A SEASON:

65

(1993/94)

FEWEST GOALS SCORED IN A SEASON:

28

(2013/14)

FEWEST GOALS CONCEDED IN A SEASON:

54

(1994/95)

MOST GOALS CONCEDED IN A SEASON:

77

(2004/05)

TOP GOALSCORER:

33

Chris Sutton

MOST APPEARANCES:

125

Russell Martin

OWN GOALS:

16

RED CARDS:

15

LOWEST ATTENDANCE:

12,452

v Southampton
(5th Sep, 1992)

HIGHEST ATTENDANCE:

27,137

v Newcastle
(2nd Apr, 2016)

NORWICH CITY

FIRST PREMIER LEAGUE MATCH: 15TH AUGUST, 1992
ARSENAL 2 (BOULD, CAMPBELL)
NORWICH 4 (ROBINS 2, PHILLIPS, FOX)

HIGHBURY 24,030

*Bryan Gunn, Ian Culverhouse, Mark Bowen, Ian Butterworth,
John Polston, Gary Megson (Ian Crook), Ruel Fox, Rob Newman,
Chris Sutton (Mark Robins), Jeremy Goss, David Phillips,
Manager: Mike Walker*

Life in the Premier League could hardly have started more sweetly for the Canaries. In the first match with little over 20 minutes left they were 2-0 down at Arsenal. Inspired by Mark Robins who, not content with becoming the first substitute to score in the Premier League having replaced Chris Sutton, added another in netting a brace as Norwich turned the game on its head. They scored four without reply and were the very first table toppers and the only team to win their opening fixture away from home and also by more than one goal. Robins went on to become the club's top scorer that season with 14.

They maintained their form throughout that first season, which became by far their most successful out of the eight they have spent in the Premier League. By the end of August they led the table and despite being hammered 7-1 by Blackburn in early October they were in the top two throughout the first half of the season and by the 5th December were eight points clear. Their form dipped in the second half of the season and they were overtaken by both Manchester United and Aston Villa but they still qualified for Europe and their famous win in Munich against the mighty Bayern courtesy of tousle-haired Jeremy Goss followed in October 1993.

They won exactly 50% of their matches in the 1992/93 season and amassed 72 points in claiming a very creditable third place despite having a negative goal difference of -4. By contrast, Blackburn finished one place below them in fourth and had a positive goal difference of +22. The following season the Canaries finished 12th but registered a positive goal difference of +4, mainly down to the exploits of Chris Sutton who weighed in with an impressive 25 goals. Having established this curious achievement in the very first Premier League season, Norwich remain the highest-placed side to have conceded more than they scored, with Everton's 4th place in 2004/05 which came despite a goal difference of -1 being the closest.

That first season was by some distance Norwich's zenith and within two years they were relegated in 20th place in the last 22-club season after Sutton departed in the summer to spearhead Blackburn's title challenge. The Canaries struggled to replace Sutton's goals and Grant Holt was the only leading scorer to manage double figures in the other seasons. They have never reached the top half since, with their next highest finish of 11th achieved in 2012/13. They hold the joint record along with Crystal Palace, Middlesbrough, Sunderland and West Bromwich Albion for the most Premier League relegations at four but like Middlesbrough they have never finished bottom of the table. The longest Premier League spell they have enjoyed is three years, which they achieved twice—1992/93-1994/95 and 2011/12-2013/14, alongside a couple of single seasons stays.

By coincidence their win ratio of 28% is the same as their East Anglian neighbours, Ipswich. Also, like the Tractor Boys, Norwich have finished in the top six once—in that inaugural season—while Ipswich were 5th in 2000/01. They even share the same average finishing position of 14th so they are almost inseparable, with bragging rights between the Old Farm rivals pretty even. The Canaries might claim that they have spent more seasons in the Premier League—eight compared to five—but then again they have been relegated those four times as opposed to twice for the Portman Road club.

Amazingly Norwich have been involved in two 5-4 reverses at Carrow Road, the first in April 1994 at the hands of Southampton courtesy of a Matthew Le Tissier hat-trick in the space of 15 minutes. The Saints were languishing in the relegation zone at the time but they eventually beat the drop by a single point. The second in January 2016 was against Jurgen Klopp's Liverpool when they lost to an Adam Lallana strike in the 95th minute and Norwich were eventually relegated. The Canaries clearly relish mining nine goal matches.

Finally, the next time Chris Sutton rankles you with one of his more controversial statements, which probably won't be too far away, here is a fact that you can throw back at him. On 24th January, 1994 Sutton opened the scoring for Norwich against West Ham in the fifth minute at Upton Park but later he became the first player to score at both ends with an own goal in the 37th minute. Sutton did redeem himself somewhat with a 56th minute goal to draw Norwich level at 2-2 and the game ended 3-3.

ONE HIT WONDER

Kyle Lafferty has had a colourful career spent mostly in the Championship and the Scottish Premiership, including two spells at Glasgow Rangers. The Northern Irishman was such a key element in his country's progress to Euro 2016 scoring seven times in qualification, but he never really convinced Norwich boss Alex Neil that he could replicate the form he showed internationally in the Premier League. Even though he was given the number 9 shirt at Carrow Road, the 13 solitary minutes he spent as a substitute after replacing Cameron Jerome against Leicester on 3rd October, 2015 offered him scant opportunity. He ended up going out on loan to Birmingham in March 2016 and that was that as far as Lafferty and his Norwich Premier League career was concerned. Lafferty was playing for Glasgow Rangers in the 2018/19 season.

FOOTNOTE

LOWEST GOAL DIFFERENCE FOR TOP SIX FINISH

CLUB	POSITION	GD	SEASON
West Ham	5th	-7	1998/99
Norwich	3rd	-4	1992/93
Everton	4th	-1	2004/05
Wimbledon	6th	+3	1993/94
Chelsea	6th	+3	1996/97
Tottenham	6th	+3	2006/07
Aston Villa	6th	+4	2003/04
Liverpool	6th	+4	2014/15
Tottenham	6th	+4	2013/14
Blackburn	6th	+5	1997/98
Bolton	6th	+5	2004/05
Newcastle	5th	+5	2011/12
Tottenham	5th	+5	2014/15

A VIEW FROM THE STANDS

Andrew Lawn

What was your club's 'Sliding Doors' moment, that seemingly inconsequential action, which actually became a turning point in their fortunes, for either good or bad?

On 18th October, 2015 Alex Neil took his newly promoted Norwich side to St James' Park. Having been appointed less than a year earlier, Neil had built an attack-minded side that went for the jugular. In the Championship it had worked wonders and the Canaries had flown up the table from stodgy mid-table inconsistency, to a three-way race for the title. While City ultimately lost out on automatic promotion to Bournemouth and Watford, they glided through the play-offs swatting aside local rivals Ipswich 4-1 on aggregate and then dismissing Middlesbrough with two early goals at Wembley. Back in the top flight, Neil insisted his team continue to attack, resulting in big wins, including 3-1 victories over Bournemouth and Sunderland, or heavy defeats such as the 3-0 tonkings at Southampton and at home to Crystal Palace.

In that vein City went north to St James' and duly lost an even and entertaining game 6-2, with Gigi Wijnaldum grabbing four. At the time most fans shrugged their shoulders, accepting the defeat as another example of Neil's Keegan-esque desire to go all guns blazing, but the result scarred the Scot. Almost overnight, he tore up the blueprint that had served him so well, instructing his team to crawl into their shell. Three goals in the next six games was the result. Unsurprisingly points became harder to come by as the goals dried up and City slid into the relegation zone. The slide down the table was mirrored in a slide in morale, compounded by City responding to two 3-0s and a 3-1 defeats, with an attempt to regain their attacking devil-may-care approach in a home game with Liverpool, during which City went 3-1 up, then 4-3 behind. A last minute Seb Bassong volley looked to have grabbed a valuable point, before Adam Lallana nicked a fifth for Liverpool, causing Jurgen Klopp to lose his glasses celebrating. Seven winless games would follow, as would relegation.

Back in the Championship, Neil again took his team to St James' Park, where this time they let a 3-1 lead slip and lost 4-3, with two goals in injury-time, bringing all those memories of 10 months earlier back to the fore. Five months later and with Norwich back in mid-table where he'd found them two years previously Alex Neil was gone and Delia and the board were back to square one. Their response was to change their model entirely. Stuart Webber was brought in as the club's first ever Sporting Director, with Daniel Farke following later that summer. *Der rest ist geschichte.*

NOTTINGHAM FOREST STATS

NUMBER OF SEASONS:

5 (3 spells)

1992/93, 1994/95-1996/97, 1998/99

NUMBER OF MATCHES:

198

Wins 60 (Home 35 Away 25)
Draws 59 (Home 32 Away 27)
Losses 79 (Home 32 Away 47)

[Win ratio 30%]

Goals F 229
(Home 115 Away 114)

Goals A 287
(Home 118 Away 169)

Goal Difference: -58

TOTAL POINTS

239

(Home 137: 57%; Away 102: 43%)
Average per season: 48

BEST POSITION:

3rd

1994/95

WORST POSITION:

22nd

(1992/93)
20th (1996/97 & 1998/99)
All 3 bottom-placed (RELEGATED)

BIGGEST WIN:

1-7

v Sheffield Wednesday
(1st Apr, 1995)

BIGGEST LOSS:

7-0 (2)

v Blackburn (18th Nov, 1995)
v Manchester United (6th Feb, 1999)

LONGEST UNBEATEN RUN:

25 matches

(26th Feb, 1995-6th Nov, 1995)

LONGEST WITHOUT A WIN:

19 matches

(8th Sept, 1998-16th Jan, 1999)

ALL TIME RANKING

33rd

MOST GOALS SCORED IN A SEASON:

72

(1994/95)

FEWEST GOALS SCORED IN A SEASON:

31

(1996/97)

FEWEST GOALS CONCEDED IN A SEASON:

43

(1994/95)

MOST GOALS CONCEDED IN A SEASON:

69

(1998/99)

TOP GOALSCORER:

24

Bryan Roy

MOST APPEARANCES:

174

Steve Chettle

OWN GOALS:

4

RED CARDS:

10

LOWEST ATTENDANCE:

17,525

v Blackburn
(25th Nov, 1996)

HIGHEST ATTENDANCE:

30,025

v Manchester United
(6th Feb, 1999)

NOTTINGHAM FOREST

DID YOU KNOW?

Players from eleven countries outside the United Kingdom have played for Nottingham Forest with the four hailing from Norway being the largest contingent. It is a Dutchman though who holds the Forest record for most Premier League appearances by a foreign player. Bryan Roy played 85 times, 13 more than second-placed Alf-Inge Håland from Norway. Roy is also Forest's leading Premier League scorer with 24 goals.

FIRST PREMIER LEAGUE MATCH: 16TH AUGUST, 1992
NOTTINGHAM FOREST 1 (SHERINGHAM)
LIVERPOOL 0

CITY GROUND 20,038

Mark Crossley, Brian Laws, Stuart Pearce, Terry Wilson, Steve Chettle, Roy Keane, Gary Crosby, Scot Gemmill, Nigel Clough (Kingsley Black), Teddy Sheringham, Ian Woan, Manager: Brian Clough

This was the very first Premier League match to be televised live and the first one to be played on a Sunday

It was appropriate that two of the greatest managers in English club football should field their sons in their opening Premier League matches. As Darren Ferguson did his father proud in Manchester United's very first game at Bramall Lane so did Nigel Clough at the City Ground the following day. The two legendary managers' paths then took sharply different trajectories as Ferguson amassed 13 titles while Clough retired at the end of the season following relegation. The pain was almost too much for him to bear but he bowed with characteristically brutal honesty: "Can't avoid the truth. Can't make it look better than it is. Only one thing to be said. We're in the shit."

After scoring Forest's first Premier League goal against Liverpool in August 1992 Teddy Sheringham also managed to emulate the feat for

Portsmouth in 2003 when he scored the opening goal in 42nd minute against Aston Villa. Sheringham remains the only player to have scored the first Premier League goal for two different clubs. Unfortunately for Forest within a week of that opening goal Sheringham was on the move as he was snapped up by Tottenham. That Sheringham ended up as the season's top scorer with a further 21 goals while Forest's top scorer was Nigel Clough with just ten as Forest finished bottom, left little doubt that this was a massive mistake.

Forest were the very first club to be relegated from the Premier League when they lost at home to Sheffield United on the 1st May, 1993, providing a sad epitaph to the managerial career of Brian Clough. They subsequently became the second club after Palace to be relegated three times. As those three relegations came in the space of eight seasons, Forest also became the second club to be relegated three times before 2000. It is interesting to note that along with Middlesbrough, the first three clubs to be relegated have amassed 11 relegations between them. All three times Forest have been relegated they have finished bottom of the table, which is a record for any club with a minimum of three relegations.

After being relegated in the 1992/93 season Forest did reclaim their Premier League status at the first time of asking and in 1994/95 under Frank Clark they achieved a highly creditable 3rd place, which is the highest position for a newly promoted club, alongside Newcastle in 1993/94. Having topped the table at the end of August they were never out of the top six. Their performance raised hopes of another sustained spell at the top of English football, however, this newfound optimism did not last as they slipped down the table to 9th the following season and then ended up bottom in 1996/97. Yet again Forest bounced straight back after relegation but their next stay was another single season and as of 2019/20 they have yet to return.

Curiously Forest's biggest victories in four out of their five seasons were away from home with the 7-1 drubbing of Sheffield Wednesday on April Fool's Day in 1995 at Hillsborough, in which both Bryan Roy and Stan Collymore scored twice, a particular highlight. Only two other clubs have scored seven or more goals away from home: Manchester United, who beat Forest 8-1 (more of which below) and Tottenham who beat Hull 7-1 in May 2017.

Blackburn Rovers will be considered by most to be Forest's bogey team, having inflicted their worst defeats in three different seasons: 1992/93, 1994/95 and 1995/96. The last of those reverses, a 7-0 drubbing at Ewood Park, was their joint worst defeat in all of their 198 games. To compound matters it was followed in the same season by a 5-1 defeat away at The

City Ground. The aggregate of 1-12 is the equal worst season aggregate alongside Wigan's against Tottenham in 2009/10.

Forest's other calamitous defeat was the 8-1 loss to Manchester United at the City Ground in February 1999, which constitutes the worst loss at home by any club. As if matters could not get much worse Ole Gunnar Solksjaer came on as a substitute and proceeded to notch four times in 12 minutes—the first and still the quickest hat-trick by a substitute but also the most goals scored by a substitute. This was all part of a depressing home winless run for Forest that started in August and only ended in May once relegation had been confirmed. Ironically their last three matches of that season yielded three wins but it was a case of too little too late.

One positive record Forest can lay claim to is the lowest own goal per season ratio of any club to have spent at least three seasons in Premier League. They have conceded just four in five seasons for a ratio of 0.8. Only Sheffield Wednesday come close to this and are the only other club to have a ratio of less than 1 per game with seven in eight seasons. Which all goes to prove that Forest can certainly see the woods for the trees.

ONE HIT WONDER

Gary Bull is one of the select few who have made just a single appearance for a club in the Premier League and scored in that game. He spent three years at the City Ground between 1993 and 1995 after joining from Barnet but made just the one fleeting appearance in January 1995 when Stan Collymore pulled out on the morning of the match because of illness. Bull scored the only goal of the game against Crystal Palace but unfortunately for him Collymore returned to the starting line-up the next week and Bull's services were not required again. Eventually he went out on loan to Birmingham and Brighton before leaving on a free transfer to the former.

Like another ex-Forest player, Neil Webb, Bull ended up being a postman.

FOOTNOTE

BIGGEST AWAY VICTORIES

MATCH	DATE	
Sheffield Wednesday 1 Nottingham Forest 7	Apr 1	1995
Nottingham Forest 1 Manchester United 8	Feb 6	1999
Hull City 1 Tottenham 7	May 21	2017

There have been nine 6-0 away victories and Liverpool have inflicted this humbling four times: Ipswich 9th September, 2001, West Brom 26th April 2003, Newcastle 27th April, 2013 and Aston Villa 14th February, 2016.

A VIEW FROM THE STANDS

Daniel Storey

What was your club's 'Sliding Doors' moment, that seemingly inconsequential action, which actually became a turning point in their fortunes, for either good or bad?

Nottingham Forest have been out of the Premier League for almost four years when they qualify for the playoffs for the first time in their history. Having drawn the home leg 1-1 against Sheffield United, Forest go 2-0 up at Bramall Lane through goals from David Johnson and Andy Reid. Immediately after the second goal is scored, Sheffield United win a free-kick.

If that free-kick is missed, Forest's future changes drastically. Sheffield United are not given a necessary jolt of belief and momentum and so Forest head to the Millennium Stadium after winning on aggregate. There they beat Wolves and return to the Premier League once again, meaning that they are able to keep hold of Marlon Harewood, Michael Dawson and Reid. That crop of academy graduates forms the spine of a top-flight team that enjoy the new-found riches of the Premier Lea...

But of course we're dreaming. Michael Brown scores the free-kick, Sheffield United pull level to force extra-time where a Des Walker own goal kills Forest's hopes—just like in the 1991 FA Cup final. Reid, Dawson and Harewood are eventually sold to the Premier League and manager Paul Hart, who developed those youngsters, is sacked the following February. Two years later and Forest have tumbled into League One. They have never been back to the Premier League.

OLDHAM ATHLETIC STATS

NUMBER OF SEASONS:

2

1992/93-1993/94

NUMBER OF MATCHES:

84

Wins 22 (Home 15 Away 7)
Draws 23 (Home 14 Away 9)
Losses 39 (Home 13 Away 26)

[Win ratio 26%]

Goals F 105
(Home 67 Away 38)

Goals A 142
(Home 63 Away 79)

Goal Difference: -37

TOTAL POINTS

89

(Home 59: 66%; Away 30: 34%)
Average per season: 44

BEST POSITION:

19th

1992/93

WORST POSITION:

21st

1993/94 (RELEGATED)

BIGGEST WIN:

6-2

v Wimbledon
(3rd Apr, 1993)

BIGGEST LOSS:

5-0

v Tottenham
(18th Sept, 1993)

LONGEST UNBEATEN RUN:

4 matches (3)

(20th Mar, 1993-7th Apr, 1993; 22nd
Jan 1994-28th Feb, 1994; 19th Mar,
1994-2nd Apr, 1994)

LONGEST WITHOUT A WIN:

10 matches

(21st August–23rd October, 1993)

ALL TIME RANKING

42nd

MOST GOALS SCORED IN A SEASON:

63

(1992/93)

FEWEST GOALS SCORED IN A SEASON:

42

(1993/94)

FEWEST GOALS CONCEDED IN A SEASON:

68

(1993/94)

MOST GOALS CONCEDED IN A SEASON:

74

(1992/93)

TOP GOALSCORER:

16

Graeme Sharp

MOST APPEARANCES:

81

Mike Milligan

OWN GOALS:

3

RED CARDS:

4

LOWEST ATTENDANCE:

9,633

v Wimbledon
(28th Aug, 1993)

HIGHEST ATTENDANCE:

17,106

v Manchester United
(9th Mar, 1993)

All statistics and records supplied by

OLDHAM ATHLETIC

DID YOU KNOW?

Having appeared in the first two Premier League seasons and none since, Oldham Athletic have fielded very few non-British players in the competition. Two Norwegians, one Irishman and a Dutchman (who played just 45 minutes) played for the Latics. Mike Milligan appeared most frequently, playing in 81 of Oldham's 84 matches.

FIRST PREMIER LEAGUE MATCH: 15TH AUGUST, 1992
CHELSEA 1 (HARFORD)
OLDHAM ATHLETIC 1 (HENRY)

STAMFORD BRIDGE 20,699

Jon Hallworth, Steve Redmond, Andy Barlow, Nick Henry, Richard Jobson, Ian Marshall, Gunner Halle, Roger Palmer (Neil Tolson), Graeme Sharp, Mike Milligan, Paul Bernard, Manager: Joe Royle

Oldham's two games against Wimbledon in 1992/93 did not lack goals or excitement and strangely featured both The Latics' biggest win and largest loss of the season. The 6-2 hammering they gave the Dons in early April effectively became their salvation as they stayed up courtesy of a goal difference that was two superior to Crystal Palace's. Their survival was one of the more unlikely escapes from the clutches of relegation. They had to win all their final three games, which took in the space of a week, to have any chance of staying up and hope that Palace did not collect more than a point from their two remaining fixtures.

To add to the size of the task, two of Oldham's matches were against strong opposition. After managing to notch up only their third win away from home against second-placed Aston Villa, three days later they overcame Liverpool 3-2 at Boundary Park courtesy of an Ian Olney double. Then on the last day they beat Southampton 4-3 at despite a Matthew Le Tissier hat-trick. Meanwhile Palace, who had drawn with Manchester City in mid-week, lost 3-0 at Arsenal and the unlikeliest of escapes was complete. This was the only time in their two seasons in the Premier League that Oldham won three successive games and it could not have been better timed. Very few seasons have ended as dramatically as this first one and this is the second smallest margin by which a club has survived after Wigan avoided relegation by one goal at Sheffield United's expense in 2006/07. Oldham had certainly made their own mark on Premier League history.

In stark contrast to their final flourish in the first season The Latics ended their second, and to date last, in the Premier League with a whimper enduring an eight-match winless run, only picking up three points and being relegated by three points. Prior to that poor ending Oldham had just enjoyed their best spell in the Premier League, collecting 18 points from nine matches which included five victories, away at Villa again, at home to Chelsea and QPR and both home and away against Southampton as well as notable draws against Arsenal, Leeds and Manchester City. This spell also included their two longest unbeaten runs of four matches each.

Of all 49 clubs to have played in the Premier League Oldham have, along with Swindon, fallen the furthest. As of the 2019/20 season they are plying their trade in League Two and they have spent the majority of the 25 years since their relegation from the top flight in 1993/94 in the third tier. They are the lowest-ranked club of the original 22 Premier League teams, and the only one in League Two. Of the rest ,12 are still in the Premier League, six are in the Championship and three are in League One (this is assuming that AFC Wimbledon are the true successors to the old Wimbledon). In recent times the Latics have been laid low by a depressingly familiar tale of shoddy ownership and a lack of financial clout.

ONE HIT WONDER

For someone with a name that appears to be more suited to an opera singer than a footballer, Orpheo Keizerweerd certainly could not have chosen a grander stage to make his single appearance as a substitute for Oldham. On 10th April 1993 he came on at halftime for Ian Olney at Anfield. It may have been a narrow loss but within a few weeks Oldham would wreak their revenge on Liverpool with their victory in that dramatic, turbulent and ultimately glorious last week of the season.

Keizerweerd was born in Suriname, the small South American country, a former Dutch colony with a population of just over 500,000. Suriname has produced many incredible players who have gone on to play for the Netherlands, such as Clarence Seedorf, Edgar Davids and Jimmy

Floyd Hasselbaink. Keizerweerd did not quite emulate the footballing prowess of his illustrious countrymen, but surely with his middle name of Henk he is worthy of an inclusion in any list of the Premier League's most wonderful/bizarre names.

His last club before retirement in 2000 was AFC DWS, a Sunday league outfit from Amsterdam.

FOOTNOTE

GREAT ESCAPES ON GOAL DIFFERENCE

CLUB	SEASON	MARGIN OF GOAL DIFF
Wigan	2006/07	1
Oldham	1992/93	2
Fulham	2007/08	3
Everton	1997/98	5
Southampton	1995/96	7

A VIEW FROM THE STAND

Chris Stringer, host @d3d4football

Your club's spell in the Premier League was brief and while there was the odd glorious moment ultimately it was short-lived. Looking back now, one question remains - Was it really worth it? What would you do differently and what were the long-term consequences of your moment in the sun?

Oldham's period in the Premier League is still, to this day, a source of great pride for Latics fans. Their relatively small club from Lancashire got a taste of the big time and became the country's "second team" for three top division (including two Premier League) seasons. In the pure sense of footballing achievement, there is no question that reaching the top division of English football is the ultimate goal of domestic football. However, when you dig a little deeper into the effects of that period it becomes clear that the financial excesses of those years made Oldham the fourth-tier club they are today. To truly appreciate the implications of those seasons, it is important to look at the timeline of events leading up to, and following, Oldham's time in the Premier League.

The Latics had been in the second tier since the start of the 1974/75 season, recording relative success in the middle and top half of the league. The club eventually won promotion to the old 'First Division' in 1991 and, in the following season, became founder members of the Premier League. After two seasons in the newly formed league, the club tumbled into the second tier of English football and utterly underwhelmed, suffering from the financial stresses of paying large wages and having an inexperienced manager in Graeme Sharp. This was before the time of "parachute payments" that would have supported the finances of the club. Three disappointing seasons were spent in the second tier, before the club eventually fell to the third in 1997. The rapid fall from the Premier League, and the potential for a quick return, made the club an attractive prospect for would-be investors. In 2001 the club was bought out by Chris Moore, who promised a Premier League return within five years. Of course, this plan didn't come to completion and Moore left after just two years with the club losing £50,000 per week due to high wage expenditure. As a result, Oldham entered administration and were eventually bought out by a consortium of three businessmen. This purchase also ultimately fell apart when two of the three left the club during the financial crash and what followed was more than two decades in the third tier, before dropping into League Two in 2018. The club now sits in the hands of controversial owner Abdallah Lemsagam; a former football agent who, in his brief tenure, has already come under criticism from supporters. Once again Oldham fans are left hoping for change, whilst witnessing difficult times both on and off the pitch. Three seasons in the top flight have been paid for by almost three decades of struggle since.

It is clear, on balance, that the years in the Premier League ultimately weren't worth it from both a financial and footballing point of view; after all, the club had been a settled 'Second Division' side prior to that and is now rooted in the fourth tier. However, it is difficult to put a price on the excitement and pride of seeing your club play in what is, arguably, the best league in the world. That period of time still burns brightly in the history of the club and, ultimately, gives fans hope that it is possible for a small-town team to reach the big time. I don't think there will be many fans that witnessed those years who would be willing to trade the excitement and pride for anything. It wasn't financially worth it, but ultimately football is about success—you can't put a price on that era in the history of Oldham Athletic.

If it were possible to turn back time and alter the course of the club, there are many key things that could have been changed. Greater relegation clauses in players contracts may have made life in the second tier a little easier. But in terms of the club's time in the Premier League it is simply a case that Oldham were not big enough to sustain the quality required for any length of time; after all the club has the second smallest stadium in Premier League history—only surpassed by Bournemouth's Dean Court—in a time when the financial rewards of being in the Premier League were good, but not nearly as great as they are today. Nothing can be changed about those Premier League years, but perhaps better decisions following relegation would have seen Oldham Athletic stand a chance of returning to the top flight rather than descending into the oblivion of Division Four.

PORTSMOUTH STATS

NUMBER OF SEASONS:

7

2003/04-2009/10

NUMBER OF MATCHES:

266

Wins 79 (Home 54 Away 25)
Draws 65 (Home 34 Away 31)
Losses 122 (Home 45 Away 77)

[Win ratio 30%]

Goals F 292
(Home 184 Away 108)

Goals A 380
(Home 159 Away 221)

Goal Difference: -88

TOTAL POINTS

302

(Home 196: 65%; Away 106: 35%)
Average per season: 43

BEST POSITION:

8th

2007/08

WORST POSITION:

20th

2009/10 (RELEGATED)

BIGGEST WIN:

6-1

v Leeds
(8th Nov, 2003)

BIGGEST LOSS:

6-0

v Manchester City
(21st Sept, 2008)

LONGEST UNBEATEN RUN:

11 matches

(15th Sept, 2007-8th Dec, 2007)

LONGEST WITHOUT A WIN:

9 matches

(7th Dec, 2008-7th Feb, 2009)

ALL TIME RANKING

30th

MOST GOALS SCORED IN A SEASON:

48

(2007/08)

FEWEST GOALS SCORED IN A SEASON:

34

(2009/10)

FEWEST GOALS CONCEDED IN A SEASON:

40

(2007/08)

MOST GOALS CONCEDED IN A SEASON:

66

(2009/10)

TOP GOALSCORER:

28

Yakubu

MOST APPEARANCES:

144

Matthew Taylor

OWN GOALS:

15

RED CARDS:

20

LOWEST ATTENDANCE:

16,207

v Blackburn
(3rd Apr, 2010)

HIGHEST ATTENDANCE:

20,821

v Tottenham
(17th Oct, 2009)

All statistics and records supplied by

PORTSMOUTH

DID YOU KNOW?

In total 11 French players appeared for Portsmouth during their seven-season spell in the Premier League with Sylvain Distin heading the list with 77 appearances. Distin also holds the Premier League record for most appearances (469) without ever being capped at senior international level.

In all, players from a dizzying 37 non-Home Nation countries represented Portsmouth in the Premier League, including 18 European nations and 11 African countries. Pompey were truly a League of Nations. Nigerian Nwankwo Kanu is the foreign player with most appearances in the competition and is the only non-British player to have played 100 times in the Premier League for the club (101). Fellow Nigerian Yakubu heads the scoring charts with 28.

FIRST PREMIER LEAGUE MATCH: 16TH AUGUST, 2003
PORTSMOUTH 2 (SHERINGHAM, BERGER)
ASTON VILLA 1 (BARRY)

FRATTON PARK 20,101

Shaka Hislop, Arjan De Zeeuw, Hayden Foxe, Boris Zivkovic, Dejan Stefanovic, Patrick Berger, Steve Stone, Nigel Quashie, Amdy Faye (Sebastien Schemmel), Teddy Sheringham, Yakubu (Vincent Pericard), Manager: Harry Redknapp

In Portsmouth's first ever Premier League game Teddy Sheringham completed the unique feat of scoring the winning goal for five different clubs on the opening day of the season. Sheringham had scored in 1-0 wins for Forest in 1992 and Tottenham in 1993. He had a prodigious record on the opening day of the season as he also scored for Tottenham on the opening days in 1994 and 1995 as well (see Tottenham section).

He achieved the same feat for both Manchester United in 1998 and West Ham in 2005. Additionally at the ripe old age of 38, Sheringham became the oldest player to score a hat-trick, for Pompey against Bolton.

During their seven-season stay Portsmouth were remarkably consistent in the number of goals they scored with a variance of only 14 between the worst of 34 in 2009/10 and the best 48 in 2007/08. This is also reflected in their top scorers which varied from the peak of Yakubu's 16 in 2003/04 to the lowest being Lomana LuaLua's seven in 2005/06.

LEGS ELEVEN

SATURDAY SEPTEMBER 29 2007

PORTSMOUTH 7 (2) BENJANI 6,' 37', 70' HREIDARSSON 55',
KRANCJAR 75', INGIMARSSON (OG) 81', MUNTARI 92' (PEN)
READING 4 (1) HUNT 45', KITSON 48', LONG 79', CAMPBELL (OG) 94'

FRATTON PARK (20,102)

There are some games that not only defy any logic but also almost defy description. Portsmouth's encounter with Reading on 29th September, 2007 very much fall into that category. Apart from being the highest-scoring Premier League game there were enough sub-plots to furnish a whole book about the events of that day. You do not get that many 7-4 score lines to the pound and this one came pretty much out of the blue. The home side's main threat, Nwanko Kanu was declared unfit before the game and having only scored eight goals in their first seven matches and with Reading having scored only one goal in their three away games at that point, the prospects of an avalanche were not promising.

The game itself started with Portsmouth taking a comfortable 2-0 lead courtesy of two Benjani goals, the second of which was driven in expertly after a mazy run. As half-time approached, the home side appeared to be in complete control, with no hint of the mayhem that was to follow. In added time Stephen Hunt brought the visitors back into the game after a hectic bit of pinball in the box involving the bar and a desperate David James clawing back a shot. If this sowed a seed of doubt into Pompey fans' previously serene disposition, that seed bloomed into full-blown anxiety early in the second half. James marked the occasion of his 600th League appearance with one of his characteristic rash decisions. He raced out of goal in the 48th minute and was easily bypassed by Dave Kitson who was left to score into the unguarded net to even things up.

The game then descended into the sort of free scoring jamboree that is more prevalent on a basketball court. Hermann Hrediarsson restored Portsmouth's lead with a header before James made some amends for his senior moment by saving a Nicky Shorey penalty that would have brought Reading back into the game. After Benjani completed his hattrick in the 70th minute the shackles were well and truly loosened and even Niko Krancjar popped up with a header. To add to the fun there was a trio of deflected goals, one off Shane Long's back in the right net plus two own goals by Ivar Ingimarsson and finally one from Sol Campbell to end the carnage in the 94th minute. The scruffy nature of the last couple of goals summed up the quality of the match as it descended into farce.

As a postscript to this ridiculous match and to highlight its freakish nature it is worth looking at the games before and after. The previous game at Fratton Park had been a goalless draw with Liverpool, and the three that followed were also goalless, against West Ham, Manchester City and Everton. Clearly exhausted by the glut of goals, Portsmouth actually failed to score in their next six home games, playing nearly ten hours of football before Benjani popped up with another hat-trick in mid-January against that season's patsies, the woeful Derby team. Portsmouth finished a creditable 8th and won the FA Cup while Reading were relegated on a goal difference margin of just three goals after Fulham snatched a last day victory at, where else but, Fratton Park.

If everything was rosy in the garden at that point for Portsmouth, things started to take a turn for the worst in the next few years. Within the space of six months the ownership changed hands three times and this dangerous game of pass-the-parcel ended in administration in February 2010, followed by a nine-point deduction in March. They never fully recovered from the heaviest sanction levied on a Premier League club and were already on their way to the Championship in early April. They ended up 16 points adrift of safety and 10 points away from the other two relegated sides, so they would have been gone down anyway.

In 2010, in a sideshow to their troubles off and on the pitch they did make it to the FA Cup Final for a second time but lost to Chelsea. Pompey became the second club to reach the FA Cup Final only to be relegated from the Premier League after Middlesbrough's unfortunate double in 1996/97. Wigan followed suit three years later although at least they had the consolation of winning the FA Cup. Within three years, following a second administration, Portsmouth had dropped all the way down to League Two before gaining promotion to League One in 2017/18 as they begin to "Play Up Pompey".

ONE HIT WONDER

When Harry Redknapp bought the 18-year-old Richard Duffy from Swansea City there were high expectations that he would become an established member of the first team. Like many one hit wonders, his only Premier League appearance came as a substitute, on 1st May, 2004 when he replaced the injured Linvoy Primus. Although he stayed at Fratton Park for the best part of five years, after that one game he spent nearly his entire career on loan to Coventry City where he enjoyed four separate spells alongside one at Burnley and another back at this first club, Swansea City.

Duffy played for Notts County during 2018/19 season.

FOOTNOTE

Portsmouth fielded the oldest Premier League starting line-up in a 2-0 defeat at Tottenham Hotspur on 27th March, 2010. The average age of the team was 32 years and 104 days with only two of the starting line-up aged under 30 - Anthony Vanden Borre and Aaron Mokoena who was eight months shy of his 30th birthday. David James was the oldest player as he was just short of his 40th birthday and it just happened to be Hayden Mullins' 31st birthday

PLAYER	AGE
David James	39
Hermann Hreidarsson	35
Steve Finnan	33
Anthony Vanden Borre	22
Aaron Mokoena	29
Hayden Mullins	31
Michael Brown	33
Richard Hughes	30
Angelos Basinas	34
Frederic Piquionne	31
Kanu	33

A VIEW FROM THE STANDS

Adam Darke

What was your club's 'Sliding Doors' moment, that seemingly inconsequential action, which actually became a turning point in their fortunes, for either good or bad?

Pompey's entire history has been a breathless rollercoaster of improbable highs and frightening lows so in many ways their seven years in the Premier League was a microcosm of what had gone before. Looking back it all seems rather surreal with star names like Sol Campbell, Lassana Diarra and Sulley Muntari wearing the red, white and blue. I suppose deep down we always knew it couldn't last long, not with a 19,000 capacity in a crumbling stadium without even a single corporate box.

The moment that stands out for me is the game against Manchester City at home in 2006 when we were staring relegation in the face. Two outstanding goals from Pedro Mendes, another player we felt so fortunate to call our own even for a short period, kickstarted a remarkable run of form. We would accumulate 20 points from a possible 27 and secure Premier League survival. It wasn't just Mendes' goals, it was the feeling they generated inside the stadium: absolute euphoria and a hopeful sense that all wasn't lost. Of course, that team went from strength to strength, culminating in the FA Cup victory two years later. Strange times, maybe never to be repeated, but certainly never forgotten.

QUEENS PARK RANGERS STATS

NUMBER OF SEASONS:

7 (3 spells)

1992/93-1995/96, 2011/12 -
2012/13, 2014/15

NUMBER OF MATCHES:

278

Wins 81 (Home 51 Away 30)
Draws 65 (Home 38 Away 27)
Losses 132 (Home 50 Away 82)

[Win ratio 29%]

Goals F 339
(Home 194 Away 145)

Goals A 431
(Home 190 Away 241)

Goal Difference: -92

TOTAL POINTS

308

(Home 191: 62%; 117: 38%)
Average per season: 44

BEST POSITION:

5th

1992/93

WORST POSITION:

20th

2012/13 2014/15 (RELEGATED)

BIGGEST WIN:

5-1

v Coventry City
(23rd Oct, 1993)

BIGGEST LOSS:

6-0 (2)

v Fulham (2nd Oct, 2011)
v Manchester City (10th May, 2015)

LONGEST UNBEATEN RUN:

7 matches

(3rd Apr, 1993-11th May, 1993)

LONGEST WITHOUT A WIN:

17 matches

(13th May, 2012-8th Dec, 2012)

ALL TIME RANKING

29th

MOST GOALS SCORED IN A SEASON:

63

(1992/93)

FEWEST GOALS SCORED IN A SEASON:

30

(2014/15)

FEWEST GOALS CONCEDED IN A SEASON:

55

(1992/93)

MOST GOALS CONCEDED IN A SEASON:

73

(2012/13)

TOP GOALSCORER:

60

Les Ferdinand

MOST APPEARANCES:

142

Andy Impey

OWN GOALS:

22

RED CARDS:

26

LOWEST ATTENDANCE:

9,875

v Swindon
(30th Apr, 1994)

HIGHEST ATTENDANCE:

21,267

v Manchester United
(5th Feb, 1994)

All statistics and records supplied by

QUEENS PARK RANGERS

FIRST PREMIER LEAGUE MATCH: 17TH AUGUST, 1992
MANCHESTER CITY 1 (WHITE)
QPR 1 (SINTON)

MAINE ROAD 24,471

Jan Stejskal, David Bardsley, Ian Holloway , Alan McDonald, Clive Wilson, Darren Peacock, Andy Impey, Andy Sinton , Ray Wilkins, Les Ferdinand, Dennis Bailey (Garry Thompson), Manager: Gerry Francis

QPR started life in the Premier League with aplomb, having been an established Division One side for almost a decade before they only lost one of their opening 11 games and were in the top six all season before finishing fifth. Three top 10 finishes in the first three Premier League seasons made QPR the most consistent London club in the top flight during that initial period with no other club from the capital managing. Between 1992/93 and 19994/95 Arsenal and Tottenham both featured twice in the top ten.

They certainly ruled West London as on each occasion were comfortably ahead of their rivals Chelsea. QPR finishing on 63 points in the first season, followed by 60 in each of the next two seasons, their relegation in 1995/96 was somewhat of a shock to the system and they have not been in touching distance of the top half of the table since. They finished the 2018/19 season as only the fourth best club in West London behind Chelsea, Fulham in the Premier League and Brentford in the Championship. Add in Arsenal, Palace, Tottenham and West Ham and they were eighth highest London club—a far cry from the early 1990s.

It has been a sorry decline and they have accumulated some of the more miserable records including for example the longest winless run from the start of a season. In the 2012/13 season they did not record their first victory until the 15th December, 2012 when they beat their West London neighbours Fulham 2-1 in what was their 17th league game. The season started with their heaviest Premier League defeat at Loftus Road when they were hammered 5-0 by Swansea and they never truly recovered from that wretched start and were duly relegated in 20th place with only four wins and 14 points below safety.

Alongside Sunderland, QPR hold another sorry record for the most red cards in a single season with a hefty toll of nine dismissals in 2011/12. Unsurprisingly the most high profile of those sending-offs was Joey Barton's on the last day of the season. Although this was the game that delivered the Premier League to Manchester City in that famous, frenetic finale, Barton, the team's captain, had left his indelible mark on proceedings by performing his own hat-trick. Not only did he poleaxe Carlos Tevez off the ball but he also kicked Sergio Aguero and for good measure aimed a head-butt at Vincent Kompany following his dismissal. Never to do things by halves Barton ended up with a 12-match ban, the lengthiest meted out by the FA for an on-pitch misdemeanour. It did not quite take the shine off the most exciting final day but it was close.

Barton was also sent off that season against Norwich in January 2012 for head-butting Bradley Johnson but at least he restricted himself to one fracas. His partner in crime that season was Djibril Cisse who matched Barton's two dismissals. The other five to be sent off were Clint Hill, Shaun Derry, Armand Traore, Adel Taarabt and Samba Diakite as Neil Warnock's side fought their way to survival by a single point.

QPR's propensity to shoot themselves in the foot was never more prevalent tha when they scored two own goals that allowed Liverpool to win 3-2 at Loftus Road in October 2014. One of those was an own-goal from Richard Dunne, the record-breaking tenth of his career as his haphazard record for Manchester City and Aston Villa continued at QPR. Dunne's ten own goals puts him well clear of Liverpool pair Jamie Carragher and Martin Skrtel who are on seven each. Dunne ended up running rings around the Hoops.

ONE HIT WONDER

Danny Simpson's finest hour was being part of that Leicester title-winning team in the 2015/16 season. The former Manchester United youth graduate spent time on loan to a variety of clubs before joining Newcastle and then QPR. Simpson helped Rangers regain their Premier League status via the play-offs and started the first game at home to Hull in August 2014. He lasted just over an hour before being substituted and within days he was transferred to Leicester and became a regular fixture for their League-winning side the following season.

Danny Simpson was still at Leicester during 2018/19 but lost his place after suffering an injury in the early part of the season and only played half a dozen times. His sixth game in the final match of the season against Chelsea was his last for the Foxes as he was released.

FOOTNOTE

HIGHS AND LOWS: ATTENDANCES

QPR's highest attendance of 21,267 in their 139 matches at Loftus Road was reached in February 1994 against Manchester United and only two months later they recorded their lowest crowd at Loftus Road when a measly 9,875 watched them lose 3-1 to Swindon.

A VIEW FROM THE STANDS

Ash Rose, editor of KiCK! Magazine
and host of The 90s Football Podcast

What was your club's 'Sliding Doors' moment, that seemingly inconsequential action, which actually became a turning point in their fortunes, for either good or bad?

Under Gerry Francis QPR finished fifth in the inaugural Premier League season. Despite a relatively restricted budget and a team with no superstars other than Les Ferdinand, they were London's top club finishing above big hitters such as Arsenal, Tottenham and Chelsea. It was a side built on a solid worth ethic, some outstanding coaching and players who were vastly underrated, and there was a genuine belief that the team was ready to push onto the next level. However, midway through the 1993-94 season the then chairman Richard Thompson sought out the services of ex-Rangers legend Rodney Marsh about a chief executive role at the club—a position above Francis' head. Seeing this as undermining his authority and a lack of faith in him from above, Francis resigned from his role and his talented R's team never really recovered. Key assets were sold and his replacement Ray Wilkins was unable to replenish his squad with adequate replacements, ultimately leading to Rangers' relegation in 1996. Players of the era and fans now look back and wonder how far the team could have progressed if Gerry hadn't left the club that fateful November.

READING STATS

NUMBER OF SEASONS:

3 (2 spells)

2006/07-2007/08, 2012/13

NUMBER OF MATCHES:

114

Wins 32 (Home 23 Away 9)
Draws 23 (Home 12 Away 11)
Losses 59 (Home 22 Away 37)

[Win ratio 28%]

Goals F 136
(Home 71 Away 65)

Goals A 186
(Home 78 Away 108)

Goal Difference: -50

TOTAL POINTS

119

(Home 81: 68%; Away 38: 32%)
Average per season: 40

BEST POSITION:

8th

2006/07

WORST POSITION:

19th

2012/13 (RELEGATED)

BIGGEST WIN:

6-0

v West Ham
(1st Jan, 2007)

BIGGEST LOSS:

0-4

v Arsenal
(22nd Oct, 2006)

LONGEST UNBEATEN RUN:

6 matches

(1st Jan, 2007-10th Feb, 2007)

LONGEST WITHOUT A WIN:

10 matches (2)

(18th Aug, 2012-10th Nov, 2012;
9th Feb 2013-28th Apr, 2013)

ALL TIME RANKING

41st

MOST GOALS SCORED IN A SEASON:

52

(2006/07)

FEWEST GOALS SCORED IN A SEASON:

41

(2007/08)

FEWEST GOALS CONCEDED IN A SEASON:

47

(2006/07)

MOST GOALS CONCEDED IN A SEASON:

73

(2012/13)

TOP GOALSCORER:

19

Kevin Doyle

MOST APPEARANCES:

90

Nicky Shorey

OWN GOALS:

5

RED CARDS:

9

LOWEST ATTENDANCE:

21,379

v Wigan
(22nd Sep, 2007)

HIGHEST ATTENDANCE:

24,374

v Blackburn
(29th Mar, 2008)

READING

DID YOU KNOW?

Reading's Premier League sojourns were heavily supported by players from the Republic of Ireland with a total of eight, headed by top scorer Kevin Doyle. This is twice as many as the second most represented non-UK nation, Jamaica, with four. Reading's record foreign appearance maker was Marcus Hahnemann from the United States who played 76 Premier League matches for the club.

FIRST PREMIER LEAGUE MATCH: 19TH AUGUST, 2007
READING 3 (KITSON, SIDWELL, LITA)
MIDDLESBROUGH 2 (DOWNING, YAKUBU)

MADEJSKI STADIUM 23,802

Marcus Hahnemann, Graeme Murty, Nicky Shorey, Ivar Ingimarsson, Ibrahima Sonko, Steve Sidwell, James Harper, Bobby Convey (Stephen Hunt), Seol Ki-Hyeon (Brynjar Gunnarsson), Kevin Doyle, Dave Kitson (Leroy Lita), Manager: Steve Coppell

Not many clubs have enjoyed such an exciting and rewarding debut as Reading did against Middlesbrough in August 2006. They had romped to the Championship title the previous season, winning at a canter with a record 106 points and scoring 99 goals in the process, but had a rude awakening in the opening 20 minutes in the Premier League after Stewart Downing and Yakubu put the away side in control at the Madejski. Approaching half-time Reading were still two goals behind but then scored twice in the space of a couple of minutes, through Dave Kitson and Steve Sidwell, to go in level at the break.

Within ten minutes of the restart Kitson's replacement Leroy Lita scored their third as they ended up 3-2 winners. The Royals continued the momentum from this barnstorming opening match, finishing a highly creditable 8th. They also joined the select list of eight teams out of the 80 which have been promoted to the Premier League since 1992 to have won more games than they lost in their first season following promotion. They were the last team to achieve this before Wolves did so in 2018/19.

Reading's most impressive performances that season were both against London clubs, beating Tottenham 3-1 in their first ever encounter in the top flight, having been 1-0 down and an even more impressive dismantling of West Ham. The New Year's Day massacre in 2007 was as comprehensive as it was surprising when the hapless Hammers were 4-0 down within 36 minutes and eventually succumbed 6-0, comfortably Reading's biggest Premier League victory.

Reading were involved in their fair share of high-scoring games in their second season and can lay claim to be one of only a few clubs who have scored four goals away from home three times in the same season although unfortunately they did manage to lose two of those games, in the space of a few months. Following their 7-4 demolition at the hands of Portsmouth in September 2007, they capitulated 6-4 at White Hart Lane in December.

On the last day of the season they completed their treble when they won 4-0 at beleaguered Derby but were still relegated as Fulham won their last game at Fratton Park and stayed up on a goal difference, three goals better off than Reading. So while the Royals may have provided great entertainment in those high-scoring defeats, they were ultimately ruinous.

Reading did play one more season in the Premier League after being promoted in 2012. They started with a rash of draws—six in the opening ten fixtures—but had to wait until their 11th match on 17th November, 2012 to gain their first victory. They only won six games overall but yet again the goals flowed, 116 in their 38 games, a healthy average of three per game with nine featuring at least five goals. Yet again Reading scored four goals away when they beat Fulham 4-2 in early May but it could not save them as they had already been relegated.

Over their 114 Premier League matches there were 322 goals, which averages out at 2.82 per game. Reading deserve the accolade of being one of the most entertaining clubs as that is the 6 highest average of any club, with Swindon, Blackpool and Barnsley, all one season wonders, as the top 3 and Oldham who had two seasons in fifth place and after last season Bournemouth are now 4th. They certainly were Royal entertainers.

ONE HIT WONDER

John Halls spent four seasons at Arsenal, including playing in the team that won the FA Youth Cup, but he never made the transition to the first team apart from a couple of League Cup games. Halls moved to Stoke in 2003 where he made more than 50 appearances before joining Reading in January 2006. He had to wait over a year for his Premier League debut which came against Bolton in August 2007 when he replaced the Ecuadorean Ulises de la Cruz in the 83rd minute of the 3-0 defeat. But then it was back out on loan for Halls before he left at the end of the 2007/08 season.

Halls is now a model and has appeared in advertisements with Armani and Dolce & Gabbana.

FOOTNOTE

List of promoted clubs to have won more games than they lost in their first season following promotion.

CLUB	SEASON	WINS/ LOSSES
Blackburn	1992/93	20/11
Newcastle	1993/94	23/11
Nottingham Forest	1994/95	22/9
Middlesbrough	1998/99	12/11
Sunderland	1999/2000	16/12
Ipswich	2000/01	20/12
West Ham	2005/06	16/15
Reading	2006/07	16/15
Wolves	2018/19	16/13

A VIEW FROM THE STANDS

Rob Langham, from The Two Unfortunates

What was your club's 'Sliding Doors' moment, that seemingly inconsequential action, which actually became a turning point in their fortunes, for either good or bad?

The watershed moment in the first of Reading's two Premier League sojourns is probably the one that most people will remember the Berkshire club for. In the first half of a gripping encounter against the reigning Premier League champions, Chelsea, in October 2006, tenacious midfielder

Stephen Hunt slid in to challenge for the ball against the Blues' goalkeeper Petr Čech. The Chelsea player underwent surgery for a depressed fracture of the skull and took three months to recover. The injury meant he had to wear a headguard for the rest of his career.

Amid a febrile inquest into the game, the notion of Reading as a plucky, welcome newcomer to the top-flight party was blown out of the water with journalists, fans of the big clubs and commentators quick to voice their condemnation of Hunt despite the challenge being in no way conclusively deliberate. Most notoriously of all, José Mourinho called into question the response time of the South Central Ambulance Service in an early foreshadowing of fake news. While Reading would go on to enjoy a fine season, the feeling from the soccer establishment was of a team that would be welcome in the Premier League provided they were willing to provide cannon fodder. This incident changed all that.

SHEFFIELD UNITED STATS

NUMBER OF SEASONS:

3 (2 spells)

1992/93-1993/94, 2006/07

NUMBER OF MATCHES:

122

Wins 32 (Home 23 Away 9)
Draws 36 (Home 22 Away 14)
Losses 54 (Home 16 Away 38)

[Win ratio 32%]

Goals F 128
(Home 81 Away 47)

Goals A 168
(Home 63 Away 105)

Goal Difference: -40

TOTAL POINTS

132

(Home 91: 69%; Away 41: 31%)
Average per season: 44

BEST POSITION:

14th

1992/93

WORST POSITION:

20th

1993/94 (RELEGATED)

BIGGEST WIN:

6-0

v Tottenham
(2nd Mar, 1993)

BIGGEST LOSS:

4-0 (2)

v Newcastle (24th Nov, 1993)
v Liverpool (24th Feb, 2007)

LONGEST UNBEATEN RUN:

8 matches

(5th Mar, 1994-4th Apr, 1994)

LONGEST WITHOUT A WIN:

12 matches

(28th Aug, 1993-24th Nov, 1993)

ALL TIME RANKING

40th

MOST GOALS SCORED IN A SEASON:

54

(1992/93)

FEWEST GOALS SCORED IN A SEASON:

32

(2006/07)

FEWEST GOALS CONCEDED IN A SEASON:

53

(1992/93)

MOST GOALS CONCEDED IN A SEASON:

60

(1993/94)

TOP GOALSCORER:

15

Brian Deane

MOST APPEARANCES:

72

Carl Bradshaw

OWN GOALS:

4

RED CARDS:

9

LOWEST ATTENDANCE:

13,646

v West Ham
(28th Mar, 1994)

HIGHEST ATTENDANCE:

32,604

v Wigan
(13th May, 2007)

All statistics and records supplied by

SHEFFIELD UNITED

DID YOU KNOW?

Keith Gillespie's sending off in Sheffield United's match away to Reading in 2007 after coming on as a substitute in the 53rd minute was unusual and in fact unique. Gillespie trotted on to the pitch as United were preparing to take a throw-in and after making a beeline for Stephen Hunt, the Irishman proceeded to elbow the Reading midfielder as an act of retaliation for something that had occurred before he entered the fray. The referee, Mark Halsey was unaware of Gillespie's immediate impact but the linesman had spotted it, informed Halsey and Gillespie was off before the game had restarted. As Gillespie was leaving the pitch he gave Hunt another cuffing just for good measure and then disappeared off down the tunnel with a record that will never be challenged—sent off after no seconds of action. In the aftermath there was even a ruckus between the two benches that led to Wally Downes and Neil Warnock joining Gillespie on the rather crowded naughty step.

FIRST PREMIER LEAGUE MATCH: 15TH AUGUST, 1992
SHEFFIELD UNITED 2 (DEANE 2)
MANCHESTER UNITED 1 (HUGHES)

BRAMALL LANE 28,070

Simon Tracey, Carl Bradshaw, Dave Barnes , Paul Beesley, Alan McLeary, Kevin Gage, John Gannon (Charlie Hartfield), Glyn Hodges (Ian Bryson), Michael Lake, Alan Cork, Brian Deane, Manager: Dave Bassett

DEANE AT THE DOUBLE

SATURDAY 15 AUGUST 1992

SHEFFIELD UNITED 2 (1) DEANE 5', 50' (PEN)
MANCHESTER UNITED 1 (0) HUGHES 61'

BRAMALL LANE - (28,070)

Brian Deane will be forever remembered as the scorer of the first ever Premier League goal when he opened the scoring after just five minutes of the match against Manchester United on 15th August 1992, the first day of Premier League action. It was a typical effort from a Dave Bassett team. Following a long throw by Carl Bradshaw that flummoxed United's defence, Deane nipped in to beat Gary Pallister and Peter Schmeichel to the ball on the edge of the six-yard box and head into the empty net. It was not a particularly aesthetic opener, but they all count. Deane secured Sheffield United's opening day win with his second of the match after Pallister was again at fault after being outrun by Alan Cork before clumsily bringing him down and Deane duly scored the first penalty in Premier League history as well. That was the Blades' first penalty for 50 matches since March 1991.

Ironically, Manchester United's only goal in response was straight out of the agricultural handbook that might have been written by Bassett and edited by a young Neil Warnock. A massive punt by Schmeichel cleared everyone and befuddled Alan McLeary so much that he allowed Mark Hughes free passage on the edge of the area and the Welshman ran on to slot the ball past the keeper. Manchester United had not won the top division for quarter of a century and it looked as though Alex Ferguson would have his work cut out ending that interminable wait. At least Schemeichel was off the mark for assists.

Manchester United were one of several notable scalps at Bramall Lane that season, which included Liverpool, Chelsea and a 6-0 hammering of Tottenham, which is still the Blades' biggest Premier League victory. But that opening game was their one and only defeat of Manchester United in the Premier League, they lost the other five fixtures, so it could be viewed as something of a false dawn. Deane went on to score 15 goals that season before his departure to Leeds and he remains the Blades' record goalscorer.

If their debut was memorable then their last appearance in 13th May 2007 was equally so but for entirely different reasons. It was a do or die game with Wigan, in which United just had to avoid defeat to beat the drop. Wigan had only won once away since early December while United had beaten the likes of Arsenal, Spurs and seemingly crucially West Ham over that same period. With the omens looking so good their biggest ever Premier League crowd of 32,604 arrived in full expectation of survival. That the winning goal for the away side came from a former player was bad enough but the fact that David Unsworth had just come on as a substitute before striking the decisive penalty past Paddy Kenny added a particularly piquant sauce to an already bubbling pot. Even when Wigan were reduced to ten men after the dismissal of Lee McCulloch United could not take advantage.

The Blades' relegation in 2006/07 will always have a bitter taste for Blades fans for of a variety of factors. The main one centred on the Carlos Tevez/ Javier Mascherano affair. West Ham were found guilty of transgressing third party ownership rules but escaped with a hefty but manageable £5.5m fine rather than the points deduction, for which Sheffield United made a strong case. For once it was hard not to feel sorry for Neil Warnock and the fact that Tevez scored the only goal of the game on the final day of the season at Old Trafford, the home of the champions, to secure West Ham's survival would not have been good for Warnock's blood pressure.

A further point of irritation for Warnock's men was their relegation was by the slightest margin in Premier League history. Warnock expressed his disbelief in his characteristically curmudgeonly style: "I don't even feel like I've been relegated but the statistics tell us we have been." There have been five relegations that have been decided by goal difference (see Footnote), but United's was the narrowest with just a solitary goal between them and their final day conquerors, Wigan. The fact that West Ham's goal difference was one worse than Sheffield United's provides a further ironic bone of contention for the Bramall Lane club.

Their other relegation in 1993/94 was also a tantalisingly close affair, with just one point separating them from Ipswich. The point they needed seemed to have been secured as their final match at Stamford Bridge entered the final minute. United had been ahead twice only to be pegged back but they were denied by a late Mark Stein winner, which condemned them to the drop after Everton's recovery from 2-0 down against Wimbledon. For both their relegations the Blades' future teetered on a knife-edge but ultimately suffered a fatal cut.

ONE HIT WONDER

Alan Wright is probably best known for being one of the shortest players to play in the Premier League, at 5' 4". The diminutive full back made more than 250 appearances for Aston Villa in an eight-year spell, having joined from Blackburn as Rovers were on the cusp of winning the Premier League in 1995. Initially joining Sheffield United on loan from Villa before earning a permanent transfer in 2004 and helping them to gain promotion in 2006. He started his solitary Premier League game for the Blades against Arsenal in a 3-0 defeat at the Emirates in late September 2006.

He was then sent out on loan to a variety of clubs including Leeds United before he joined Cheltenham in 2007. 'The Mighty Atom' finished his career at Fleetwood Town.

FOOTNOTE

RELEGATIONS ON GOAL DIFFERENCE

1992/93	49 points	20th Crystal Palace - 13	19th Oldham -11
1995/96	38 points	18th Manchester City - 25	17th Southampton - 18
1997/98	40 points	18th Bolton - 20	17th Everton - 15
2006/07	38 points	18th Sheffield United - 23	17th Wigan - 22
2007/08	36 points	18th Reading - 25	17th Fulham - 22

A VIEW FROM THE STANDS

Ian Rands

What was your club's 'Sliding Doors' moment, that seemingly inconsequential action, which actually became a turning point in their fortunes, for either good or bad?

Saturday 8th April, 2006. The dying seconds of injury time. Sheffield United, pegged back to 2-2 by Hull City after being 2-0 up, win a corner. The usual corner taker David Unsworth hasn't the energy or time to run out to take it. Following a header and a blocked shot the ball falls free, just yards out. As one, three sides of the ground lean forward in anticipation and anguish. Unsworth, the right man in the wrong place, slams the ball into the back of the net. Bedlam.

A win at Cardiff and defeat for Leeds the following weekend confirmed United's promotion to the Premiership. At the time Unsworth said: "I've never scored a more important goal." A view that was to change 12 months later.

He fell out of favour during the following season and was allowed to join Wigan Athletic on a free in January. Roll forward four months and following an inexplicable handball by Phil Jagielka, Unsworth slammed home the decisive penalty that was to condemn United to relegation back to the Championship on the final day of the season and save Wigan. In some ways he had a double role to play in United's relegation, having been one of two United players to have missed penalties in a 0-0 draw at home to Blackburn earlier in the season. United were relegated on goal difference. It felt like a loss on penalties.

SHEFFIELD WEDNESDAY STATS

NUMBER OF SEASONS:

8

1992/93 - 1999/2000

NUMBER OF MATCHES:

316

Wins 101 (Home 63 Away 38)
Draws 89 (Home 50 Away 39)
Losses 126 (Home 45 Away 81)

[Win ratio 32%]

Goals F 409
(Home 234 Away 175)

Goals A 453
(Home 187 Away 266)

Goal Difference: -44

TOTAL POINTS

392

(Home 239: 61%; Away 153: 39%)
Average per season: 49

BEST POSITION:

7th (3)

1992/93, 1993/94, 1996/97

WORST POSITION:

19th

1999/2000 (RELEGATED)

BIGGEST WIN:

5-0 (2)

v West Ham (18th Dec, 1993)
v Bolton (8th Nov, 1997)

BIGGEST LOSS:

8-0

v Newcastle
(19th Sept, 1999)

LONGEST UNBEATEN RUN:

12 matches

(19th Oct, 1996-11th Jan, 1997)

LONGEST WITHOUT A WIN:

9 matches (2)

(8th May, 1993-13th Sep, 1993;
7th Aug, 1999-25th Sep, 1999)

ALL TIME RANKING

23rd

MOST GOALS SCORED IN A SEASON:

76

(1993/94)

FEWEST GOALS SCORED IN A SEASON:

38

(1999/2000)

FEWEST GOALS CONCEDED IN A SEASON:

42

(1998/99)

MOST GOALS CONCEDED IN A SEASON:

70

(1999/2000)

TOP GOALSCORER:

48

Mark Bright

MOST APPEARANCES:

264

Des Walker

OWN GOALS:

7

RED CARDS:

19

LOWEST ATTENDANCE:

16,229

v Coventry
(4th Dec, 1995)

HIGHEST ATTENDANCE:

39,640

v Manchester United
(2nd Feb, 2000)

SHEFFIELD WEDNESDAY

FIRST PREMIER LEAGUE MATCH: 15TH AUGUST, 1992
EVERTON 1 (HORNE)
SHEFFIELD WEDNESDAY 1 (PEARSON)

GOODISON PARK 27,687

Chris Woods, Phil King, Roland Nilsson, Nigel Pearson, Paul Warhurst, Graham Hyde, Carlton Palmer, Chris Waddle (Chris Bart-Williams), Nigel Worthington, David Hirst (Gordon Watson), Paul Williams, Manager: Trevor Francis

After being promoted in 1990/91 Wednesday became an established top flight club throughout the next decade, only losing their place at the turn of the millennium. They finished 7th three times in the first seven seasons and were never seriously threatened by relegation until they went down in 1999/2000. They have yet to return, leading to their longest spell outside the top flight.

Seven is clearly the Owls' lucky number as they won seven on the trot between 28th December, 1992 and 23rd February, 1993, a feat not matched by too many clubs. Their overall win ratio of 32% is a testament to their generally positive record and by coincidence that is exactly the same ratio as their Steel City rivals, Sheffield United and ranks both in the top five of clubs who are no longer in the Premier League as of 2018/19 but the Blades did gain promotion and will have a chance to better the Owls in 2019/20.

Wednesday started their relegation season badly, only collecting one point from their first nine matches, which included an 8-0 humbling at St. James' Park. Alan Shearer bagged five goals, including a first-half hattrick, as Wednesday joined the sorry bunch of eight clubs who have conceded at least eight goals in a match.

The first two seasons are the only ones when both Sheffield clubs were in the Premier League. The first three meetings were typical tense, tight derby struggles and all ended in 1-1 draws. The fourth match saw Wednesday run out 3-1 winners at Hillsborough, a game in which they scored three goals in the space of 12 minutes to give them the Steel City bragging rights. Twenty five years on and there has been no repeat in the Premier League and there has not been a Sheffield club in the Premier League for a dozen years until United's promotion in 2019/20.

The game that most Wednesday fans will remember for differing reasons was in September 1998 when they entertained champions Arsenal who went into the game unbeaten. As a pretty mundane first half was meandering towards its close a flare-up between Patrick Vieira and Paolo Di Canio enlivened proceedings and when Martin Keown got involved Di Canio took exception and manhandled the Arsenal centre back. The referee Paul Alcock was left with little choice but to send off the Italian but Di Canio did not quite see it that way and gave Alcock a shove in his annoyance.

As Alcock lost his balance and went down in instalments, Di Canio waved his hand dismissively at the official before chuntering off down the tunnel. He subsequently picked up an 11-match ban for his troubles and was soon on his way to West Ham. From Rome to Glasgow, from Sheffield to London his career was laden with controversy and this was another in a long line of disciplinary flash points.

Few remember that Wednesday took all three points thanks to a last-minute strike and fewer still will recall the name of the man who scored goal. Lee Briscoe not only grabbed the winner but also his one and only goal for the Owls in 78 appearances. Undoubtedly to his eternal frustration, Briscoe's moment of fame was overshadowed by the furore created by the Di Canio-Alcock spat.

ONE HIT WONDER

For certain players who are associated with certain clubs it is often difficult to believe they played for any other club, especially when it is just a fleeting appearance. This is true of Nigel Clough who will always be thought of as a Forest player and then very much in a lesser way as representing Liverpool and latterly Manchester City. It was while Clough was at City that he went on loan to Sheffield Wednesday for a month in September 1997.

It seems slightly incongruous to imagine him playing in the blue and white stripes of Wednesday but on 24th September Clough did just that at Hillsborough against, of all teams, Derby County where his father forged his reputation as a manager. Despite going 2-1 up as early as the 12th minute, Wednesday lost 5-2 and Clough was substituted at half time, to be replaced by David Hirst. It is a pity that such a talented player's last ever Premier League appearance should end in such an underwhelming and anti-climatic fashion. At the end of that season he became player-manager at Burton Albion and went on to establish his managerial credentials over the next 11 years in charge of the Brewers. After spells at Derby and Sheffield United he returned to Burton in December 2015 and led them during 2018/19 season.

FOOTNOTE

As of 2018/19 the clubs who were not in
Premier League with the highest win ratio

CLUB	WIN RATIO
Leeds	40%
Blackburn	38%
Aston Villa	34%
Sheffield United	32%
Sheffield Wednesday	32%

A VIEW FROM THE STANDS

Alan Biggs

What was your club's 'Sliding Doors' moment, that seemingly inconsequential action, which actually became a turning point in their fortunes, for either good or bad?

It should be noted that Alan is not a Wednesday fan and was asked to contribute as an experienced journalist who has covered both Sheffield clubs and other clubs in the area for many years and so has consummate knowledge of the goings-on at many Yorkshire clubs, including Wednesday.

As sliding doors moments go, none was bigger than one that actually occurred just BEFORE Wednesday's near-decade in the top flight.

It happened just as they were sliding OUT of it in 1990. I was at a stunned Hillsborough for Radio 5 Live to report on a shock 3-0 home defeat to Nottingham Forest that combined with other results to down Ron Atkinson's side.

Big Ron, whose bright yellow tea shirt was in total contrast to the mood, rounded on his players afterwards by insisting all of them would stay to face the consequences.

It went beyond punishment because Atkinson knew relegation was a crime with the talent in that team - Hirst, Sheridan, Nilsson, Palmer, Wilson, Worthington etc. And virtually the same side roared back with an immediate promotion, not to mention winning the League Cup.

Indeed, it was that team, too—now under Trevor Francis after Atkinson was lured to Aston Villa—that competed strongly in the top division.

Come the Premier League, another huge moment with Francis's capture of one of England's top players. Unprompted, Francis announced to me for the Daily Express that summer of '92: "I want to sign Chris Waddle."

It was a bizarre and, by current standards, unthinkable tactic to use the media in that way. But, sure enough, Francis landed Waddle from Marseilles and Wednesday reached the final of both domestic cups in 1993.

The former Newcastle and Spurs winger took the Owls' profile and ambitions to another level. He was utterly brilliant, the peak of his career and, having kept his home in Sheffield, he enjoys rightful legendary status in the steel city. A living monument to better days.

Later, Waddle would be at the heart of a contentious set of circumstances that began Wednesday's spiral to relegation in 2000.

Francis was harshly sacked for finishing 13th in the Premier League in 1995. David Pleat was appointed to the thorny task of managing a dressing room of accomplished senior players whose best days were arguably behind them.

Whether Pleat tried to shake up that side too early is open to debate. But the sensitive nature of rebuilding a great team amid high expectations—and with outside investment needed to prop up the club's overstretched finances—was a cocktail for the sack.

So it proved and Pleat's demise brought back Atkinson for a successful mission to save the Owls from relegation. Big Ron was controversially dispatched afterwards ... and Wednesday's subsequent relegation meant that their spell in the elite ended almost back where it started.

SOUTHAMPTON STATS

NUMBER OF SEASONS:

20 (2 spells)

1992/93-2004/05, 2012/13-2018/19

NUMBER OF MATCHES:

772

Wins 238 (Home 158 Away 80)
Draws 214 (Home 111 Away 103)
Losses 320 (Home 117 Away 203)

[Win ratio 33%]

Goals F 937
(Home 556 Away 381)

Goals A 1087
(Home 458 Away 629)

Goal Difference: -150

TOTAL POINTS

928

(Home 585: 63%; Away 343: 37%)
Average per season: 46

BEST POSITION:

6th

2015/16

WORST POSITION:

20th

2004/05 (RELEGATED)

BIGGEST WIN:

8-0

v Sunderland
(18th Oct, 2014)

BIGGEST LOSS:

7-1

v Liverpool
(16th Jan, 1999)

LONGEST UNBEATEN RUN:

9 matches

(23rd Nov, 2002-11th Jan, 2003)

LONGEST WITHOUT A WIN:

12 matches (3)

(26th Dec, 1994-18th Mar, 1995;
29th Nov, 2017-31st Jan, 2018;
17th Sept, 2018-8th Dec, 2018)

ALL TIME RANKING

12th

MOST GOALS SCORED IN A SEASON:

61

(1994/95)

FEWEST GOALS SCORED IN A SEASON:

34

(1995/96)

FEWEST GOALS CONCEDED IN A SEASON:

33

(2014/15)

MOST GOALS CONCEDED IN A SEASON:

66 (2)

(1993/94 & 2004/05)

TOP GOALSCORER:

100

Matthew Le Tissier

MOST APPEARANCES:

329

Jason Dodd

OWN GOALS:

36

RED CARDS:

54

LOWEST ATTENDANCE:

9,028

v Ipswich Town
(8th Dec, 1993)

HIGHEST ATTENDANCE:

32,151

v Arsenal
(29th Dec, 2003)

All statistics and records supplied by  gracenote.
A NIELSEN COMPANY

SOUTHAMPTON

FIRST PREMIER LEAGUE MATCH: 15TH AUGUST, 1992
SOUTHAMPTON 0
TOTTENHAM HOTSPUR 0

THE DELL 19,654

Tim Flowers, Francis Benali, Micky Adams, Richard Hall, Jason Dodd, Steve Wood, Matthew Le Tissier, Glenn Cockerill, Terry Hurlock, David Speedie, Kerry Dixon, Manager: Ian Branfoot

Southampton have become the opening match draw specialists with 50% of their 20 games ending in draws—the second highest proportion of any club with at least 10 seasons in the Premier League behind Leeds who drew seven of their 12. Of those 10 games five have ended goalless which is the most of any club, curiously all those 0-0s have been when playing at home.

Claus Lundekvam racked up the second most appearances for the Saints with 290 matches over nine seasons between 1996/97 when he joined the club and 2004/05 when they were relegated. The Norwegian centre back only managed to score one goal in that but it was a landmark one. It came in his 250th game, making him the outfield player with the most appearances before scoring.

On 3rd April, 2004 he made the breakthrough in an emphatic 4-1 win away at Wolves, then managed by former Saints boss, Dave Jones. "It was fantastic to score after seven or eight years," Lundekvam told Norwegain television. "It felt like a shock. I have waited for this and it was wonderful that it happened today. The goal was a tap-in from short-range, after a free kick from [David] Prutton. There has been a bit of stick about this, but I haven't been bothered after all not to score—that is my job. I'm a man for the big occasions, this was my 250th league game for Southampton."

Unfortunately for Lundekvam the following season ended in relegation so his last Premier League game was in the 2-1 defeat to Manchester United that consigned Southampton to their only relegation from the Premier League, in 2005. Southampton finished bottom of the pile although he did stay on to play for them in the Championship, but had to retire following a serious ankle injury. Four years later they were wallowing in League One for a couple of seasons before climbing back up to the Premier League in 2012/13.

When Ralph Hasenhuttl took over the reigns at St. Mary's in December 2018 he became their 18th permanent manager during their 20 Premier League seasons, which is quite a turnover even in the hiring/firing frenzy that is the Premier League. Alongside the nine Englishmen, there have been three Scots, two Argentinians, and one each from the Netherlands, France, Wales and Austria.

ONE HIT WONDER

There is only one Ali Dia, which for Graeme Souness and all those associated with Southampton at the time is probably just as well. His solitary appearance against Leeds is probably the most (in)famous of all One Hit Wonders, not just in the Premier League but in all of world football. It seems incredible that somebody managed to persuade Souness, who does not appear to be the sort of person easily hoodwinked, into believing Dia was a cousin of then FIFA World Player of the Year George Weah, or that he had represented Senegal a dozen times and been at Paris St. Germain in the dim, distant past.

And so it was that Dia replaced Southampton legend Matt Le Tissier in the 32nd minute of the game against Leeds on 23rd November, 1996. It quickly became apparent that Dia was not quite who he claimed to be and was in fact a charlatan. It was no doubt through incredulity that he was allowed to stay on the pitch so long until eventually being replaced by Kenneth Monkou in the 85th minute. To have lasted over 50 minutes was an achievement in itself as Le Tissier who had watched him train prior to the match commented: "He joined us in the five-a-side on the Friday morning, and was introduced as a triallist. I remember at the time thinking: 'He's not very good. He's probably not going to make it'."

Incredibly Dia was presented with a golden chance to score and make a name for himself with his first touch of the ball. But he fluffed the opportunity and ultimately Le Tissier's intuition was spot. "He ran around like Bambi on ice," Le Tissier said. "It was very, very embarrassing to watch. We were like: 'What's this geezer doing? He's hopeless.' Graeme named him as sub and we couldn't believe it. I got injured after 20 minutes and when I saw him warming up, I'm going: 'Surely not?' Graeme put him on and he was fucking hopeless, so he took him off again. It was crazy." Le Tissier recalls "The mood was pretty sombre in the dressing-room afterwards, so we didn't really discuss him then." Oh to be a fly on the wall of that dressing room when Souness eventually got hold of him.

After that truncated Premier League debut Dia left Southampton a week later with his contract torn into shreds (by an enraged Souness perhaps) and made the seamless switch to the Football Conference with Gateshead, having previously been at near-neighbours Blyth Spartans of the Northern Premier League prior to his brief dalliance with the top flight. At least Dia proved his worth to Gateshead when he scored on his debut but even that illusory moment of fame was curtailed after just eight matches. Just as he had arrived he then disappeared off the radar and after reluctantly turning his back on his football career he graduated with an MBA from San Francisco State University in 2003 before pursuing a career in business in Qatar.

FOOTNOTE

THE LONG AND SHORT OF IT

Shane Long continued a rich vein of form when he scored his third goal in four matches on 23rd April, 2019 at Vicarage Road but the wider significance of the goal was that it took just over seven seconds for the Irish striker to break the deadlock and he entered the record books for the fastest Premier League goal. The previous holder of the record Ledley King scored the very first Premier League goal under 10 seconds back in December 2000 against Bradford. Curiously Long's record-breaking goal came from a Watford kick-off.

FASTEST PREMIER LEAGUE GOALS

TIME (SECS)	PLAYER	MATCH	SEASON
07.69	Shane Long	Watford v Southampton	2018/19
09.82	Ledley King	Bradford v Tottenham	2000/01
10.52	Alan Shearer	Newcastle v Man City	2002/03
10.54	Christian Eriksen	Tottenham v Man Utd	2017/18
11.90	Mark Viduka	Charlton v Leeds	2000/01

A VIEW FROM THE STANDS

Alex Stewart

What was your club's 'Sliding Doors' moment, that seemingly inconsequential action, which actually became a turning point in their fortunes, for either good or bad?

Southampton have had their fair share of sliding doors moments in the last 15 or so years, mostly involving the boardroom. But when Brett Ormerod's shot was saved on the final day of the 2004/05 season, and Ruud van Nistelrooy scored shortly afterwards, a 1-2 defeat condemned us to relegation from the top flight for the first time in 27 years.

Southampton needed to win the final fixture to stay up. If Ormerod, contentiously picked over Kevin Phillips by Harry Redknapp, had scored at 1-1, relegation would have been avoided if we'd held on, even with West Brom's victory over Portsmouth. Van Nistelrooy's header made it 2-1 shortly afterwards and there was no way back.

But without relegation, we would also likely have avoided the ructions that saw constant flux behind the scenes in the boardroom—the financial impact of relegation and mismanagement left the club in serious, and potentially, irreparable straits. Administration and another relegation was the beginning of rebirth, with Marcus Liebherr taking over the club, before Alan Pardew, then Nigel Adkins, steered us back to the Premier League.

Ormerod's saved shot, and van Nistelrooy's goal, effectively began the process that stopped a merry-go-round of bad managerial appointments, iffy signings, and boardroom complacency. Who's to say where we would have been if we'd stayed up? Harry might have stayed. We could have had a Jamie Redknapp/Graeme Le Saux Indian summer and won something.

My sneaking suspicion is, though, that without that Ormerod miss, we would have just deferred crisis and resurrection, perhaps without the good bit.

STOKE CITY STATS

NUMBER OF SEASONS:

10

2008/09-2017/18

NUMBER OF MATCHES:

380

Wins 116 (Home 81 Away 35)
Draws 109 (Home 54 Away 55)
Losses 155 (Home 55 Away 100)

[Win ratio 30%]

Goals F 398
(Home 248 Away 150)

Goals A 525
(Home 213 Away 312)

Goal Difference: -127

TOTAL POINTS

457

(Home 297: 65%; Away 160: 35%)
Average per season: 46

BEST POSITION:

9th (3)

2013/14, 2014/15, 2015/16

WORST POSITION:

19th

2017/18 (RELEGATED)

BIGGEST WIN:

6-1

v Liverpool
(24th May, 2015)

BIGGEST LOSS:

7-0

v Chelsea
(25th Apr, 2010)

LONGEST UNBEATEN RUN:

10 matches

(10th Nov, 2012-29th Dec, 2012)

LONGEST WITHOUT A WIN:

13 matches

(31st Jan, 2018-5th May, 2018)

ALL TIME RANKING

20th

MOST GOALS SCORED IN A SEASON:

48

(2014/15)

FEWEST GOALS SCORED IN A SEASON:

34 (2)

(2009/10, 2012/13)

FEWEST GOALS CONCEDED IN A SEASON:

45 (2)

(2012/13, 2014/15)

MOST GOALS CONCEDED IN A SEASON:

68

(2017/18)

TOP GOALSCORER:

45

Peter Crouch

MOST APPEARANCES:

317

Ryan Shawcross

OWN GOALS:

20

RED CARDS:

31

LOWEST ATTENDANCE:

22,690

v West Ham
(2nd Mar, 2013)

HIGHEST ATTENDANCE:

30,022

v Everton
(17th Mar, 2018)

STOKE CITY

FIRST PREMIER LEAGUE MATCH: 16TH AUGUST, 2008
BOLTON WANDERERS 3 (STEINSSON, DAVIES, ELMANDER)
STOKE CITY 1 (FULLER)

MACRON STADIUM 22,717

*Thomas Sorensen, Andy Griffin, Andy Wilkinson (Carl Dickinson),
Leon Cort, Ryan Shawcross, Seyi Olofinjana,
Glenn Whelan (Liam Lawrence), Richard Cresswell, Rory Delap,
Mamady Sidibe (Ricardo Fuller), Dave Kitson, Manager: Tony Pulis*

In the season in which they were relegated, their goal difference of -33 matched their points tally providing some quirky as well as unique statistical symmetry, the only occasion that this has happened. Pulisball was middling in many ways.

Ryan Shawcross probably symbolises everything about Stoke. He played in their first Premier League game in 2008 and their last in 2018. In the intervening 10 years he racked up more than 300 appearances playing in 83% of Stoke's matches which is amongst the highest percentages for any player of a club with a minimum of seven seasons in the Premier League. For the majority of those games he was captain, having been appointed skipper in 2010.

Stoke may not have been the most talented or attractive side during their ten-year tenure in the Premier League but, as mentioned above, for sheer consistency they have very few rivals. After Aston Villa (24) and Leeds (12), Stoke have the third longest spell in the Premier League of a club to subsequently be relegated. Apart from their relegation in 2017/18 they finished no lower than 14th and no higher than 9th (which they achieved three times in a row under Mark Hughes), with the highest tally of points 54 and the lowest 42, so they became the epitome of solid, mid-table respectability.

Tony Pulis gorged himself on such comforts and forged a reputation for the ultimate in effective football. He became a firm favourite amongst the Potters fans for his sheer, curmudgeonly determination to not be moved by anyone from his target of securing another season at the top table, which he did successfully until his departure in 2013. Indeed they became such a tough nut to crack that the acid test of a team's or an individual player's endurance was whether they could do it on a rainy Tuesday night in Stoke. Pulis would have regarded that as the highest of compliments and rejoiced in such a reputation.

Expansive football was not high on the agenda, in six out of their ten seasons their biggest winning margin was by two goals and the greatest margin of victory was 4-0 against Newcastle in 2010/11. Indeed in a total of 322 matches as a Premier League manager, including spells at Crystal Palace and West Brom, 4-0 was Pulis' biggest win, which he also achieved with the Baggies against Burnley in 2016/17. Under Pulis Stoke were not blessed with prolific marksmen, with the most goals scored by an individual in a single season being 11, which was achieved by Ricardo Fuller (2008/09), Mame Diuof (2014/15) and Marko Arnautovic (2015/16). Their all-time leading goalscorer, the recently retired, Peter Crouch was top scorer in three separate seasons—2011/12, 2013/14 and 2016/17—a rare feat, which puts Crouch amongst the Premier League's sharpest shooters including Alan Shearer, who not only was Blackburn's top scorer four times in a row, he also was Newcastle's for ten consecutive seasons; Ian Wright who was Arsenal's leading marksman for the first five seasons of the Premier League and Thierry Henry, who surpassed Wright's record by racking up seven on the trot, as has Sergio Aguero who was Manchester City's highest scorer for the seventh successive time last season.

One performance that stands out as it was strangely both typical as well as being out of the ordinary was on the last day of the 2014/15 season. Stoke had a curious record in their final matches of the season as their comprehensive victory over Liverpool was one of five consecutive wins, having lost their first three and drawing the next two. It was Steven Gerrard's farewell appearance after more than 500 games for Liverpool and Stoke did allow him the pleasure of scoring in his last match. But their generosity did not extend much beyond that as The Potters recorded the biggest win of their 380 Premier League matches by thrashing the visitors 6-1. It was only the third time in their ten Premier League seasons that they had scored more than three goals. In typically unsentimental fashion they raced into a 5-0 lead before half-time and after affording Gerrard that one valedictory moment his former teammate Peter Crouch added the sixth, thus completing a thoroughly miserable day for the Liverpool captain who could not even do it on a sunny Sunday afternoon in Stoke.

ONE HIT WONDER

Oliver Shenton joined the Stoke academy in 2004 at the age of seven. He has been on the verge of the first team squad and came on in added time for Stephen Nzonzi during the 4-1 home defeat to Manchester City in February 2015. Since that fleeting glimpse of first team action he was loaned out to Wrexham.

Shenton is contracted to Stoke until the summer of 2020.

FOOTNOTE

Stoke's reputation as a hard nut to crack is not really borne out by the number of red cards they received: 31 in 10 seasons, which is the same as West Brom, where Pulis was in charge briefly. Out of the 20 teams to have scored the most Premier League points, Stoke's average of 3.1 red cards per season is only the eighth highest while at 3.3 their bête noire Arsenal have a higher average. Blackburn are the black sheep of the family, the only club averaging more than 4 red cards per season.

Of all-time top 20 clubs the ten with most red cards per season.

CLUB	RED CARDS	AVG PER SEASON
Blackburn	77	4.3
Sunderland	62	3.9
Leicester	47	3.6
Bolton	44	3.4
Everton	93	3.4
Newcastle	82	3.4
Arsenal	88	3.3
Stoke	31	3.1
West Ham	31	3.1
Middlesbrough	45	3.0

A VIEW FROM THE STAND

Mark Holmes, Planet Football

What was your club's 'Sliding Doors' moment, that seemingly inconsequential action, which actually became a turning point in their fortunes, for either good or bad?

On paper, the 2015-16 season was a good one for Stoke. It was the third in a row in which they finished ninth in the Premier League, and in January 2016 they came within a penalty kick of making the League Cup final.

But that night at Anfield was also the night the wheels came loose before eventually falling off altogether as Stoke skidded back into the Championship a couple of years later. And the club have Liverpool's Joe Allen to blame.

Nine days before that League Cup semi-final second leg at Liverpool, Stoke had drawn 0-0 with Arsenal and were seventh in the Premier League, just a couple of wins off the top four, with 22 games gone. A few weeks later they would break their transfer record to sign Giannelli Imbula. It looked like a club on the up.

But in the meantime, little did he know, Allen had already pulled the brake on the club he would go on to join that summer. All by scoring a penalty.

Stoke had lost the home leg of the League Cup semi but were the better team at Anfield, won in normal time, agonisingly hit the post in extra-time, then lost 5-4 on penalties in front of the away fans, with Allen scoring the decisive spot-kick.

The Potters lost their next two league games 3-0, suffered even bigger hidings at the hands of Spurs and Manchester City, and won just three of their final 15 games as a crisis began which Hughes was ultimately never able to stop.

And it's all because of Joe Allen.

SUNDERLAND STATS

NUMBER OF SEASONS:

16 (4 spells)

1996/97, 1999/2000-2002/03,
2005/06, 2007/08-2016/17

TOTAL POINTS

618

(Home 381: 62%; Away 237: 38%)
Average per season: 39

NUMBER OF MATCHES:

608

Wins 153 (Home 98 Away 55)
Draws 159 (Home 87 Away 72)
Losses 296 (Home 119 Away 177)

[Win ratio 25%]

Goals F 612
(Home 336 Away 276)

Goals A 904
(Home 371 Away 533)

Goal Difference: -292

BEST POSITION:

7th (2)

1999/2000, 2000/01

WORST POSITION:

20th (2)

2002/03, 2005/06, 2016/17
(RELEGATED)

BIGGEST WIN:

0-5

v Derby
(18th Sept, 1999)

BIGGEST LOSS:

8-0

v Southampton
(18th Oct, 2014)

LONGEST UNBEATEN RUN:

10 matches

(25th Aug, 1999-6th Nov, 1999)

LONGEST WITHOUT A WIN:

26 matches

(21st Dec, 2002-17th Sept, 2005)

ALL TIME RANKING

15th

MOST GOALS SCORED IN A SEASON:

57

(1999/2000)

FEWEST GOALS SCORED IN A SEASON:

21

(2002/03)

FEWEST GOALS CONCEDED IN A SEASON:

41

(2000/01)

MOST GOALS CONCEDED IN A SEASON:

69 (2)

(2005/05 & 2016/17)

TOP GOALSCORER:

61

Kevin Phillips

MOST APPEARANCES:

189

John O'Shea

OWN GOALS:

39

RED CARDS:

62

LOWEST ATTENDANCE:

18,581

v West Ham
(8th Sept, 1996)

HIGHEST ATTENDANCE:

48,355

v Liverpool
(13th Apr, 2002)

SUNDERLAND

FIRST PREMIER LEAGUE MATCH: 17TH AUGUST, 1996
SUNDERLAND 0
LEICESTER CITY 0

ROKER PARK 19,262

Tony Coton, Dariusz Kubicki, Michael Gray (Sam Aiston), Richard Ord, Andy Melville, Martin Scott, Steve Agnew (Michael Bridges), Paul Bracewell, Kevin Ball, David Kelly (Niall Quinn), Paul Stewart, Manager: Peter Reid

Sunderland have averaged almost exactly a goal per game with 612 in 608 matches and they boast the last English player to score 30 goals in a Premier League season when Kevin Phillips did so in 1999/2000, scoring over half the team's 57 goals and claiming the top scorer spot to boot. This was only the second occasion that the outright top scorer came from a club outside the top six. Sunderland finished 7th that season and the other player to achieve the feat was Teddy Sheringham in the very first Premier League season when he played one game for Forest before switching to Tottenham, who finished 8th.

Phillips went on to top the scoring charts for the club in four successive seasons, a feat only surpassed by five other players. Arsenal's Thierry Henry did it seven times between 1999/2000 and 2005/06 as did Liverpool's Michael Owen who did it between 1997/98 and 2003/04. Matthew Le Tissier did it on six occasions from 1992/93 to 1997/98 while Spurs' Harry Kane and Manchester City's Sergio Aguero both completed their fifth successive top scoring season for their clubs in 2018/19.

However Sunderland's defensive frailties are plain to see as their record of conceding 904 goals has given them that worst overall goal difference of -292. West Brom are the nearest club to them with a goal difference of -221. Sunderland also share the ignominy of holding the record for the most red cards in a single season, along with QPR, when they received nine in the 2009/10 season. Perennial offender Lee Cattermole averaged one dismissal per season racking up eight, which was a couple more than the number of goals he managed.

Sunderland are one of five clubs to have been relegated four times along with Crystal Palace, Middlesbrough, Norwich and West Brom and on three of those occasions they have finished bottom, which has only happened to one other club, Nottingham Forest. When finishing bottom they have recorded three of the lowest points totals and they are also the only club to have recorded less than 20 points twice. In 2002/03 they accrued 19 and in 2005/06 they only scraped 15 points, the second worst tally of any team. Derby, Portsmouth, Aston Villa and Huddersfield are the only other clubs to have finished with fewer than 20 points, but have done so just the once (although Portsmouth would have finished with 28 points had it not been for a nine-point deduction due to financial irregularities). For good measure, or maybe that should be bad, the Black Cats also have the ninth worst total when amassing 24 points in the 2016/17 season. So with three entries in the bottom ten Sunderland can be considered to be the lowest of the lowest points achievers.

Their meagre total of 23 goals in 2005/06 was four fewer than Thierry Henry managed on his own that season and seven fewer than Phillips' tally six years earlier. Four players top scored for them that season but with just three goals apiece they were the lowest top scorers of all time. The famous four were Liam Lawrence, Anthony Le Tallec, Tommy Miller and Dean Whitehead. Even the Derby team of 2007/08 rustled together a striker with four goals in the shape of Kenny Miller. Mind you, Sunderland even managed to outdo themselves by scoring only 21 in 2002/03.

That season ended in a horrific run after mid-December of 20 games without a win. It included just two draws and they lost their last 15 matches, which is the worst run of successive losses in the Premier League. Unsurprisingly they never left the relegation zone after Christmas. They also managed to record the lowest points tally at home with just seven points from one win and four draws sprinkled alongside the 14 losses—the most defeats on home turf in a 38-game season.

In their last spell between 2007/08 to 2016/17 they were notoriously bad starters and did not win a match in August for the six seasons before their relegation in 2017. Their record in August over this period was played 17, drew nine and lost eight. September was marginally better with two victories, six draws and 11 losses. Their last Premier League victory in August was at the Stadium of Light against Manchester City on 29th August, 2010.

If their starts to the season were poor then they did not exactly finish with a flourish either, as they have the worst record in final day fixtures of any club with a minimum of two seasons. They won just once in 16 games, losing 12 and drawing three, so picking up just six points out of a possible 48 at an average of 0.375 points per game. Their solitary win was a surprisingly comfortable one as they beat West Ham 3-0 away in May 2011.

They became the eighth club to concede at least eight goals in a match and their humiliating 8-0 defeat to Southampton in October 2014 was compounded by scoring a hat-trick of own goals from Santiago Vergini, Liam Bridcutt and Patrick van Aanholt. No other club has managed that spectacularly awful hat-trick. Gus Poyet was nonplussed by the performance: "I can't explain what happened," their Uruguyan manager said. "I will let the players explain to you, maybe they will have better words. I don't." Exit stage right, Poyet.

ONE HIT WONDER

The brief Premier League career of Stern John as a Sunderland player is worthy of mention. His only appearance came against one of his former clubs, Birmingham City when he came on as a substitute and snatched a last-minute equaliser at St. Andrew's. The then manager Roy Keane claimed that he knew he would make his mark after seeing a picture of John scoring a goal for Birmingham on the wall of the players tunnel before the match. Within a week of this important strike, John was on his way to Championship side Southampton as part of a swap deal for Kenwyne Jones. Maybe Keane had a premonition that John would not be repeating his late heroics any time soon. At least John is part of the select bunch of players who scored on their one appearance for their club.

FOOTNOTE

TEAMS WITH LOWEST POINTS TOTAL

POINTS	TEAM	SEASON
11	Derby	2007/08
15	Sunderland	2005/06
16	Huddersfield	2018/19
17	Aston Villa	2015/16
19	Sunderland	2002/03
19	Portsmouth	2009/10 (9 points deducted)
24	Watford	1999/2000
24	Sunderland	2016/17
25	Wolves	2011/12
25	QPR	2012/13

A VIEW FROM THE STANDS

David Preece

What was the club's 'Sliding Doors' moment, that seemingly inconsequential action, which actually became a turning point in their fortunes, for either good or bad?

There's one thing supporting the football club of the city you grew up in all your young life. It's another being sat in the dressing room of that said club to witness it change in an instant before your eyes.

From the very moment Peter Reid walked through the door at Roker Park, Sunderland Football Club just wasn't the same. In with him came a shift of mentality. Here was a club that was no longer the powerhouse it had been decades previously. Brief flirtations with the old First Division aside, Sunderland were a second-tier club with a second-tier mentality.

Two crates of lager were placed in the centre of the floor and everyone was instructed to take one. From then on, it was a one-man show, the new gaffer telling us that the current league position that placed us perilously close to relegation was temporary and we would get out of trouble in the seven games that remained. Everyone believed him and we eventually did. His confidence and authority permeated the room. Things were different now.

The very next season he took us up to the Premier League as champions. Relegation after just one season followed but it laid the foundations for a fast return and successive seventh-place finishes in the top flight. Moving to the Stadium of Light may have contributed to the club entering the big league, but without Peter Reid it simply would not have happened.

SWANSEA CITY STATS

NUMBER OF SEASONS:

7

2011/12-2017/18

NUMBER OF MATCHES:

266

Wins 82 (Home 51 Away 31)
Draws 66 (Home 37 Away 29)
Losses 118 (Home 45 Away 73)

[Win ratio 31%]

Goals F 306
(Home 179 Away 127)

Goals A 383
(Home 170 Away 213)

Goal Difference: -77

TOTAL POINTS

312

Home 190: 61%; Away 122: 39%)
Average per season: 45

BEST POSITION:

8th

2014/15

WORST POSITION:

18th

2017/18 (RELEGATED)

BIGGEST WIN:

0-5

v QPR
(18th Aug, 2012)

BIGGEST LOSS:

5-0 (4)

v Liverpool (17th Feb, 2013);
v Chelsea (17th Jan, 2015);
v Tottenham (3rd Dec, 2016);
v Liverpool (26th Dec, 2017)

LONGEST UNBEATEN RUN:

7 matches

(23rd Dec, 2012-29th Jan, 2013)

LONGEST WITHOUT A WIN:

11 matches

(20th Aug, 2016-19th Nov, 2016)

ALL TIME RANKING

28th

MOST GOALS SCORED IN A SEASON:
54
(2013/14)

FEWEST GOALS SCORED IN A SEASON:
28
(2017/18)

FEWEST GOALS CONCEDED IN A SEASON:
49
(2014/15)

MOST GOALS CONCEDED IN A SEASON:
70
(2016/17)

TOP GOALSCORER:
34
Gylfi Sigurdsson

MOST APPEARANCES:
198
Wayne Routledge

OWN GOALS:
17

RED CARDS:
14

LOWEST ATTENDANCE:
18,985
v Blackburn
(14th Apr, 2012)

HIGHEST ATTENDANCE:
20,972
v Liverpool
(1st May, 2016)

All statistics and records supplied by

SWANSEA CITY

FIRST PREMIER LEAGUE MATCH: 15TH AUGUST, 2011
MANCHESTER CITY 4 (DZEKO, AGUERO 2, SILVA)
SWANSEA CITY 0

ETIHAD STADIUM, 46,802

Michel Vorm, Angel Rangel, Steven Caulker , Ashley Williams, Alan Tate, Leon Britton (Joe Allen), Stephen Dobbie (Wayne Routledge), Kemy Agustien, Nathan Dyer (Leroy Lita), Danny Graham , Scott Sinclair, Manager: Brendan Rodgers

Swansea's arrival on the Premier League scene in 2011 felt like a breath of fresh air. It was not just because they were the first Welsh club to do so but because they did so with a dash of style and élan that very few newly promoted clubs attempt and even fewer achieve. This progressive brand of football that endeared them to the neutral had proved remarkably successful in their rise to the Premier League under Roberto Martinez, Paulo Sousa and was then continued in the top flight by Brendan Rodgers, Michael Laudrup and Garry Monk.

The alacrity of Swansea's remarkable rise up the divisions was akin to that of Wimbledon in the 1980s. In less than a decade the Swans had recovered from the nadir of the early 2000s, when the club teetered on the brink of losing their Football League status. They finished 20th in the lowest tier in 2001/02 and the next season were even closer to the Conference when they were 21st. Going into the last two games the Swans were in the relegation zone but a precious win at Rochdale followed by a 4-2 victory at home over Hull in the biggest game of their 91-year history saved their skin.

As well as being the first Welsh club to compete in the Premier League they also became the most westerly club to do so. And for those who are fond of their geography the other compass points are covered thus: the most northerly club are Newcastle, the most easterly are Norwich and the most southerly are Bournemouth.

Despite an initially sticky start, which saw The Swans thumped 4-0 on their debut by an Aguero-inspired Manchester City (their heaviest defeat of the season) and fail to score until their fifth match, there was no sense of panic. After those tentative beginnings, they soon adjusted to life at the higher level to the extent that not only did they survive but finished a creditable 11th. They consolidated in the following four seasons and began to look like an established Premier League side with comfortable mid-table finishes. With an average of 10th place, over those first five years, the Swans have the second best combined period of consolidation by any club promoted via the play-offs after Blackburn's barnstorming start to life in the Premier League between 1992/93 and 1996/97. They were like ducks, or even swans, to water.

They made a virtue of their ownership model by becoming the first Premier League club to appoint an elected supporter, Huw Cooze, as a director on to the board and the close relationship with the supporters trust was widely lauded. Swansea were acclaimed by many as the perfect model and that progressive attitude remained until the summer of 2016 when chairman Huw Jenkins and other shareholders sold part of their stakes to a couple of American investors. Having bought a majority stake in the club Jason Levien and Steve Kaplan did not continue in the same vein and they soon came to represent the worst type of absentee landlords by rarely leaving the States and ruling from afar. In the process they alienated the vast majority of the supporters and they got their comeuppance in 2017/18 when Swansea were relegated. The Swansea Way had ended up in a cul-de-sac.

Their appointment of former USA national boss Bob Bradley in 2016 was an unmitigated disaster as he lasted a mere 84 days at the Liberty Stadium with a record of two wins, two draws and seven defeats. Although one of those rare wins was an extraordinary 5-4 against Crystal Palace when a relatively mundane game exploded into life in the second half. After a quickfire Leroy For double put Swansea 3-1 up with just over

20 minutes to go, they then conceded three goals in under ten minutes. Enter Fernando Llorente who came on as substitute and scored twice in added time to leave everyone speechless. It was a game that was littered with as many mistakes as there was entertainment. Within a month both Bradley and Palace manager Pardew had departed and Bradley took his place among the five shortest managerial reigns (see Footnote).

Relegation in 2018 was a painful, bitter end to the club's most successful period, when seven consecutive seasons of top-flight football came juddering to a halt. The sense of loss was exacerbated by Cardiff's unlikely promotion from the Championship as they replaced their Welsh counterparts. If one player sums up Swansea's plight that season it was one who arrived in a blaze of glory but left with his tail firmly tucked between his legs. Step forwards or maybe more aptly backwards, Renato Sanches. When the young Portuguese midfielder moved on loan from Bayern Munich to Swansea in 2017 many an eyebrow was raised at the audacity of the bid. Expectation at the Liberty soared as one of the stars of Portugal's Euro 2016 winning team would choose to move to South Wales from the Bundesliga champions for a season. Many Swans fans waited to see him prove himself to be the transfer coup of the season for Paul Clement, who had replaced Bradley.

Unfortunately for both the Swans and Sanches the anticipated heights were not reached and he was branded a dismal flop as he failed to make his mark, both literally and metaphorically. The tragic-comedy of his time in South Wales was exemplified when he was playing away at Stamford Bridge on 29th November, 2017 when under no pressure he inexplicably passed the ball out of play nowhere near a colleague. He may have been confused by the red logo of an advertising hoarding that may have looked like Swansea's away strip but that is being generous. His manager certainly wasn't when substituting the sorry Sanches at half-time. Sky Sports' Adam Bate did not hold back either with this tweet: "Renato Sanches has just served up one of the worst individual performances I have seen this season. If Paul Clement's body language is any clue, he feels the same way."

The only high point for Sanches was in his choice of shirt number when he selected the one he used to wear at his first club, Benfica. The number 85 would have given him the record over Manchester City's Jose Pozo for highest Premier League shirt number had it not been for the Premier League insisting on sticking to rules that do not allow any non-consecutive numbers so Sanches was forced to settle for the slightly more prosaic No. 35 that he had worn at Bayern. Even the club voiced its disapproval of these draconian measures and jokingly tweeted "We're still going ahead with the transfer!" However, by the end of the season the joke was most certainly on them as they were relegated and Sanches returned to Germany, a sorry and ridiculed figure.

ONE HIT WONDERS

Kenji Gorre became the second player from the small Caribbean island of Curacao to play in the Premier League, after his team mate Kemy Agustien who played in Swansea's very first Premier League game in 2011. Gorre played the last six minutes of the final match of the 2014/15 season at Selhurst Park, having joined Swansea in 2013 and after a couple of loan spells at Den Haag and Northampton Town, he left the club in 2018 to join Portuguese side Nacional.

In 2019 Gorre went out on loan to another Portuguese club, Estoril.

FOOTNOTE

SHORTEST MANAGERIAL REIGNS

#	NAME	CLUB	DAYS/MATCHES
5.	Terry Connor	Wolves	91 days - 13 matches (All PL)
4.	Bob Bradley	Swansea	84 days - 11 matches (All PL)
3.	Frank de Boer	Crystal Palace	77 days - 4 matches (All PL)
2.	Rene Meulensteen	Fulham	75 days - 17 matches (13 PL)
1.	Les Reed	Charlton	40 days - 8 matches (7 PL)

A VIEW FROM THE STANDS

Stuart James, The Athletic

What was your club's 'Sliding Doors' moment, that seemingly inconsequential action, which actually became a turning point in their fortunes, for either good or bad?

In the end, everything comes back to the summer of 2016. The club was at a crossroads and Swansea took every wrong turn possible. The calamitous takeover that was ratified in the July of that year, when Steve Kaplan and Jason Levien bought a controlling stake in the Welsh club, sowed the seeds for the self-inflicted relegation that would follow less than two years later. Kaplan and Levien were nowhere to be seen when that day came and, in many ways, that has been the story of their tenure. Detached and disengaged, the pair talked a good game but delivered on none of their promises. "We will be relentless in our determination to continually improve this club—and we have the financial resources to do so," they said on the eve of their first home game. "We will be competitive and we will outwork our opponents on the pitch and in the boardroom."

Yet there was something else that happened shortly before the takeover that could possibly have saved Swansea, even with Kaplan and Levien at the helm. Brendan Rodgers was out of work after being sacked by Liverpool, the club he left Swansea to join in 2012, and ready to come back to the Liberty Stadium after holding talks with Huw Jenkins, the chairman. Jenkins, however, made the disastrous decision to give the job to Francesco Guidolin, the Italian who had taken charge during the second half of the 2015-16 season and steered the club away from relegation. Guidolin was the first Premier League manager sacked the following season and was replaced with Bob Bradley. Swansea were in a cycle of hire and fire from which they never recovered. They were playing "survival football" too and making mistake after mistake in the transfer market. Appointing Rodgers would have prevented all of that. Eighteen months later, Jenkins more or less admitted as much. "My biggest regret is not getting Brendan back here at any cost," he said. "I'm not going to hide from that. And I told [Brendan] as well a few times."

SWINDON TOWN STATS

NUMBER OF SEASONS:

1

1993/94

TOTAL POINTS

30

(Home 19: 63%; Away 11: 37%)
Average per season: 30

NUMBER OF MATCHES:

42

Wins 5 (Home 4 Away 1)
Draws 15 (Home 7 Away 8)
Losses 22 (Home 10 Away 12)

[Win ratio 12%]

Goals F 47
(Home 25 Away 22)

Goals A 100
(Home 45 Away 55)

Goal Difference: -53

BEST POSITION:

22nd

1993/94 (RELEGATED)

WORST POSITION:

22nd

1993/94 (RELEGATED)

BIGGEST WIN:

3-1

v Coventry
(5th Feb, 1994)

BIGGEST LOSS:

7-1

v Newcastle
(12th Mar, 1994)

LONGEST UNBEATEN RUN:

2 matches (5)

(11th Sep, 1993-18th Sep, 1993;
16th Oct, 1993-23rd Oct, 1993;
20th Nov, 1993-24th Nov, 1993;
11th Dec, 1993-18th Dec, 1993;
22nd Jan, 1994-5th Feb, 1994)

LONGEST WITHOUT A WIN:

15 matches

(14th Aug, 1993-20th Nov, 1993)

ALL TIME RANKING

28th

MOST GOALS SCORED IN A SEASON:

47

(1993/94)

FEWEST GOALS SCORED IN A SEASON:

47

(1993/94)

FEWEST GOALS CONCEDED IN A SEASON:

100

(1993/94)

MOST GOALS CONCEDED IN A SEASON:

100

(1993/94)

TOP GOALSCORER:

12

Jan Age Fjortoft

MOST APPEARANCES:

42

Shaun Taylor

OWN GOALS:

1

RED CARDS:

1

LOWEST ATTENDANCE:

11,940

v Oldham Athletic
(18th August, 1993)

HIGHEST ATTENDANCE:

18,102

v Manchester United
(19th March, 1994)

All statistics and records supplied by

SWINDON TOWN

DID YOU KNOW?

Swindon's solitary venture into the uplands of top-flight football was one that was littered with unwelcome records. Having won the Division Two play-off Final in 1990 they were denied that long-awaited promotion when the Football League punished them for financial irregularities. Three years later under Glenn Hoddle, Swindon won the play-off final again in a seven-goal thriller against Leicester. However, this achievement was not enough for Hoddle to resist the allure of managing Chelsea and John Gorman was thrust into the vacant manager's hot seat. The nature of that promotion-securing victory at Wembley set a precedent for Swindon's spectacular season where goals flowed and records tumbled.

FIRST PREMIER LEAGUE MATCH: 14TH AUGUST, 1993
**SHEFFIELD UNITED 3 (FALCONER, BRADSHAW, ROGERS)
SWINDON 1 (MONCUR)**

BRAMALL LANE 20,904

*Fraser Digby, Shaun Taylor, Adrian Whitbread, Ross MacLaren,
Luc Nijholt, John Moncur, Martin Ling, Nicky Summerbee, Jan Age Fjortoft
(Kevin Horlock), Craig Maskell, Steve White, Manager: John Gorman*

The one record that will haunt them for eternity is conceding the most goals of any club and that is one that is unlikely to be broken as it was set over 42 games rather than the current 38. At a rate of just under 2.4 goals per game Swindon were on a par with Derby's pitiful 2007/08 season when they conceded 89 in 38 matches. The Robins conceded at least three goals on 18 occasions and a minimum of five goals seven times, underlined their vulnerability at the back. However, they did manage five clean sheets, which is two more than the fewest achieved by both Birmingham and Derby in 2007/08 and Blackburn and Norwich in 2011/12.

Swindon's only ever present was centre back, Shaun Taylor, who certainly earned his corn in being one of the busiest players in Premier League history. Entering the final minute of their last match they were 4-0 down against Leeds at home, and although all hope of survival had long been abandoned, they were still one shy of that dreaded 100 goal-mark, so pride was at stake. Almost inevitably the worst did happen with pretty much the last kick of the match and their sorry season was capped off as the hardly prolific centre back Chris Fairclough scored the goal that would leave this Swindon team etched into Premier League history. Having waited 115 years for their first taste of the top division their unedifying experience was as big an anti-climax as any club could have endured.

To be fair, their tally of 47 goals was a reasonable return and this was more than any of their relegation rivals, but the negative goal difference of -53 is in the three worst ever. The following season Ipswich managed to accumulate a -57 goal difference but the very worst was Derby's calamitous 2007/08 season. Even though it was a 38-game season, their goal difference was an unprecedented and ugly -69.

Jan Age Fjortoft bagged a dozen goals for Swindon, which was a pretty good return especially considering he did not score until 22 January when Swindon had already completed over half of their fixtures. That goal then sparked a hot streak for the Norwegian who scored ten goals in the space of nine games.

Swindon fans had to wait until their 16th game of the season for their first taste of victory, at The County Ground, the longest any club has had to wait for a Premier League win. On 24th November they won 1-0 against QPR, who were also coincidentally the last team they beat, 3-1 away on 30 April. Furthermore it was QPR who broke this record when in 2012/13 they did not win a game until their 17th match, against Fulham on 15th December.

It was not all doom and gloom and there were a few creditable draws away at Anfield and Highbury and against champions Manchester United when Eric Cantona was sent off. Swindon's most notable scalp were Tottenham from whom they took four points, in a 1-1 draw at White Hart Lane and a 2-1 win at home. That victory sparked a run of two wins and three draws at the County Ground but it was not enough to save them and their leaky defence. In the final reckoning Swindon will always be remembered as the first century-makers.

ONE HIT WONDERS

If you are going to make just the one appearance then you probably would not choose the one fixture that confirmed one of the longest-standing records, that of the worst defence in Premier League history. However, that was the fate of Andy Thomson, who made his debut in Swindon's fateful final match of the season. Perhaps mercifully he was substituted at half-time and was therefore not on the pitch when that dreaded 100th goal hit the back of the net. After that inauspicious start Thomson went on to make over 350 appearances with the likes of Portsmouth and Bristol Rovers, where he became captain.

After such a chastening experience it seems natural that Thomson now acts as an advisor/counsellor to sportspeople.

FOOTNOTE

MOST GOALS CONCEDED IN A SEASON
All 38 games unless stipulated

CLUB	GOALS	SEASON
Swindon Town	100	1993/94 (42 games)
Ipswich Town	93	1994/95 (42 games)
Derby County	89	2007/08
Fulham	81	2018/19
Fulham	85	2013/14
Barnsley	82	1997/98
Burnley	82	2009/10
Wolves	82	2011/12
Hull City	80	2016/17

A VIEW FROM THE STANDS

The club's spell in the Premier League was brief and while there was the odd glorious moment ultimately it was short-lived. Looking back now, one question remains - Was it really worth it?

Was it really worth it? Now there's a question.

If Glenn Hoddle had stayed with Swindon instead of taking the Chelsea job who knows how different the 1993/94 season would have gone for the club. It was the only season the club has played in the Premier League to date but his replacement John Gorman didn't have Hoddle's vision on and off the pitch. Gorman didn't have Hoddle's eye for a player, and didn't have his ability to organise a defence. Swindon finished rock bottom, conceded a record number of goals, and only won five games.

But—and it's the buts that make us love football—without that season there would be no glorious memory of Eric Cantona being wound up so much that he would get one of the more obvious red cards of a career stuffed with them. Nor would sending off have galvanised Swindon into snatching a 2-2 draw.

Without that season there's no grim pride in being able to say to QPR fans that in a season where Swindon only won just five times it was quite an achievement to have done the double over them. Or to have won 2-1 against a Spurs team that contained names like Nicky Barmby, Sol Campbell, and Darren Anderton. Or to have watched Jan Age Fjortoft's brilliant hat-trick against Coventry in a 3-1 win.

So bright lights among the doom but ultimately a slide through the leagues followed, financial troubles, managers coming and going, and much more drama besides. Was it worth it? Probably. Maybe. Just about.

TOTTENHAM HOTSPUR STATS

NUMBER OF SEASONS:

27

1992/93-2018/19

NUMBER OF MATCHES:

1,038

Wins 446 (Home 276 Away 170)
Draws 257 (Home 125 Away 132)
Losses 335 (Home 118 Away 217)

[Win ratio 43%]

Goals F 1,547
(Home 886 Away 661)

Goals A 1,306
(Home 562 Away 744)

Goal Difference: +241

TOTAL POINTS

1,595

(Home 953: 60%; 642: 40%)
Average per season: 59

BEST POSITION:

2nd

2016/17

WORST POSITION:

15th

1993/94

BIGGEST WIN:

9-1

v Wigan
(22nd Nov, 2009)

BIGGEST LOSS:

7-1

v Newcastle
(28th Dec, 1996)

LONGEST UNBEATEN RUN:

14 matches (5)

(15th Aug, 2015-5th Dec,
2015 & 23rd Dec, 2017-7th Apr, 2018)

LONGEST WITHOUT A WIN:

10 matches

(1st Jan, 1994-19th Mar, 1994)

ALL TIME RANKING

28th

MOST GOALS SCORED IN A SEASON:

86

(2016/17)

FEWEST GOALS SCORED IN A SEASON:

44 (2)

(1996/97 & 1997/98)

FEWEST GOALS CONCEDED IN A SEASON:

26

(2016/17)

MOST GOALS CONCEDED IN A SEASON:

66

(1992/93)

TOP GOALSCORER:

125

Harry Kane

MOST APPEARANCES:

299

Darren Anderton

OWN GOALS:

36

RED CARDS:

64

LOWEST ATTENDANCE:

17,452

v Aston Villa
(2nd Mar, 1994)

HIGHEST ATTENDANCE:

83,222

v Arsenal
(10th Feb, 2018)

All statistics and records supplied by

TOTTENHAM HOTSPUR

DID YOU KNOW?

Tottenham have the biggest difference between their highest and lowest attendance—65,770. Their highest attendance of 83,222 was against Arsenal at Wembley in February 2018 and is also the Premier League record. One of the few advantages of the seemingly endless delays in moving to their new ground was that it granted them the opportunity to record some of the Premier League's largest ever attendances. Their lowest gate of 17,452 against Aston Villa in March 1994 ranks 16th out of the 49 clubs and is below so-called 'smaller' teams such as Brighton, Cardiff, Reading, Stoke, WBA and Wolves. Ironically in their two seasons playing their home matches at Wembley their away record was the second and third best in the division.

FIRST PREMIER LEAGUE MATCH: 15TH AUGUST, 1992
SOUTHAMPTON 0
TOTTENHAM HOTSPUR 0

THE DELL 19,654

Ian Walker, Neil Ruddock, Justin Edinburgh, Terry Fenwick, Jason Cundy, Vinny Samways, Darren Anderton, Paul Allen, David Howells, Gordon Duire, Andy Turner (Andrew Gray), Manager: Doug Livermore

During their dogged but ultimately fruitless pursuit of Liverpool and Man City in 2018/19 they only drew two matches, one of which was their last game of the season, 2-2 with Everton. Tottenham were not the only club who seemed so averse to draws in 2018/19. The record for consecutive Premier League games without a draw was set when Brighton lost at home to Cardiff on 16 April. It was the 34th time that teams had not shared the spoils since Matt Ritchie struck an equaliser for Newcastle against Bournemouth in added time on 16 March. The draw-less spell was broken on 20 April when Wolves and Brighton played out a goalless draw on the same day that West Ham drew 2-2 with Leicester. Overall the 2018/19 season featured the lowest number of draws in Premier League history with 71 out of 380 games, or just under 19% of the total. This compares with the historical high of 1996/97 when 119 games (or 31%) were drawn.

Having lived in the shadow of their North London rivals for the vast majority of their Premier League existence Spurs revelled in the moment that they finally made it above Arsenal. In fact in the first and third seasons they did finish above the Gunners, 8th as opposed to 10th in 1992/93 and 7th compared to 12th in 1994/95 but then there were the 21 years in the wilderness. The idea of 'Spursy' [OED: looking almost certain to achieve something until falling flat on their faces at the very last possible moment] was exemplified by the 2015/16 season when they were expected to overhaul Leicester and could have exerted some pressure on Leicester if they had won at Stamford Bridge on 2nd May, 2016.

SO NEAR BUT SO SPURSY

MONDAY 2 MAY 2016

CHELSEA 2 (0) CAHILL 58', HAZARD 83'
TOTTENHAM HOTSPUR 2 (2) KANE 35', SON HEUNG-MIN 44'

STAMFORD BRIDGE (41,545)

After racing into a 2-0 half-time lead at Stamford Bridge via the trusty duo of Harry Kane and Son Heung-min Spurs finally looked like laying the hoodoo of their perennial failure to win at Chelsea, which had then stretched to 29 games in all competitions and they certainly looked like finally finishing above Arsenal.

Things got a bit feisty after Gary Cahill got one back for Chelsea and all hell broke loose when Eden Hazard equalised with a typically accomplished finish into the top corner in 83rd minute. Not only had Spurs handed Leicester the trophy but they also went into a meltdown on the pitch with some atypical aggression as Mousa Dembele was accused of poking Diego Costa in the eye amidst a whole flurry of fiery exchanges which led to nine Spurs players being booked.

They were later fined for not controlling their players while their supporters wept uncontrollably. Meanwhile Leicester's players were famously filmed at Jamie Vardy's house enjoying the moment that delivered the title on a silver platter with some gusto. To compound the sense of loss for Spurs, Arsenal eventually overhauled them to leave them in their customary position behind the Gunners.

Although he earned the rather unfortunate sobriquet 'Sick Note', Darren Anderton remained free of injuries long enough to make the most number of appearances for Spurs, just one shy of 300. From the first season in 1992/93 he was at Spurs for over a decade until he moved to Birmingham in 2004 and scored 34 goals. One of Jacques Santini's last acts as Spurs boss was to release him and Anderton was clearly not exactly chuffed at what was on the table. "The new contract gives me only a tiny rise and I won't sign it." Anderton admitted in the *News of the World*. "They have only made me one offer and they haven't come back. If they don't want me to stay then I'll go. I would love to sign a new deal but what they have put on the table simply isn't good enough." And off he went to St. Andrews in high dudgeon.

When Spurs hosted Crystal Palace on 3rd April, 2019 they finally christened their new ground, the officially titled "Tottenham Hotspur Stadium" some nine months after the intended move in date. The final cost of £1bn more than double the original budget of £400m, making it the most expensive football stadium ever built. It even dwarfing the massive over spend on rebuilding Wembley, which was finished in 2007 at a cost of £790m. Tottenham joined the handful of clubs that have moved to a new ground while in the Premier League (see Footnote).

ONE HIT WONDER

Jamie Slabber was one of many players to have turned out for Spurs just the once. He gets the nod here partly because I had never heard of him until I started research for this book, but mainly for his name. A local boy, born in nearby Enfield, Slabber got his one opportunity on 16th March, 2003 when he replaced Gary Doherty in the 79th minute in a 3-2 defeat at home to Liverpool and in those 11 minutes he picked up an assist for Teddy Sheringham's goal.

Despite this impressive debut Slabber never ventured on to the pitch again for Spurs and then became an accomplished journeyman around the non-league circuit, taking in a dozen clubs, from Aldershot Town to Woking and many in between, including a few stints at Grays Athletic, which became his last destination before retiring in 2018.

FOOTNOTE

BREAKING NEW GROUND
*List of current PL clubs that have moved into
new grounds while in the Premier League*

CLUB	NEW STADIUM	OPENING	COST
Southampton	St. Mary's	2001	£32m
Leicester City	Walkers/King Power	2002	£37m*
Manchester City	Eastlands/Etihad	2003	£154m
Arsenal	Emirates	2006	£400m
West Ham	London Stadium	2016	£760m**
Tottenham	Tottenham Hotspur	2019	£1.1bn

*Leicester were relegated in the 2001/02 season
and their first game in the stadium was in the Championship.

**(£486m original cost plus £274m renovation)

A VIEW FROM THE STANDS

Seb Stafford-Bloor

**As one of the select clubs that is an ever-present throughout
Premier League history your club has enjoyed prolonged success
so what is your favourite moment from the last 27 years?**

Amsterdam 2019 and, as the clock ticked towards the 95th minute of
Tottenham's Champions League semi-final against Ajax, most Spurs
supporters would have told you the same thing. That they had accepted
elimination but were happy that a second-half rally was sending their
side home on their shields.

That's the thing about a fan's life: it conditions you a particular way.
Spurs have been one of the Premier League's great under-achievers and,
within that context, failure has had to become a relative situation. Success?
Completely alien. A lifetime of watching Tottenham has taught us all how
to process disappointment and to reason it away with illusory positives.
It has not, however, equipped us to cope with jolts of undiluted victory.

When Lucas Moura completed his hat-trick and the visiting bench
spilled deliriously out onto the pitch, it was a mighty catharsis which
melted Spurs hearts, old and young, all over the world. Winning is always

wonderful. But winning after football has spent the last few decades punching you in the gut is so pure and so exhilarating, that it's difficult to imagine anything ever exceeding it. The richness of that moment will stay with me for as long as I'm alive.

WATFORD STATS

NUMBER OF SEASONS:

6 (3 spells)

1999/2000, 2006/07 & 2015/16
- 2018/19

NUMBER OF MATCHES:

228

Wins 59 (Home 37 Away 22)
Draws 51 (Home 32 Away 19)
Losses 118 (Home 45 Away 73)

[Win ratio 26%]

Goals F 240
(Home 141 Away 99)

Goals A 377
(Home 163 Away 214)

Goal Difference: -137

TOTAL POINTS

228

(Home 143: 62%; Away 85: 38%)
Average per season: 38

BEST POSITION:

11th

2018/19

WORST POSITION:

20th (2)

1999/2000 & 2006/07 (RELEGATED)

BIGGEST WIN:

1-5

v Cardiff
(22nd Feb, 2019)

BIGGEST LOSS:

0-6

v Manchester City
(16th Sept, 2017)

LONGEST UNBEATEN RUN:

5 matches (2)

(5th May, 2007-23rd Aug, 2015 &
28th Nov, 2015-26th Dec, 2015)

LONGEST WITHOUT A WIN:

11 matches (2)

(25th Sep, 1999-26th Dec, 1999 &
11th Nov 2006-20th Jan, 2007)

ALL TIME RANKING

34th

MOST GOALS SCORED IN A SEASON:

52

(2018/19)

FEWEST GOALS SCORED IN A SEASON:

29

(2006/07)

FEWEST GOALS CONCEDED IN A SEASON:

50

(2015/16)

MOST GOALS CONCEDED IN A SEASON:

77

(1999/2000)

TOP GOALSCORER:

37

Troy Deeney

MOST APPEARANCES:

136

Troy Deeney

OWN GOALS:

15

RED CARDS:

22

LOWEST ATTENDANCE:

13,766

v Blackburn Rovers
(23rd Jan, 2007)

HIGHEST ATTENDANCE:

21,590

v Sunderland
(27th Nov, 1999)

All statistics and records supplied by

WATFORD

FIRST PREMIER LEAGUE MATCH: 7TH AUGUST, 1999
WATFORD 2 (KENNEDY, NGONGE)
WIMBLEDON 3 (CORT, GAYLE, JOHNSON OG)

VICARAGE ROAD 15,511

Chris Day, Robert Page (Tommy Smith) (Stephen Brooker), Des Lyttle, Peter Kennedy, Steve Palmer, Mark Williams, Richard Johnson, Alexandre Bonnot, Clint Easton, Michael Ngonge, Tommy Mooney, Manager: Graham Taylor

NB Tommy Smith came on as a substitute replacing Robert Page at half time, only to then be substituted himself and replaced by Steve Brooker in the 85th minute

Having lost their first two matches in 1999, Watford sprung a surprise by winning at Anfield thanks to a Tommy Mooney goal and then repeated the dose the following week against Bradford at home. But then they went down by the same 1-0 scoreline for the next three games before beating Chelsea, by, you guessed it, 1-0. They made it seven 1-0s in a row when losing to Arsenal, who of course are the past masters at this particular score. Unfortunately that defeat to at Highbury was the start of a dismal 11-game run in which Watford picked up just two points. It left them well and truly ensconced in the relegation zone, from where they never escaped and they were rock bottom come May with just 24 points.

Watford's second tilt at the Premier League actually started far worse than their first, having been promoted after a 3-0 play-off win over Leeds in 2006 they did not manage to win a game until 4th November, when they beat Middlesbrough 2-0 at Vicarage Road. They did not recover from such a shaky beginning and never spent any time outside the bottom three, ending up bottom again. With just five wins, they racked up one fewer than the first attempt but at least they did gather more points—28 as opposed to 24.

Watford were one of three clubs which found it third time lucky (see Footnote) when they gained promotion to the Premier League in 2015/16. Having lasted just one season in their previous two attempts the Hornets are now about to embark on their fifth successive season, almost emulating the glory years under the late Graham Taylor in the early 1980s when they had six successive seasons in the top flight. In 2018/19, Watford achieved both their highest points total of 50 and highest position in finishing 11th and reached the FA Cup final to boot.

In three separate spells Taylor clocked up a total of 15 years in charge and racked up over 600 games. How things have changed, under the ownership of the Pozzo family the managerial merry-go-round at Vicarage Road has rarely been quiet and current manager Javier Garcia who took over in January 2018 is the first Watford manager out of the last ten incumbents to last longer than 18 months.

Unusually their biggest victory out of their six seasons was away, a 5-1 win at Cardiff on 22nd February, 2019, while their heaviest defeat was at Vicarage Road when they were pummeled 6-0 by Manchester City on 16th September, 2017. It was an eerie forerunner of their FA Cup final loss to City by the same scoreline in May 2019. The previous May on the last day of the 2016/17 season they lost 5-0 to City at home. In all competitions Watford has lost their last 11 matches against City by an aggregate of 38-6.

There has been a long tradition of Jamaican players at Watford. One of their greatest was John Barnes who was born in Kingston but who moved to England when he was 12 and consequently qualified for England. Barnes paved the way for a long line of Jamaicans playing for the Hornets. Watford have had seven "Reggaeboyz" players with Adrian Mariappa having made the most appearances with 80 to his name.

ONE HIT WONDER

The Brazilian Robert Kenedy Nunes Nascimento, or Kenedy for short, has not quite had as many English clubs as he has names, but he has come close. Like so many Chelsea loanees, he has been around the block a little bit and in amongst his peripatetic career he had a stop at Vicarage Road for the 2016/17 season. He did come on during a 2-0 defeat at Burnley on 26th September replacing Roberto Pereyra with quarter of an hour remaining. But that was his 15 minutes of fame as far as Watford were concerned and he was sent back to Stamford Bridge in December.

Kenedy has spent almost two seasons at Newcastle but his performance against Cardiff in August drew a fair amount of criticism as he became the first player since 2010 to play for a full 45 minutes in the first half without completing a pass. The second half was marginally better until he had his penalty saved in added time and the game petered out into a goalless draw.

FOOTNOTE

THIRD TIME LUCKY
There are three clubs that have returned to the Premier League after two single season spells

CLUB	TWO RELEGATIONS		THIRD SPELL
Bolton	1. 1995/1996	2. 1997/1998	2001/2002-2011/12
Burnley	1. 2009/2010	2. 2014/2015	2016/2017-present
Watford	1. 1999/2000	2. 2006/2007	2015/2016-present

A VIEW FROM THE STANDS

David Walker, Football editor, talkSPORT

What was the club's 'Sliding Doors' moment, that seemingly inconsequential action, which actually became a turning point in their fortunes, for either good or bad?

May 2015, Watford have just clinched promotion to the Premier League by virtue of a second-place finish. Promotion was secured on the back of a remarkable run of form that saw the Hornets win ten of their last 14 matches, and they did it while playing stylish, swaggering football.

Naturally the next step was to get rid of the man who masterminded the triumph—head coach Slaviša Jokanović. Despite the fact he was himself the fourth head coach of that season this still came as a big surprise. What was the owner Gino Pozzo thinking? This man had picked up an unmotivated, floundering squad and turned them into a ruthless winning machine, surely he deserved a crack at the big time?

Pozzo clearly had his doubts so out went Slav and in came Quique Sanchez Flores, a man whose elegance and charm off the pitch was in stark contrast to the compact defensive philosophy he preached on it. Under Flores Watford quickly found their feet and by the turn of the year had all but sealed their safety.

Fast forward to August 2018 and Slaviša Jokanović finally got his chance in the top flight with a familiarly attractive Fulham team. Although there were mitigating factors the Serb just couldn't get his team to stop shipping goals and he was gone by November, meanwhile Watford were on course for their best ever Premier League season and a run to the FA Cup final.

Never doubt the Pozzos. They know better than we do.

WEST BROMWICH ALBION STATS

NUMBER OF SEASONS:

12 (4 spells)

2002/03, 2004/05-2005/06,
2008/09, 2010/11-2017/18

TOTAL POINTS

464

(Home 279: 60%; Away 185: 40%)
Average per season: 39

NUMBER OF MATCHES:

456

Wins 112 (Home 73 Away 39)
Draws 128 (Home 60 Away 68)
Losses 216 (Home 95 Away 121)

[Win ratio 25%]

Goals F 475
(Home 280 Away 195)

Goals A 696
(Home 322 Away 374)

Goal Difference: -221

BEST POSITION:

8th

2012/13

WORST POSITION:

20th (2)

2008/09 & 2017/18 (RELEGATED)

BIGGEST WIN:

1-5

v Wolves
(12th Feb, 2012)

BIGGEST LOSS:

0-6 (2)

v Liverpool (26th Apr, 2003)
v Chelsea (14th Aug, 2010)

LONGEST UNBEATEN RUN:

7 matches

(12th Feb, 2011-9th Apr, 2011)

LONGEST WITHOUT A WIN:

20 matches

(27th Aug, 2017-2nd Jan, 2018)

ALL TIME RANKING

34th

MOST GOALS SCORED IN A SEASON:

56

(2010/11)

FEWEST GOALS SCORED IN A SEASON:

29

(2002/03)

FEWEST GOALS CONCEDED IN A SEASON:

48

(2015/16)

MOST GOALS CONCEDED IN A SEASON:

71

(2010/11)

TOP GOALSCORER:

30

Peter Odemwingie

MOST APPEARANCES:

269

Chris Brunt

OWN GOALS:

27

RED CARDS:

31

LOWEST ATTENDANCE:

21,467

v Swansea
(14th Dec, 2016)

HIGHEST ATTENDANCE:

27,751

v Portsmouth
(15th May, 2005)

WEST BROMWICH ALBION

FIRST PREMIER LEAGUE MATCH: 17TH AUGUST, 2002
MANCHESTER UNITED 1 (SOLKSJAER)
WEST BROM 0

OLD TRAFFORD 67,645

Russell Hoult, Neil Clement, Darren Moore, Phil Gilchrist, Igor Balis, Larus Sigurdsson, Sean Gregan (Bob Taylor), Derek McInnes, Andy Johnson , Danny Dichio (Scott Dobie), Jason Roberts (Lee Marshall), Manager: Gary Megson

One of the more frequent yo-yo clubs, West Brom share the record number of relegations with four but perhaps their most memorable season was when they somehow avoided the drop on the last day of the 2004/05 season under Bryan Robson. As miracles go this was among the most spectacular as they became the first side to stay up despite being bottom of the table at Christmas when they were nine points adrift of 17th. Uniquely going into that final day no club had yet been relegated so there was a four-way dogfight between the Baggies, Norwich, Southampton and Palace. West Brom were bottom and were relying on all the others to slip up, which is exactly what they did to grant Robson's men the unlikeliest of lifelines.

As the tension ratcheted up throughout the afternoon all four teams were safe at one stage. Norwich started the day clear but were doomed after collapsing to a 6-0 defeat away to Fulham. Norwich's fall briefly gave Southampton an escape route and they seemed to take it going 1-0 up at home to Manchester United after 10 minutes. However, United equalised soon after to give West Brom and Palace the sniff of safety.

It was around the hour mark that things really livened up. West Brom edged ahead of the pack when they took the lead in the 57th minute through journeyman extraordinaire Geoff Horsfield against a disinterested Portsmouth, who some even accused of lying down because of their rivalry with Southampton. A minute after West Brom took the lead, Palace equalised at Charlton as the Saints fell behind leaving West Brom in pole position. However, that changed when Palace's leading scorer Andy Johnson put them 2-1 up with less than 20 minutes to play, but they could not hold on and Jonathan Fortune scored for Charlton with eight minutes to go. At the Hawthorns Kieran Richardson added a second to ensure The Baggies' safety in front of nearly 28,000, which was appropriately their biggest ever Premier League attendance. Ironically, West Brom have one of the worst final-day records of any club that has played in a minimum of five seasons. This was their only win on the final day out of a dozen attempts, with six draws and five losses, averaging 0.75 points per game.

BAGGIES GIVE FERGIE A HIGH FIVE

SUNDAY 19TH MAY 2013

WEST BROMWICH ALBION 5 (1) Morrison 40',
Lukaku 50', 80', 86', Mulumbu 81'
MANCHESTER UNITED 5 (3) Kagawa 6', Olsson (OG) 9',
Buttner 30', van Persie 53', Hernandez 63'

In as neat a piece of 'top and tailing' as has been experienced, after their first match was at Old Trafford West Brom provided Alex Ferguson's last opponents in May 2013. Few could have predicted the result as there are not many 5-5 draws in modern football and it was certainly the highest scoring draw in Ferguson's long and illustrious United career of 1,500 games and it is still the highest scoring Premier League draw to date.

The Baggies recovered from being 3-0 down after just 30 minutes and 5-2 down midway through the second half, aided by a second half hat-trick from substitute Romelu Lukaku who was on loan from Chelsea at the time and who ended up at United the season afterwards. So it was that in the last ten minutes of Ferguson's illustrious career his side shipped three goals. This draw secured the Baggies their highest Premier League finish of 8th while putting the slightest of dents in Ferguson's reputation, and so the side from the Hawthorns proved to be a thorn in Fergie's side.

ONE HIT WONDER

Luke Daniels spent just under nine years from 2004 at The Hawthorns as a keeper but only managed 13 minutes of Premier League action when replacing the injured Ben Foster against Everton in a goalless draw in August 2013. Foster's injury meant he was out for a few months but Daniels did not get another crack of the whip as Boaz Myhill took over as the No.1. Daniels went on loan to seven clubs during his time at West Brom but eventually made a permanent move to Scunthorpe in 2015.

He is currently reserve team keeper at Brentford.

FOOTNOTE

There is no substitute for class and here is the list of players who have scored a hat-trick as a substitute, and West Brom have two of the six.

PLAYER	MATCH	YEAR
Ole Gunnar Solksjaer	Forest 1 Man Utd 8	1999
Jimmy Floyd Hasselbaink	Chelsea 5 Wolves 2	2004
Robert Earnshaw	Charlton 1 West Brom 4	2005
Emmanuel Adebayor	Derby 2 Arsenal 6	2008
Romelu Lukaku	West Brom 5 Man Utd 5	2013
Steven Naismith	Everton 3 Chelsea 1	2015

A VIEW FROM THE STANDS

Chris Lepkowski

What was your club's 'Sliding Doors' moment, that seemingly inconsequential action, which actually became a turning point in their fortunes, for either good or bad?

Sliding doors moments aren't new to West Bromwich Albion. Although not in the Premier League, Albion's match against West Ham in October 2003 was one. The Baggies were 3-0 behind after just 18 minutes a score which looked set to be the end of Gary Megson. There were many stories in the media at the time that he was set to be eased out in favour of someone else—Mark Hughes being mentioned by several. The Hammers' Jermain Defoe missed a brilliant chance to make it four but minutes later he was then sent-off for a rash challenge on Sean Gregan. Albion went onto win 4-3. Gary Megson ended up taking the Baggies up. Hughes never did get the job.

Elsewhere, Albion fans will point to a moment during the following season when the Baggies played Manchester City. Megson had been replaced by Bryan Robson and the team had lost six of his seven games in charge and were heading for another defeat at the Etihad Stadium following Nicolas Anelka's free-kick.

Ten-man Albion (Thomas Gaardsoe had been sent-off) didn't even have a shot, but secured a draw when a long ball caused confusion between Richard Dunne and David James. As James rushed off his line to claim the ball, Dunne stuck his foot out to send it past his stranded keeper. 1-1. That draw was subsequently enough to keep Albion up.

WEST HAM UNITED STATS

NUMBER OF SEASONS:

23 (3 spells)

1993/94-2002/03,
2005/06-2010/11, 2012/13-2018/19

NUMBER OF MATCHES:

882

Wins 290 (Home 191 Away 99)
Draws 228 (Home 111 Away 117)
Losses 364 (Home 139 Away 225)

[Win ratio 33%]

Goals F 1,064
(Home 635 Away 429)

Goals A 1,269
(Home 554 Away 715)

Goal Difference: -205

TOTAL POINTS

1,098

(Home 684: 61%; Away 414: 39%
Average per season: 48

BEST POSITION:

5th

1998/99

WORST POSITION:

20th

2010/11 (RELEGATED)

BIGGEST WIN:

6-0

v Barnsley
(10th Jan, 1998)

BIGGEST LOSS:

7-1 (2)

v Blackburn (14th Oct, 2001)
v Manchester United (1st Apr, 2000)

LONGEST UNBEATEN RUN:

10 matches

(13th Feb, 2016-30th Apr, 2016)

LONGEST WITHOUT A WIN:

14 matches

(27th Oct, 2002-22nd Jan, 2003)

ALL TIME RANKING

10th

MOST GOALS SCORED IN A SEASON:

65

(2015/16)

FEWEST GOALS SCORED IN A SEASON:

35

(2006/07)

FEWEST GOALS CONCEDED IN A SEASON:

45

(2008/09)

MOST GOALS CONCEDED IN A SEASON:

70

(2010/11)

TOP GOALSCORER:

47

Paolo Di Canio

MOST APPEARANCES:

349

Mark Noble

OWN GOALS:

35

RED CARDS:

72

LOWEST ATTENDANCE:

14,554

v Sheffield Wednesday
(23rd Jan, 1995)

HIGHEST ATTENDANCE:

59,988

v Everton
(30th Mar, 2019)

All statistics and records supplied by  gracenote.
A NIELSEN COMPANY

WEST HAM UNITED

FIRST PREMIER LEAGUE MATCH: 14TH AUGUST, 1993
WEST HAM UNITED 0
WIMBLEDON 2 (FASHANU, SANCHEZ)

UPTON PARK 20,363

Ludek Miklosko, Julian Dicks, Steve Potts, Tim Breacker, Tony Gale, Matt Holmes (Keith Rowland), Martin Allen, Dale Gordon, Peter Butler, Trevor Morley, Clive Allen, Manager: Billy Bonds

Mark Noble not only has the most appearances with one shy of 350 games, he also has the second most goals with 42 and is only five behind Paolo Di Canio. If he plays for most of the 2019/20 season he would be expected to overtake the Italian although it is a fair assumption he will never score a goal quite like Di Canio's right foot volley against Wimbledon in 2000. As the ball came across from a long cross from the right the Italian executed a perfect scissor-kick volley. As Martin Tyler enthused on Sky: "Di Canio. I do not believe that. That is sensational even by his standards." Andy Gray added with suitably understated awe: "Well take a bow, son. TAKE A BOW." The goal quite rightly won the Goal of the Season and although it was scored in March 2000 it beat off all other competition to be voted the goal of the decade in a Sky Sports poll.

Di Canio arrived at Upton Park in January 1999 following his controversial push on referee Paul Alcock while playing for Sheffield Wednesday. He was a tempestuous character and there were wild fluctuations between moments of sublime skill and crass stupidity. One incident which maybe reflects best the Italian's mercurial temperament came nine months after his stunning goal against Wimbledon, when West Ham were playing at Goodison Park.

THE HAND OF GOD, DI CANIO STYLE

SATURDAY 16 DECEMBER 2000

EVERTON 1 (0) Cadamarteri 75'
WEST HAM 1 (0) Kanoute 83'

GOODISON PARK (31,260)

A 1-1 draw is not necessarily something to write home about but the result of this game is pretty incidental to its significance. The devil was in the detail after Danny Cadamarteri gave Everton the lead, Frederick Kanoute equalised and then in the final minute as the game hang in the balance, the real action happened. A cross was knocked into the box with Di Canio waiting to pounce, he had the goal at his mercy as the keeper Paul Gerrard had slipped on the way out of the penalty area and the Everton faithful had their hearts in their mouths.

But to the astonishment of the 30,000 or so spectators rather than trying to head the ball into the empty net Di Canio caught it up, tucked it under his arm and pointed towards the stricken Gerrard who he had spotted, clearly in agony as he had dislocated his knee. After the Everton fans recovered, they showed their appreciation for Di Canio's gesture by giving him a standing ovation and he was also thanked profusely by other Everton players. But reportedly his manager Harry Redknapp was not so enamoured by this altruism and was apoplectic that he had surrendered the chance to seal the game.

Redknapp was very much in the minority and indeed It was considered such an extraordinary gesture that even everybody's least favourite football authority, FIFA awarded Di Canio a special mention for his act of good sportsmanship.

Mark Noble epitomises the spirit of the Irons and occasionally has allowed that to spill over, he handily also has the most red cards and infamously confronted one of the pitch invaders who were protesting about the move to the London Stadium during a game against Burnley. Cut him and he would undoubtedly bleed claret... and blue. That move away from Upton Park was not universally welcome but after that tempestuous first season, the status quo has been somewhat restored. West Ham became the fifth club to move grounds while in the Premier League.

Another captain who became a firm favourite was Kevin Nolan who moved from Newcastle to West Ham after their miserable relegation in 2011 to reunite with his former Bolton boss, Sam Allardyce. Nolan was installed as captain and instilled a fighting spirit that took The Hammers back to the Premier League at the first time of asking after beating Blackpool in the play-off final. They finished a respectable 10th following promotion and have been solidly mid-table ever since. The Allardyce/Nolan partnership may not have been the most popular but it was mightily effective.

Current manager Manuel Pelligrini is the Hammers' 13th boss in their 23 seasons, including the odd caretaker such as Kevin Keen and Sir Trevor Brooking. The Chilean is the first South American to be in charge of West Ham after eight Englishmen, one Scotsman, one Italian, one Israeli and a Croatian.

ONE HIT WONDER

Sasa Ilic is best known down in South East London, and revered by Valiants fans, for his part in securing Charlton's promotion to the Premier League in the extraordinary 1998 play-off final win against Sunderland. He had kept a record number of ten consecutive clean sheets prior to the final but that record was blown out of the water in spectacular fashion in a pulsating 4-4 draw. But the Serbian-Australian keeper crucially kept out Michael Gray's rather feeble spot kick in the shoot-out and Charlton were in the Premier League for the first time.

After relegation in that first season Ilic was second in the pecking order to Dean Kiely at the Valley and went out on loan to West Ham in February 2000. On 26 February he was picked to face Everton at Upton Park but his Hammers debut went badly awry as a Nick Barmby hat-trick contributed to a 4-0 hammering. He never regained his place and moved to Portsmouth on loan before moving to Hungary. He did come back to England and played a couple of dozen games for Barnsley and a handful for Blackpool.

Ilic is now involved in developing golf courses and was part of the organisation that opened the first course in Montenegro, the regally titled Royal Montenegro Golf & Country Club, which was opened in 2016.

FOOTNOTE

TOP 10 CLUBS IN TERMS OF NUMBER OF SEASONS

CLUB	SEASONS
Arsenal	27
Chelsea	27
Everton	27
Liverpool	27
Manchester United	27
Tottenham	27
Aston Villa	24
Newcastle	24
Manchester City	23
West Ham	23

A VIEW FROM THE STANDS

Stuart Fuller

What was your club's 'Sliding Doors' moment, that seemingly inconsequential action, which actually became a turning point in their fortunes, for either good or bad?

"Tevez and Mascherano"—three words which would change the football transfer system, certainly in this country, forever. The footballing world tried desperately to belittle the fact that two global footballing superstars had pitched up at The Boleyn Ground on transfer deadline day in 2006, suggesting that every other major club had put their arrival at their own doorstep as some kind of prank. But it was the real deal. Well, sort of. As the weeks went by and both players looked unfit and out of their depth playing in a team crafted by first Alan Pardew and then Alan Curbishley, failing to hold down regular starting places as the stories began to leak that the players weren't exactly the property of West Ham—a bit like renting a blockbuster from, well, Blockbuster and saying you owned the rights to distribute the film.

Javier Mascherano would start just five games for the Hammers, falling out of favour with Curbishley when asked to play in a defensive midfielder role (oh, the irony) and left for Liverpool in January 2007 whilst Carlos Tevez began to thrive, scoring vital goals for the Hammers, none more so than the double against Tottenham Hotspur in a 4-3 win in March 2007.

A month later it was announced by the Premier League that West Ham had breached transfer rules over the acquisition of the pair, specifically regarding the fact the deal was done as a third-party agreement, and the club were fined a record £5.5m. Both players were still free to continue to play and Tevez scored the only goal of the game away at Champions Manchester United to give the Hammers a 1-0 that saw them survive at the expense of Sheffield United.

The controversial deal which took football by surprise in August resulted in changes to the player ownership rules and subsequently transfer rules in the Premier League. It also saw the Blades launching proceedings against the Hammers for the loss of revenue resulting from their relegation, due to Tevez's influence on results that kept West Ham up. It was eventually settled out of court in March 2009 with a settlement rumoured to be between £15m and £25m.

Just suppose the taxi had gone to East Ham United by mistake—now there's your sliding doors moment...

WIGAN ATHLETIC STATS

NUMBER OF SEASONS:

8

2005/06-2012/13

NUMBER OF MATCHES:

304

Wins 85 (Home 48 Away 37)
Draws 76 (Home 45 Away 31)
Losses 143 (Home 59 Away 84)

[Win ratio 28%]

Goals F 316
(Home 169 Away 147)

Goals A 482
(Home 215 Away 267)

Goal difference: -166

TOTAL POINTS

331

(Home 189: 57%; 142: 43%)
Average per season: 41

BEST POSITION:

10th

2005/06

WORST POSITION:

18th

2012/13 (RELEGATED)

BIGGEST WIN:

0-5

v Hull
(30th August, 2008)

BIGGEST LOSS:

9-1 (2)

v Tottenham (22nd Nov, 2009)
v Chelsea (9th May, 2010)

**LONGEST
UNBEATEN RUN:**

9 matches

(27th Aug, 2005-5th Nov, 2005)

**LONGEST
WITHOUT A WIN:**

13 matches

(25th Aug, 2007-9th Dec, 2007)

ALL TIME RANKING

10th

MOST GOALS SCORED IN A SEASON:

47

(2012/13)

FEWEST GOALS SCORED IN A SEASON:

34

(2007/08 & 2008/09)

FEWEST GOALS CONCEDED IN A SEASON:

25

(2008/08)

MOST GOALS CONCEDED IN A SEASON:

79

(2009/10)

TOP GOALSCORER:

24

Hugo Rodallega

MOST APPEARANCES:

194

Emmerson Boyce

OWN GOALS:

14

RED CARDS:

27

LOWEST ATTENDANCE:

14,007

v Middlesbrough
(15th Aug, 2007)

HIGHEST ATTENDANCE:

25,133

v Manchester United
(11th May, 2008)

All statistics and records supplied by  gracenote.
A NIELSEN COMPANY

WIGAN ATHLETIC

FIRST PREMIER LEAGUE MATCH: 14TH AUGUST, 2005
WIGAN 0
CHELSEA 1 (CRESPO)

DW STADIUM 23,909

Mike Pollitt, Arjan de Zeeuw, Pascal Chimbonda, Stephane Henchoz, Leighton Baines, Damien Francis, Jimmy Bullard, Alan Mahon, Gary Teale, Jason Roberts, Henri Camara (Andreas Johansson), Manager: Paul Jewell

Having reached the top-flight for the first time in their history in 2005, Wigan showed that they could acclimatise at the highest level without too much trouble. Even though they lost their first match at home to Chelsea through a Hernan Crespo injury-time winner they soon settled into life at the highest echelon of English football. They had an excellent run of form from late August to early November winning eight out of their nine games after losing their first two and were second in the table behind their opening day conquerors and eventual champions Chelsea. They finished 10th in that first season and this was the highest they reached in their eight seasons. No other promoted club which has lasted more than five seasons have ever recorded their highest position in their first season. Wigan scored 45 goals, which was their highest total until, ironically, they scored 47 in their final season when they were relegated in 2012/13.

Maynor Figueroa may not have scaled the greatest of heights in his time at Wigan but he will be forever remembered for one outstanding moment when he managed to emulate David Beckham by scoring from inside his own half, direct from a free-kick. Figueroa spotted Stoke keeper Thomas Sorensen straying off his line and quick thinking was rewarded when his shot sailed serenely over Sorensen as he flailed in desperation at the ball. Over his five years at the DW Stadium Figueroa managed just four goals but that one outstanding effort against Stoke will remain the one that Wigan fans will cherish.

In 2009/10 Wigan achieved a unique and unwanted double by losing two matches in the same season by eight goals, in November they fell foul of a handful of goals from Jermaine Defoe in a 9-1 defeat against Spurs and then on the last day of the season Chelsea wrapped up their title with an 8-0 win over the hapless Latics. They also lost 5-0 twice to Manchester United and suffered a pair of 4-0 losses to Arsenal and Portsmouth. In those six matches they conceded the not-so-princely sum of 35 goals and consequently ended up with a goal difference of -42, the worst in the division. But even after all this significant damage they were not relegated, finishing six points clear of Burnley in 18th.

This means that Wigan are the only club to not be relegated despite having the season's worst goal difference and they have the worst goal difference of any club that has not been relegated. The next closest to them are Bradford in 1999/2000 and Huddersfield in 2017/18 who both survived with a goal difference of -30 each.

The Latics' finest victory came against a team that were their customary tormenters—Chelsea. In their 16 Premier League encounters Wigan lost 13and drew two with a goal aggregate of 10-40 but their one and only victory was a sweet one to savour. In 2009/10 Chelsea won the title under Carlo Ancelotti and handed out that final day 8-0 shellacking but earlier in the season the champions fell foul of an inspired Wigan side who comprehensively beat them 3-1 at the DW Stadium. The goals came from the unlikely trio of Titus Bramble, Hugo Rodallega and Paul Scharner after Petr Cech had been sent off for bringing down Rodallega early in the second half. Chelsea only lost six games that season and only two by more than one goal, so this represented a considerable feather in Roberto Martinez's cap and was some compensation for their generally poor record against Chelsea as Wigan finally banished the Blues.

ONE HIT WONDER

Fraser Fyvie, or FF as he should have been known, arrived from Aberdeen in 2012 and had to wait until the final day of the 2012/13 season before he took his Premier League bow. He replaced Ben Watson for the last 21 minutes of the 2-2 draw with Aston Villa in what was Wigan's last match in the Premier League to date. A week earlier he had been an unused substitute when Wigan won the FA Cup. Fyvie went on loan to Yeovil and Shrewsbury before returning to his native Scotland joining Hibernian in February 2015.

He was a member of Dundee United's squad in the 2018/19 season.

FOOTNOTE

Of the three FA Cup Finalists that have been relegated from the Premier League in the season they reached the final, Wigan are the only one to have lifted the trophy. A further two clubs Hull, in 2015, and Aston Villa, in 2016, were relegated the season after they lost in the final, Arsenal being the victors on both occaisions.

FA CUP FINALIST	YEAR
Middlesbrough lost to Chelsea	1997
Portsmouth lost to Chelsea	2010
Wigan beat Manchester City	2013

A VIEW FROM THE STANDS:

Danny Jamieson, presenter/reporter Premier League Productions

What was your club's 'Sliding Doors' moment, that seemingly inconsequential action, which actually became a turning point in their fortunes, for either good or bad?

Going to Craven Cottage to face Fulham on 12th January, 2013, Wigan were in the relegation zone. The point gained that weekend in west London would take them out of the bottom three, but the final minute played a large part in that season's relegation. Iván Ramis, a summer signing, had become a pillar in central defence but was stretchered off with what would turn out to be damaged knee ligaments. Out for the season, his absence caused defensive turmoil.

Eight other players would spend time in Martínez's back three—including midfielders Ben Watson and James McArthur. Only two clean sheets followed in the league. It would force club captain Gary Caldwell to return far too early from the severe hip injury, which eventually ended his career, for a must-win Tuesday evening game with Swansea in May. Clearly unfit, he gave the ball away minutes after taking a 2-1 lead for Swansea's equaliser. The 3-2 home defeat was what ultimately consigned them to the Championship, relegation that was confirmed by losing at Arsenal three days after winning the FA Cup. But for Ramis's injury and subsequent unavailability, the whole season may have panned out differently—not that you'll find a single Wigan fan who would swap the Cup win for anything.

WIMBLEDON STATS

NUMBER OF SEASONS:

8

1992/93-1999/2000

NUMBER OF MATCHES:

316

Wins 99 (Home 62 Away 37)
Draws 94 (Home 46 Away 48)
Losses 123 (Home 50 Away 73)

[Win ratio 31%]

Goals F 384
(Home 218 Away 166)

Goals A 472
(Home 198 Away 274)

Goal Difference: -88

TOTAL POINTS

391

(Home 232: 59%; Away 159: 41%)
Average per season: 49

BEST POSITION:

6th

1993/94

WORST POSITION:

18th

1999/2000 (RELEGATED)

BIGGEST WIN:

5-0

v Watford
(4th Dec, 1999)

BIGGEST LOSS:

7-1

v Aston Villa
(11th Feb, 1995)

LONGEST UNBEATEN RUN:

14 matches

(4th Sept-14th Dec, 1996)

LONGEST WITHOUT A WIN:

14 matches

(16th Sept-23rd Dec, 1995)

ALL TIME RANKING

10th

MOST GOALS SCORED IN A SEASON:

56

(1992/93 & 1993/94)

FEWEST GOALS SCORED IN A SEASON:

34

(1997/98)

FEWEST GOALS CONCEDED IN A SEASON:

46

(1997/98)

MOST GOALS CONCEDED IN A SEASON:

74

(1999/2000)

TOP GOALSCORER:

58

Dean Holdsworth

MOST APPEARANCES:

244

Robbie Earle

OWN GOALS:

14

RED CARDS:

27

LOWEST ATTENDANCE:

3,039

v Everton
(26th Jan, 1993)

HIGHEST ATTENDANCE:

30,115

v Manchester United
(9th May, 1993)

All statistics and records supplied by

WIMBLEDON

FIRST PREMIER LEAGUE MATCH: 15TH AUGUST, 1992
LEEDS UNITED 2 (CHAPMAN 2)
WIMBLEDON 1 (BARTON)

ELLAND ROAD 25,795

*Hans Segers, Warren Barton, Scott Fitzgerald,
John Scales (Dean Blackwell), Roger Joseph, Lawrie Sanchez,
Robbie Earle, Gary Elkins, Paul Miller, Dean Holdsworth,
Andy Clarke (Gerald Dobbs), Manager: Joe Kinnear*

On 26th January, 1993 3,039 hardy souls gathered together at Selhurst Park to watch Wimbledon play Everton. Little did they know at the time that this was going to be a match that would go into the history books. This is still, and will probably remain, the lowest ever Premier League attendance. In each of their eight seasons Wimbledon managed to record the lowest crowds of the season and in only one of those seasons did they not record an attendance of less than 10,000.

Remarkably there were over 100 occasions out of their 158 home fixtures when their crowds did not reach five figures and this can be partly explained by their nomadic existence. Having left Plough Lane in 1991 Wimbledon's entire Premier League life was spent in exile at Selhurst Park, something which many of their fans resented and consequently the shunned the games.

Wimbledon's reputation as an iconoclastic club was summed up by their sobriquet, "The Crazy Gang" and led by forthright characters such as Vinnie Jones and John Fashanu, the club enjoyed nothing more than cocking a snook at the establishment. In 1992/93 they enjoyed doubles over both Arsenal and Liverpool as well as winning at Old Trafford. The club reached its peak in 1993/94 when they finished 6th, the second-highest London club behind Arsenal and with Chelsea and Tottenham marooned some distance away in 14th and 15th respectively. With their robust style and those uncompromising players few would associate Wimbledon with a spotless reputation but in one sense they were the most spotless as they went an astounding 91 games between 1st November, 1997 and 4th March, 2000 without being awarded a penalty. The deadlock was broken in 32nd minute on 11th March, 2000 against Leicester City and Neal Ardley converted, just as he had done with their previous spot kick against Leeds on 25th October, 1997. Those Ardley conversions were a staggering 1,166 days apart.

Wimbledon ended their eight-year Premier League tenure with a whimper that was so uncharacteristic of their generally forthright and feisty approach. They endured one of their longest runs without a win at just the wrong time, going 10 matches without a victory. This was the moment that Sam Hammam decided to leave the club having overseen their dramatic rise from non-League to top flight in the space of ten years. Having looked comfortably mid-table in January they slipped away alarmingly, gathering just five points from a possible 45 as they dropped into 18th on the last day of the season and allied to Bradford's unexpected win over Liverpool, that was that. Further salt was added to their wounds as they were left marooned on 99 Premier League wins.

ONE HIT WONDER

In October 1992 Aidan Newhouse became the first of that rare breed who managed to score on their only appearance for a club. It was unfortunate for Newhouse that his moment of glory was somewhat overshadowed by Dalian Atkinson's strike for Villa , which was rightly voted the goal of the season. By comparison Newhouse's effort was very much the ugly sister, a scruffy shot that ricocheted off a defender before ending up in the net. Despite the lack of aesthetics of the goal at least Newhouse can claim he was the Premier League's original One Hit Wonder.

Newhouse is now a maths teacher and even in his next career he has yet again been outshone as one of his former pupils is Welsh international Ben Woodburn, who just happens to be Liverpool's youngest-ever scorer.

FOOTNOTE

LOWEST CROWDS

Seven clubs have recorded attendances of less than 10,000. Six of these seven attendances were in the first two years of Premier League, Bournemouth being the exception.

CLUB	ATTENDANCE	MATCH	DATE
Wimbledon	3,036	vs Everton	26 Jan 1993
Chelsea	8.923	vs Coventry	4 May 1994
Southampton	9,028	vs Ipswich	8 Dec 1993
Coventry	9,509	vs Ipswich	10 Oct 1994
Oldham	9,633	vs Wimbledon	28 Aug 1993
QPR	9,875	vs Swindon	30 Apr 1994
Bournemouth	9,980	vs Huddersfield	4 Dec 2018

A VIEW FROM THE STANDS

What was the club's 'Sliding Doors' moment, that seemingly inconsequential action, which actually became a turning point in their fortunes, for either good or bad?

The name Joe Kinnear may mean different things to different people but to Wimbledon fans he will always be remembered fondly. Taking over after Peter Withe's brief spell in charge, he was the last manager who really got the Dons playing above their level. Dave Bassett and Bobby Gould created the modern Wimbledon 'Crazy Gang' but Kinnear steered them through the early Premier League years all the way to 1999. They remained a difficult club to beat, kept their identity, and stayed a little crazy along the way.

In March of 1999 Kinnear suffered a heart attack and had to walk away from the job he had held for 364 games. The club's Norwegian owners replaced him with their compatriot Egil Olsen. He was sacked before the end of the 1999/00 season with the club heading for a relegation that new manager Terry Burton couldn't avoid.

The slide continued, ownership issues took the headlines from what was actually happening on the pitch and in 2004 the club was renamed the Milton Keynes Dons and moved to the city. Wimbledon may be gone but they'll never be forgotten, but for a heart attack who knows where they'd be today.

WOLVERHAMPTON STATS

NUMBER OF SEASONS:

5 (3 spells)

2003/04, 2009/10-2011/12, 2018/19

NUMBER OF MATCHES:

190

Wins 48 (Home 33 Away 15)
Draws 49 (Home 22 Away 27)
Losses 93 (Home 40 Away 53)

[Win ratio 25%]

Goals F 203
(Home 113 Away 90)

Goals A 327
(Home 151 Away 176)

Goal Difference: -124

TOTAL POINTS

193

(Home 121: 63%; Away 72: 37%)
Average per season: 39

BEST POSITION:

7th

2018/2019

WORST POSITION:

20th (2)

2003/04, 2011/12 (RELEGATED)

BIGGEST WIN:

4-0

v Blackpool
(26th Feb, 2011)

BIGGEST LOSS:

0-5 (3)

v Chelsea (20th Sep, 2003)
v Fulham (4th Mar, 2012)
v Manchester Utd (18th Mar, 2012)

LONGEST UNBEATEN RUN:

6 matches

(25th Aug, 2018-6th Oct, 2018)

LONGEST WITHOUT A WIN:

17 matches

(12th Feb, 2012-25th Aug, 2018)

ALL TIME RANKING

37th

**MOST GOALS SCORED
IN A SEASON:**

47

(2018/19)

**FEWEST GOALS
SCORED IN A SEASON:**

32

(2009/10)

**FEWEST GOALS
CONCEDED IN A SEASON:**

46

(2018/19)

**MOST GOALS
CONCEDED IN A SEASON:**

82

(2011/12)

TOP GOALSCORER:

22

Steven Fletcher

MOST APPEARANCES:

108

Matt Jarvis

OWN GOALS:

12

RED CARDS:

13

LOWEST ATTENDANCE:

22,657

v Fulham
(21st Aug, 2011)

HIGHEST ATTENDANCE:

31,436

v Arsenal
(24th Apr, 2019)

All statistics and records supplied by

WOLVERHAMPTON WANDERERS

FIRST PREMIER LEAGUE MATCH: 16TH AUGUST, 2003
BLACKBURN ROVERS 5 (AMORUSO, THOMPSON, EMERTON, COLE 2)
WOLVERHAMPTON WANDERERS 1 (IVERSEN)

EWOOD PARK 26,270

Matt Murray, Paul Butler, Denis Irwin, Lee Naylor, Jody Craddock, Shaun Newton (Henri Camara), Paul Ince , Colin Cameron, Silas (Oleg Luzhny), Steffen Iversen, Dean Sturridge (Nathan Blake), Manager: Dave Jones

In their first four seasons Wolves managed to accumulate a total of 32 wins and in the 2018/19 season they managed to add half as many again with 16 victories. Two of Wolves' biggest defeats of 5-0 were against West London clubs, Chelsea at home in 2003/04 and Fulham away in 2011/12.

When Wolves were relegated in 2004 Nathan Blake was completing an unwanted quintuple. It was his fifth relegation in the space of ten years, having gone down with Sheffield United in 1993/94, Bolton twice in 1995/96 and 1997/98, and Blackburn in 1998/99. Blake joined Hermann Hreidarsson as the only player to suffer five relegations [see list below].

Wolves' return to the Premier League in 2018 was an unqualified triumph. Not only did they stay up with ease but they finished in a lofty seventh place, which was also the highest position a promoted club had reached since Ipswich's 5th place in 2000/01. To cap it all off, they secured European football at Molineux for the first time since 1970s courtesy of Watford's loss in the FA Cup Final. When they won their fourth fixture back in the Premier league with a 1-0 victory at West Ham they had stopped the winless streak of 17 matches that they had endured since February 2012. They also achieved that rare feat for promoted clubs of winning more games than they lost with 16 wins as opposed to 12 losses.

Most impressively they more than held their own against the top six, gaining more points against that leading group than any other team with 16 points, including beating Tottenham, Chelsea and Arsenal as well as drawing with Manchester City. However, they reserved some of their best displays for Manchester United. A well-deserved draw at Old Trafford was followed by two victories at Molineux, with a win in the FA Cup quarter final preceding victory in the League. Remarkably, this was the first time that United had taken the lead and ended up losing, since they lost against Swansea on 30th August, 2015 a run of 68 matches that featured 64 wins and just 4 draws.

Weirdly Wolves record against the bottom six was appreciably worse. They gained only 14 points out of a possible 36, including having the double done over them by the bottom club, Huddersfield, who won only three games all season. Wolves scored only nine goals, conceding 12, in their games against the clubs that finished 15th or below.

ONE HIT WONDER

Matt Murray came through the club's academy and spent 20 years at Molineux, with a dozen of those, between 1998 and 2010, as a full-time professional. He played 89 times for Wolves but most of that time was outside the Premier League. He starred in their 2003 play-off final win over Sheffield United, notably saving Michael Brown's penalty, and he played in their debut match in the Premier League on 16th August, 2003 at Ewood Park. The unlucky Murray saw five goals put past him in what proved to be his one and only Premier League appearance. After this he was dogged by a series of injuries including a broken foot and shoulder.

Michael Oakes then took over from Murray and although he conceded four goals in the following match at Charlton the club stuck with Oakes and Paul Jones for the remainder of the season, in which they were relegated. When they finally returned in 2009 Murray had been supplanted by Wayne Hennessey and he finally called it a day after another serious injury, this time to his knee.

Murray now works as a pundit for Sky Sports and is the goalkeeping coach at the Nike Academy and at Barnsley.

FOOTNOTE

TEAMS TO FINISH IN THE TOP EIGHT AFTER PROMOTION

SEASON	CLUB	POSITION
1992/93	Blackburn Rovers	4th
1993/94	Newcastle United	3rd
1994/95	Nottingham Forest	3rd
1999/00	Sunderland	7th
2000/01	Ipswich Town	5th
2006/07	Reading	8th
2018/19	Wolves	7th

GOING DOWN, GOING DOWN, GOING DOWN ETC.
11 players who have been relegated more than three times with different clubs

NATHAN BLAKE (5) Sheffield United, Bolton (twice), Blackburn, Wolves

HERMANN HREIDARSSON (5) Crystal Palace, Wimbledon, Ipswich, Charlton, Portsmouth

MARCUS BENT (4) Crystal Palace, Ipswich, Leicester, Charlton

ROB GREEN (4) Norwich, West Ham, QPR twice

CURTIS DAVIES (4) West Brom, Birmingham, Hull City (twice)

SEBASTIEN BASSONG (4) Newcastle, Wolves, Norwich (twice)

ASHLEY WARD (4) Norwich, Barnsley, Blackburn, Bradford

NIGEL QUASHIE (4) QPR, Nottingham Forest, Southampton, West Brom

MARC EDWORTHY (4) Crystal Palace, Coventry, Norwich, Derby

DES LYTTLE (4) Nottingham Forest (twice), Watford, West Brom

PAUL ROBINSON (4) Watford, West Brom, Bolton, Leeds

A VIEW FROM THE STANDS

Dan Weaver, Official Wolves Fan twitter

What was your club's 'Sliding Doors' moment, that seemingly inconsequential action, which actually became a turning point in their fortunes, for either good or bad?

Late January 2012 and Wolves host local rivals Villa at Molineux. Emmanuel Frimpong, on loan from Arsenal, starts for Wolves in only his fifth appearance for the club. He had drive, determination and no fear, attributes we undisputedly lacked. He had a brilliant first half, energised the fans and was instrumental in us being 2-1 up at half time. The scoreline should've been more as we had battered them. You could sense the energy he gave the team. It felt like we were turning a corner as we were struggling in the league at the time. However, he got injured second half and was out for the rest of season. We proceeded to lose 3-2 courtesy of two spectacular goals from who else but Robbie Keane. Then Karl Henry got sent off to top it off. But, that Frimpong injury changed the game and ultimately the direction of the season—we won just once more in the league. It killed us and our survival hopes.